AF478111

How Britain Works

Also by Michael Temple

COALITIONS AND COOPERATION IN LOCAL GOVERNMENT

COMMUNITY IDENTITY AND PARTICIPATION IN LOCAL DEMOCRACY
(*co-author*)

How Britain Works

From Ideology to Output Politics

Michael Temple
Senior Lecturer in Politics
Staffordshire University
Stoke-on-Trent

Consultant Editor: Jo Campling

 First published in Great Britain 2000 by
MACMILLAN PRESS LTD
Houndmills, Basingstoke, Hampshire RG21 6XS and London
Companies and representatives throughout the world

A catalogue record for this book is available from the British Library.

ISBN 0–333–73885–3

 First published in the United States of America 2000 by
ST. MARTIN'S PRESS, LLC,
Scholarly and Reference Division,
175 Fifth Avenue, New York, N.Y. 10010

ISBN 0–312–23539–9

Library of Congress Cataloging-in-Publication Data
Temple, Michael, 1949–
How Britain works : from ideology to output politics / Michael Temple.
p.   cm.
Includes bibliographical references (p.) and index.
ISBN 0–312–23539–9
1. Central-local government relations—Great Britain. 2. Local government—Great
Britain. 3. Great Britain—Politics and government—1979–1997. 4. Great
Britain—Politics and government—1997– I. Title.

JS3137 .T45   2000
320.8'0941—dc21

00–036913

This book is printed on paper suitable for recycling and made from fully managed and sustained
forest sources.

10   9   8   7   6   5   4   3   2   1
09   08   07   06   05   04   03   02   01   00

Printed and bound in Great Britain by
Antony Rowe Ltd, Chippenham, Wiltshire

To Shirley Kliment-Temple, with love

Contents

List of Tables

List of Abbreviations

BBC	British Broadcasting Corporation
BNP	British National Party
CBI	Confederation of British Industry
CCT	Compulsory Competitive Tendering
CIPFA	Chartered Institute of Public Finance and Accountancy
CSA	Child Support Agency
DHA	District Health Authority
DETR	Department of the Environment, Transport and the Regions
DLO	Direct Labour Organisation
EAZ	Education Action Zone
ERDF	European Regional Development Forum
ESF	European Social Fund
EU	European Union
FHSA	Family Health Service Authority
GLC	Greater London Council
GOWM	Government Office for the West Midlands
GP	General Practitioner
HAT	Housing Action Trust
HAZ	Health Action Zone
IMF	International Monetary Fund
NDPB	Non-Departmental Public Body
NHS	National Health Service
NPM	New Public Management
MEP	Member of the European Parliament
MP	Member of Parliament
OECD	Organisation for Economic Cooperation and Development
PCG	Primary Care Group
PR	Proportional Representation
QUANGO	Quasi-Autonomous Non-Governmental Organisation
QUELGO	Quasi-Elected Local Government Organisation
RDA	Regional Development Agency
RHA	Regional Health Authority
SDP	Social Democrat Party

SEM	Single European Market
SOLACE	Society of Local Authority Chief Executives
SRB	Single Regeneration Budget
TEC	Training and Enterprise Council
UDC	Urban Development Corporation

Acknowledgements

If you contributed to this book, your omission from this list is an oversight. So many people gave help and feedback. Mike Brereton's input was paramount. As well as his contribution to Chapter 6, where he helped give coherence to my ideas and made some crucial improvements, our discussions usually threw up some fruitful (and occasionally fruity) suggestions. His initial guidance, especially on the book's structure, was invaluable. Jim Radcliffe was a wonderfully supportive and sympathetic reader of my final drafts and his encouragement was vital. He suggested a number of significant improvements. Jo Campling knows how important she was to this project; without her, it would not be in print. Emma Clarence provided valuable assistance and helped carry out the early research. Shirley Kliment-Temple, in addition to her practical help, made a significant intellectual contribution to this book. Thanks are also due to Nigel Ashford, David Denver, Steve Griggs, Brian Jacobs, David Newton, Colin Rallings, Michael Thrasher and Brian White, who all, whether they remember it or not, made some input, and to Karen Brazier at Macmillan. None of the people I've mentioned are responsible for any errors and some would dispute my arguments.

The nominated elite of 24 people that I interviewed, helped by Mike Brereton and Emma Clarence, also deserve my thanks. Some of them are mentioned in the book. Others requested anonymity for some of the things they said and to list them here would be to provide considerable clues to the provenance of those comments. As you will see, they were often incredibly candid about their role in the central and local governance system and I therefore thank them without mentioning their names. I also interviewed and spoke off-the-record to many people active in local governance between 1994 and 1999 and their insights, introductions and suggestions are gratefully acknowledged. Chapter 6 is a reworking of an article 'The New Public *Service* Ethos: an Ethical Environment for Governance' that originally appeared in *Public Administration*, 1999, Vol. 77 (3), pp. 455–74.

1
Thatcher's Legacy to Blair

> Economics are the method, the object is to change the soul.
> Margaret Thatcher, *The Sunday Times*, 3 May 1981

Introduction

Margaret Thatcher was that rarity in British politics, a politician with a clear mission to change the way we thought about the role of state. However much critics such as Gamble (1990) may dispute the existence of a coherent body of thought which could be called 'Thatcherism', her aim throughout was clear. She sought to make 'Britain safe from Socialism' (Mayo, 1994, p. 2). The new right claimed the Thatcher decade marked an electoral, ideological and policy watershed in which Thatcherism had 'broken the hold of collectivism' on 'intellectuals and policy-making elites'. Economic decline had been reversed, the authority of the state restored and British sovereignty reasserted (see Gamble, 1990, p. 335). At its most populist, she had 'put the Great back in Britain'. Has the soul of the British polity been changed? Is socialism dead? By the end of Mrs Thatcher's reign in 1990 most commentators had no doubt that the effects of Thatcherism, of eleven years of strife and confrontation, was nowhere near as significant as new right ideologues had been claiming. As well as dismissing the economic and political claims of Thatcherism, sceptics disputed the claims of widespread public support for her policies. In this view, popular support for Thatcherism was not widespread and her governments had failed to instil the values of the 'enterprise culture'. Despite new right rhetoric the basic structure of the welfare state remained untouched and public support for the welfare state was undiminished (British Social Attitudes, 1990; Le Grand, 1990).

The consensus when Thatcher left office was that either nothing much had changed or that change had been relatively insignificant (Glennerster and Midgely, 1991: Gamble, 1990). As Mayo points out, such beliefs overlooked the major changes that had taken place in the way services were being provided and the challenges to 'fundamental assumptions' about the role of state, private sector, community and voluntary organisations (Mayo, 1994, pp. 4–5). These changes – especially the introduction of a strong market ethos into the local governance system – were to have a fundamental impact on the provision of public services in Britain. The impact of those changes was largely felt at local level as quangos and government agencies were created but the culmination was to come in New Labour's realisation of the enormous coordinating power the removal of local democratic control from many services potentially gave to central government (see also Jenkins, 1995). The creation of arm's-length agencies allowed the executive to concentrate on policy matters and also introduced a newly 'rationalised' local 'quasi-civil service' more receptive to meeting centrally set targets. As the Cabinet Secretary Richard Wilson notes, there is 'now a much sharper focus on the outcomes that the government wishes to deliver in the community' (Wilson, 1999). Centrally determined outcomes require strong central control of local service deliverers. Thanks to the changes instituted by Thatcher's governments and his emphasis on achieving measurable outputs, Tony Blair is in control of a government machinery which has unprecedented peacetime power over the actions of local actors. In part, his power is due to a widespread new consensus on the need for public, private and voluntary sectors to work together in a 'positive welfare' system encouraging autonomy and initiative as its prime focus (Giddens, 1998a, p. 128).

The politics of uncertainty

At the end of the 1980s, the old certainty of the 'cradle to the grave' welfare state had been successfully challenged but it had not been replaced by a new Thatcherite certainty of the necessity for a large private sector providing 'social' services. People are bound to be confused when deeply cherished beliefs in the supremacy of institutions like our education system and the National Health Service (NHS) are challenged by a new orthodoxy. The impact of Thatcherism had replaced certainty, albeit a certainty that had become constricting and unpopular, with uncertainty, reflected in the findings of Social Attitude surveys which revealed a population increasingly racked by insecurity.

The public wanted the new 'economic freedoms' provided by Thatcher, but they wanted to keep at least the possibility of the state's security blanket. Citizens appeared unwilling to accept everything the market threw at them and still saw an important role for government. John Major's Conservative government, in hock to its right wing, struggled to understand these feelings and despite attempts to reassure the population, failed to convince them that, for example, the NHS was safe in Major's hands. Its history assured voters that Labour would probably protect the weak in society but in order to win an election, Labour had to prove its acceptance of 'market disciplines'. Therefore, New Labour sought a philosophy which embraced capitalism but also addressed the need for 'realism with a heart' (Dionne, 1999, p. A17). So, out of the uncertainty, out of the clash of two apparently mutually exclusive positions, a 'synthesis' has emerged in the shape of the Third Way, which attempts to reconcile themes such as 'the promotion of enterprise and the attack on poverty and discrimination' which have 'wrongly been regarded as antagonistic' (Blair, 1998a, p. 1). The Third Way promises that, where appropriate, the state will continue to *fund* provision but services will be *provided* by any mixture of public–private actors. Crucially, although public–private partnerships seem most favoured, the superiority of any approach will not be a given, prompting accusations that New Labour has replaced principles with pragmatism (Maude, 1998). Although pragmatism about means was a key factor, the driver of the Thatcherite revolution was ideological; it achieved necessary change but that change was also dysfunctional. In the words of a senior local Labour politician, 'what it did was achieve the dislocation required to allow things to be put together again' (interview, 1999). This prompts the thought that, rather than the Third Way's stated aim of a rebirth of social democracy, Blair's true 'historic project' might be adjusting us to Thatcherism (Hall, 1998).

At the beginning of the twenty-first century the assertion that 'we are all Thatcherites now' appears to some force but the reality is more complex. Blair's reciprocal admiration of Margaret Thatcher, and his acceptance that there were 'good things' done in the 1980s that New Labour had 'not to dismantle' but build upon (Blair, 1996) may have been mainly for the purpose of reassuring both Middle England and working class converts to private ownership that the changes Thatcher initiated were safe in his hands, but it also indicated the widespread acceptance of those policies. By the mid-1990s, the British Social Attitudes survey was finding a more libertarian and self-interested population, but, apparently paradoxically, a population still favouring state provision of services like health, education and social benefits. However, that apparent paradox is easily explainable – Britain was becoming richer, but more insecure (*Social Trends*, 1995). The changes Thatcherism ushered in were seen as essential but had introduced, *inter alia*, economic insecurity; in such circumstances, people want to feel that, if the worst happens, a state safety net exists to protect them and their family. Tony Blair and his advisers recognised this. Their promise was that New Labour would not abandon economic rectitude but that in times of trouble the state would still be there to help. Blair's apparent control of his party and his successful modernisation were key factors in New Labour's 1997 General Election victory (Worcester and Mortimore, 1999). Blair was seen as a safe and strong ruler, who would protect the hard fought gains of the Thatcher years but deliver a more compassionate capitalism than the Tories.

It is difficult to disagree with Hall (1998) that Blair has been shaped and formed by his experience of Thatcherism, and that the 'Blair project' is 'framed by and moving on terrain defined by Thatcherism' (Hall, 1998). Hall represents this as reprehensible, and, perhaps rightly, deplores what he sees as Blair's acceptance of the inevitability of wider forces. What Hall characterises as the Blair view of politics – managing events rather than directing them – is also lamented. Hall's anguish is a reflection of just how deep Thatcher's triumph really went. It may pain the old left to admit it but, if we judge political greatness by the extent to which you achieve your ends, Margaret Thatcher was a great prime minister. British politics at the beginning of the 21st century is unrecognisable from the class war rhetoric that dominated the political discourse in 1979. Along the way there were casualties; those at the 'bottom' of society suffered disproportionately while others were unfairly rewarded (for example, British Rail middle managers, city traders, former Conservative ministers); trade unionists whose contribution to the wealth of this country is inestimable were classified as 'the enemy within'; and whole communities were left unemployed by 'rationalisation' and then made to feel it was their own fault. Without meaning to be callous, the broad sweep of history will barely record such pain but will it have been, as the former Chancellor of the Exchequer Norman Lamont put it, 'a price worth paying'? If Tony Blair succeeds in his aim of a reformulation of social democracy which values entrepreneurship but rewards less obvious contributions to the nation's wealth, then perhaps even opponents of Thatcherism will regard the pain as an acceptable price. Control of the local governance system is crucial if Blair is to achieve his goals.

The book's approach

This book looks at the local governance system that Thatcher 'created' and draws some general conclusions about the way Britain is governed, using data drawn from a decision-making elite from a representative section of Britain, namely Staffordshire.[1] It is necessary to discuss briefly what I mean by 'governance'. It is generally acknowledged that 'local government', where the majority of local services are directly provided by employees of the elected system of local government, has given way to local 'governance' in which a variety of public and private sector actors deliver services (John, 1997, pp. 255–7). Rhodes (1997b, p. 57), while noting the multiple meanings of 'governance' in the literature, argues that governance defined as the new and largely self-organising networks of public and private actors now delivering a wide range of services at local and regional level offers the best explanation for the changes to British government. However, despite his seminal contribution to understanding the new systems of governance, I disagree with some of Rhodes' arguments on the ability of such networks to resist central guidance and dispute his view that there has been a 'hollowing out' of the British state in which central control has necessarily been weakened (see also Saward, 1997). Governance is about more than 'networks', and other changes, especially the creation of arm's-length agencies and New Labour's concentration on measurable outputs, have limited the autonomy of local 'self-organising' actors.

'Governance' has at least six separate uses; 'as the minimal state; as corporate governance; as the new public management; as "good governance"; as a socio-cybernetic system; [and] as self-organising networks' (Rhodes, 1996, p. 653). All of these definitions offer clues to the complexity of the new system. 'Governance' is too complicated a phenomenon to be reduced to one simple dimension and I offer an uncomplicated and very general use of the term without seeking to refine it. As I use the term, governance is emphatically *not* 'governing without Government' (Rhodes, 1996, p. 667). As Chapter 2 points out, actors from the voluntary and private sectors have always had a role in delivering 'public' services, but post-Thatcher it is the scope of such involvement that has really changed. From being clearly the dominant actor, elected local government is now just one of the actors in the system. So, throughout this book, 'local governance' refers to the whole community of public, quasi-public, private, quasi-private and voluntary actors and institutions delivering publicly funded services at local and regional level while 'local government' refers specifically to the elected tier of government.

The title *How Britain Works* implicitly makes a big claim. Obviously, the scope of this book is partial. While acknowledging global forces, it makes no attempt to examine the intricacies of central government or explore the growing power of the European Union. A key argument is that what happens at local level offers the best picture of how Britain works. It is here that the mass of citizens interact with the state. It is where they make their judgements about the sort of political system they live in, and given that most public or quasi-public services are provided at the local level it is where they judge the success or otherwise of national governments. The local governance system is critical in the operation of the British state. Central government could shut down tomorrow and it would be a long time before we noticed; indeed much of central politics closes down for the summer (the journalistic 'silly season') and the lack of central directives and policy pronouncements bothers no-one but news reporters. By contrast, the networks of local governance are vitally important to our everyday lives and the decisions made by local representatives of the state have a direct impact on the quality of, for example, the health, leisure and education we enjoy. How Britain works is largely through local governance actors delivering (and influencing the content of) the functions our taxes have largely paid for. This does not necessarily mean they have a great degree of autonomy. I argue that the changes introduced by Thatcherism, far from creating a more pluralistic local political system, have facilitated a potential for greater central control which Tony Blair and New Labour have utilised in their attempt to deliver 'joined-up' government.

No account of the way local services are delivered can overlook the history of local government. Chapter 2 examines the process up to 1974, when the local government system was fundamentally reformed. What a historical survey reveals is that, unsurprisingly, local government has always been a potential source of friction with the centre. Likewise, networks of actors from all sectors of society have always been involved in providing local services. However, until the mid-1970s, the need for local democratic institutions had never been seriously questioned. It took an economic recession fuelled by the world oil crisis of 1974, and the election of a government determined to reverse the post-war progression of government towards 'from the cradle to the grave' provision, to bring a fundamental change in attitude. Chapter 3 looks at the changes introduced by the new right attack on local government and assesses the nature of the new system. The attacks on the legitimacy of local government inspired fierce opposition to Margaret Thatcher's governments, yet her reforms contributed to an environment in which public–private cooperation could prosper.

However, the growth of government quangos and agencies, which accelerated from the 1980s onwards, has weakened local democratic accountability and helped to facilitate central control. The Blair government's move from a concentration on ideology towards setting state actors deliverable targets is critically examined in Chapter 4, as are the claims that New Labour is decentralising authority after the centralisation of the Thatcher years. Subtle and often ephemeral networks of influence exist in which new actors now engage; elite actors are in no doubt that the really important networks of influence are effectively undetectable by outsiders. Most importantly, I propose that the current governance system can best be characterised by a movement from a concern with ideology and processes to one in which it is outputs that matter. The new local governance system has raised many questions and the book explores three areas – the lack of community participation in decision-making; the concern with the decline of the public sector ethos; the weakening of local democratic accountability – in some depth. One commonly raised merit associated with multi-agency local governance is that, for many reasons, an allegedly more pluralistic approach has allowed local community groups to impact on local decision making more effectively than before. Chapter 5 assesses the relevance of such claims. Chapter 6 looks at the impact of private sector practices on the public sector and proposes that the process has had a more complex effect than is commonly acknowledged. Public–private partnership has impacted on both sides of the 'divide', offering a new ethos of public service for both public and private actors which can underpin an ethical environment for governance. The removal of many services from direct democratic control has raised concerns about democratic accountability. Chapter 7 looks at this 'crisis of accountability' and finds that private sector perceptions of responsibility are more complex than often acknowledged. That said, the decline of political accountability is real and is not compensated for by mechanisms such as citizen's charters and other procedures which ape the market.

The election of New Labour in 1997 introduced a new factor into the equation. The importance of the local governance system to New Labour's project is clear and Chapter 8 explores the relationship between the changing local governance system and (especially) the development by New Labour of the Third Way. The thrust of the Third Way requires greater community empowerment which could act against the central control of local actors which is needed given Blair's emphasis on centrally determined but locally delivered outputs.

Finally, Chapter 9 draws some general conclusions from the evidence of the substantive chapters. Any attempt at understanding the changes in British governance as a whole must acknowledge the importance of New Labour's move from a concern with processes and ideology towards 'output politics'. When combined with the structural and attitudinal changes largely initiated by the Thatcher governments, the potential power of the core executive is considerable.

Is local governance important?

Central to this book is the view that what happens in the networks of local governance has had and continues to have significance beyond the local, but is this really the case? After all, I contend that the mechanisms and institutions of local service delivery are increasingly under central control and, beyond that, most writers appear to have little doubt that it is decisions taken beyond our national boundaries which now have the greatest impact on all our lives (for example, see Dunleavy, 1997). As Massey chillingly puts it:

> The new global and European realities have locked British policy makers into a position as inimical to independent national action as at any time since the most glacial periods of the Cold War. The administration is cordoned and corralled by treaty obligation, declining national power and economic interdependence.
>
> (Massey, 1997, p. 21)

In addition, many of the fundamental changes in government of the 1980s, such as the raft of reforms under the broad framework of New Public Management, are seen as largely a response to wider global and technological developments (Massey, 1997b). If this is the case, then the changes identified by observers such as Rhodes (1996), in which 'steering' rather than 'rowing' is proposed as the correct way for governments to govern, may be more accurately seen as 'an unwitting description of current British governmental ability' (Massey, 1997a, p. 21) rather than as a prescription for reform. Also, my study of local governance would be telling us less than it seemed about prime ministerial power. I maintain that such arguments underestimate the *possibility* of local autonomy and considerably underplay the role of charismatic and driven individuals at both local and national level. As Hall's comments on Blair's debt to her indicates, Thatcher *counted*, but so does Blair. He has modernised and led his party in a way his 'uninspiring' (Rogaly, 1993) predecessor, the late John Smith, could never have done. It is almost inconceivable that 'New Labour' would exist under Smith's leadership. Even if he could have ditched key elements of old Labour gospel it would not have been his style and it was only when he was succeeded by Blair in July 1994 'that the thrust of the modernisation project was resumed' (Kavanagh, 1997, p. 217). With Blair as leader, the idea of 'New Labour' has caught the public imagination and is a much cleverer piece of re-branding than it seemed initially. The freedom the simple addition of 'New' gives Blair is considerable. Arguably, a Bevan (or even a Bevin) would not recognise Blair's party as the descendant of the post-war Labour party which launched the welfare state. In many ways, Blair's election as leader marks a transition from old to new as significant as the West German Social Democrat's ditching of Marxism in 1959. Both events signalled a fundamental change to sceptical electorates. Indeed, throughout this book I use 'New Labour' to describe Blair's party and to distinguish it from the old Labour party precisely because of the movement away from the ideological imperative of the old Labour party.

The argument that governments are powerless in the face of global economic forces may contain much truth, but we must remain sceptical of explanations which so considerably underplay the role of national and local actors. The game of 'what if?' is not just an intellectual exercise; it can show us that what appears to be a natural succession of events is anything but. At national level, whatever the global forces demanding a re-evaluation of the state's role in western democracies, can anyone seriously doubt that a different policy agenda would have dominated British politics during the 1980s with another prime minister? Margaret Thatcher only stood for her party's leadership because the right-wing's preferred candidate Sir Keith Joseph was forced to withdraw from the first ballot after an embarrassing gaffe. 'What if', for example, William Whitelaw, the 'obvious successor' to Ted Heath (Blake, p. 318), had become party leader in 1975 and prime minister in 1979? Almost certainly, there would have been a much less extensive process of privatisation; the political will to implement the Next Steps programme would probably not have existed and the functions exercised by agencies would still come under central departmental control; government would have shown a greater degree of accommodation towards worker interests; central–local relations could not possibly have been as antagonistic and the poll tax would never have been introduced; and perhaps there would have been no Falklands War following the Argentinean invasion. Given Michael Heseltine's involvement with quango creation during the early 1980s, it could be argued that there would have been an acceleration of appointed government but without the driving force of Thatcher behind the programme it is difficult to see the process being as far-reaching. Consequently, the Labour opposition would not have had the same imperative to change fundamentally and British politics, whatever the forces of global change, would look considerably different. The current system of local governance, which affords Blair considerable centralising powers, would not exist and the prime minister's ability to coerce local actors would be much weaker.

I make no comment about the pros and cons of the policies referred to and the speculation is not merely academic but carries a serious point. In short, meso and micro level politics matter, and the decisions made by national, local and regional actors directly affect people's lives and are worth studying. As Giddens (1998b) points out, globalisation does indeed pull upwards away from the nation state and the state loses some control over decision making in areas where it was once more powerful, but globalisation also 'pushes downwards, creating pressures towards greater local autonomy below the level of the state' (Giddens, 1998b, pp. 27–8) and thereby (perhaps) helping to promote decentralisation. We have seen some effects of this impact since joining the European Union, as regions have often bypassed national parliaments to lobby the supra-national institutions (Benington, 1994). Such developments possess the capacity to counter the central government control inherent in the British governance system.

Individuals matter – for better or worse, Margaret Thatcher helped to change the world and it might not have changed if she hadn't seized the imperative. For many, her charisma was a crucial contributory factor to breaking down the Cold War barriers and her advocacy of new right ideology was popular and effective. And just as significantly, both for the long-term benefits and for the short-term misery her policies inflicted on many communities, she changed the way we interact with government, especially in her reorganisation of the local state. Her tactics were often crude and unnecessarily confrontational and she made mistakes. Also, some of the benefits were not ones she might have intended. Her policies and tactics provided the platform for a growth in the informal and ephemeral networks characterising the local governance system, enhancing the possibility of 'joined-up government' with local and national actors in all sectors working together in an apparently more fragmented but actually more coordinated system.

Tony Blair may turn out to have been a similarly crucial individual in the development of the British state but we will have to wait to find out if the Third Way resonates like Thatcherism. What is indisputable is that local actors are important to achieving the Third Way and the move to output politics requires their assistance and cooperation. Despite the political and institutional moves towards centralisation there are other forces in addition to the power of supra-national organisations (for example, community politics, a more individualistic polity, local Conservative councils) which may counter Blair's wish for 'joined-up government'. However, the new consensus provides the possibility of Blair achieving his stated goals, both in output targets and reformulating a social democracy in which the apparently antagonistic strands of modern life are finally reconciled. Given his dependence on it, he must be careful not to take the local governance system for granted.

2
Before the Flood: Local Government up to 1974

Introduction

Local government has always had an ambiguous position within the British constitution. In a unitary state, local government theoretically exists only by the good grace of central government. Our unwritten (or more accurately, 'part-written') constitution gives the institutions of local government no special protection, as the abolition of the Greater London Council and other metropolitan authorities in 1986 graphically illustrates. However, one of the quirks of a 'flexible' constitution is that practices and conventions tend to acquire an almost mystical force. Local democratic institutions may be an anomaly in a unitary system, but their long existence has endowed them with a legitimacy almost the equal of any codified mention in a written constitution. The concept of local democracy, no matter how tarnished or under siege the institutions of local government may have become, continues to hold a special place in Britain's political culture. Central governments can attack the institutions of local government, although it's a dangerous pastime, but the principle of local democracy itself remains sacrosanct.

After a brief review of local government history, this chapter will outline the principles which underpinned the 1974 local government reorganisation in England and Wales. I will examine the new structural arrangements which were introduced at that time and review the managerial doctrine which characterised the internal workings of the reorganised local authorities. A number of assumptions about local power and decision making, both implicit and explicit, informed the 1974 reform; those assumptions, which to some extent still dominate the public discourse of local elites, are identified and placed in theoretical and historical context. An assessment is offered of the decision-making practices which grew out of the 1974 reform. The chief characteristics of these practices are presented as a 'local state' model of power in communities, with local authorities seen as distinct, if semi-autonomous, political systems possessing considerable democratic legitimacy. This perception structured debate and action about local government for a number of years. Throughout, the desirability of 'local democracy' has rarely been seriously questioned, and the assumption that local services are best delivered by directly elected local councils dominated the discourse until 1979.

A brief history of British local government

This is not the place for a detailed history of the development of local government but as Byrne (1994) pertinently notes, an historical perspective enables one to go a long way towards understanding the present system. Byrne conveniently (for our purposes) divides the history of local government in four phases, concluding his examination in 1974 (1994, pp. 13–34). Utilising Byrne's chronology, while not necessarily agreeing with his interpretations, some common characteristics can be identified.

Before 1800, 'local government' had evolved naturally from local communities, with leaders either emerging from local officials and worthies or being appointed by the monarch. The management of activities was carried out by networks not all that dissimilar to the public–private networks we regard today as innovative; 'self-help groups, voluntary associations … commercial undertakings [and] formal legal authorities' (ibid., p. 14) carried out a variety of functions, with significant local variations in both the mix of actors involved and in the ways officials and agents were appointed or sometimes elected. The 'system', if the *ad hoc* set of bodies and individuals could be so described, was characterised, like so much of state and civil society of that time, by corruption, inefficiency and unfairness.

Byrne's second period, from 1800–1880, covers the surprisingly substantial, if incoherent, local response to industrialisation. As for so much of the history of local service provision, private enterprise was to the fore in meeting (however inadequately by present-day standards) some of the problems of society which an increasingly mobile population exacerbated, such as law and order, health and housing. In addition, further *ad hoc* bodies were set up, which included poor law boards and independent commissioners with powers to provide services such as paving, cleansing, street lighting and watchmen (Stoker, 1988, p. 3). Not only were these bodies unable to meet the growing demands of an industrial society, they were also resented by the new ruling class emerging in the increasingly prosperous towns and cities who desired more control over their own environment. Largely in response to local elite pressure, in 1835 the Municipal Corporations Act created elected municipal councils and introduced a greater measure of uniformity than ever before. However, a number of Acts of Parliament created even more *ad hoc* bodies administering health, education, sanitation and policing (Keith-Lucas and Richards, 1978). The result was such a proliferation of bodies that local government was ineffectively 'carried out by an intricate network of unintegrated local authorities' (Harrison, 1996, p. 115) and contemporary accounts of the 1870s describe the resulting system as 'a chaos of areas, a chaos of authorities and a chaos of rates' (in Byrne, 1994, p. 17).

Recognising this, the Local Government Act 1888 created multi-purpose and directly elected county councils and county borough councils. This was an effective solution to many of the problems and further reorganisation along similar lines soon followed, establishing a range of directly elected multi-purpose urban, rural and non-county borough councils. The stability and administrative harmony that followed this period of reorganisation means the period from 1888 to the mid 1930s is often seen as a 'golden age' for local government (see Harrison, 1996, pp. 115–20, for an elegant assessment). It is certainly the case that the system enjoyed a high degree of democratic legitimacy and that central government was prepared to trust it with delivering important services. As well as being a generally harmonious time for central–local relations, the period is also characterised by harmony and cooperation between local political and business elites, perhaps because the two groups were often essentially the same people. The role played by local businessmen in building civic pride during those years is often overlooked; although ratepayers might express concern over the cost of poor relief, leaders like Joseph Chamberlain in Birmingham ruled cities where 'the local middle class elite set the pace…[and] civic pride required town halls with high towers and splendid facades' (ibid., p. 116). There were still conflicts between local and central government, and still concerns of an over-centralisation of power (see below) but the relationship was largely uncontroversial and central government was seen as having 'no general power of interference in local government' (Maud, 1932, p. 194). It is important to note that, historically, the centralising tendencies of the state may often have been overstated.

As the state assumed more responsibilities many of these were handed to local government in the early years of the twentieth century. For example, the development of public utilities such as gas, water and electricity were taken over by local authorities as well as responsibility for town and country planning, housing and a number of important welfare services (Richards, 1973, pp. 27–31). Essentially, there was a compromise, with local government accepting more interference as its share of state spending increased (see Pickvance, 1991, p. 51). The cordial relations between centre and periphery in those days may have reflected the close relationship between the backgrounds of central and local elites, with many distinguished parliamentarians having established their credentials in municipal government.

In contrast, the period of the post-Second World War years has been most often characterised in terms of a decline in the status and power of local government (Byrne, 1994). Even before the Second World War, in the so-called 'golden age', concerns were raised (especially during the 1920s and 1930s) that increasing legal controls and the removal of some functions was contributing to a centralisation of power. Stoker disputes the general idea of a 'decline', pointing out that while local government did lose some functions it also gained further responsibilities (1988, p. 6). Certainly, during the immediate post-war period, when following the inauguration of the Welfare State by the Labour government of 1945–51 central government introduced wholesale nationalisation, fears of a loss of local democratic control were supported by the removal of key services from local government control (Robson, 1954); for example, gas and electricity services were nationalised and the National Health Service (NHS) created. Balancing this undeniable centralisation, elected local government was given the task in an expanding state of developing many of the new services introduced. Newton and Karran (1985, p. 59) point to nearly 50 separate pieces of legislation which enlarged the scope of local government and from 1955 to 1975 local government current expenditure increased by three times in real terms (Stoker, 1988, p. 9). This hardly paints a picture conforming to Byrne's characterisation of the post war years as 'a period of decline' (1994, p. 22) and others have characterised those years as local government's time of 'greatest affluence' (Newton and Karran, 1985, p. 52). The truth may lie somewhere in between. Certainly, while local government budgets increased and it gained new roles, local councils also lost some important services and the rise in the number of quangos was already causing some concern to local government actors. Dunleavy estimates that 'a total of 85 organisational "births" in the period 1946–75 were based on powers transferred from local authorities' (Dunleavy, 1980, p. 103) while there were very few transfers of responsibility back to local government. In general, however, the period could be classified as one of central–local cooperation and the relationship was seen that way by most contemporary observers (Mackenzie and Grove, 1957, p. 405).

While we can see that there is no consensus among observers on the strength of local government's position in relation to central government, especially in the post-war years of the Welfare State, it is undeniable that central government has needed local government to deliver high quality and equitable local services. What this brief history also demonstrates is that *local governance* – a situation where local authorities are not the only or indeed dominant actor in their locality but merely one of a number of agencies involved in service provision – is not a new phenomenon. Local government has always been just one member (admittedly, for a long period the most important) of a network of different organisations delivering local services.

The pre-1974 quango state and its relationship with local government

Although its current scale may be a new phenomenon, quasi-government has a long history. Crown Agents date from the mid-nineteenth century and the Horserace Totalisator Board (popularly known as the Tote) was instituted in 1928 (in passing, John Major's dying Conservative government had shrunk from privatising the Tote in 1996, but it has now been privatised by New Labour, an example of the party's acceptance of Thatcherite philosophy). Ever since the beginning of the British local government system the 'motivation, characteristics and political behaviour' of local councillors has been a matter for examination and public debate. However, despite the long history of quasi-government, there have been almost no similar investigations into the motives and activities of quango members until very recently (Skelcher and Davis, 1996, p. 8).

This is understandable; the relationship between local government and quangos has not always been as stormy as an examination of recent years would suggest. In general, although many local actors would have disagreed, the situation by 1974 was that quangos were widely seen as dealing with specialised tasks which both local and central government were not well equipped to perform (see Greenwood and Wilson, 1984). Central government retained a measure of control over appointments to nationalised companies and local authorities generally had an input into quango appointments. The appointing of 'good chaps' by other 'good chaps' and the post-war consensus over the role of the state limited the scope for conflict in the ways quangos operated and local government's relationship with quangos was not seen as a significant problem (Jackson, 1963, p. 99). Textbooks largely ignored quangos as influences on local government actors, although it was being recognised by some commentators that the 'challenge of rival institutions' which would be established following the 1974 reforms (such as the area health authorities proposed in a 1970 Green Paper on the NHS) did have the capacity to make local government's case for providing future new services 'increasingly difficult to sustain' (Richards, 1973, pp. 33–4). Hill (1970) had already sounded a prescient warning, pointing out that not only was the variety of bodies providing local services often proving a barrier to participation, the consequences of this could be catastrophic for the future of local democracy:

> the danger is not so much that a centralised bureaucracy will take the responsibility for all services, but that local affairs may gradually wither away through inertia and unawareness of what is happening. Over a period of time we might find that the reality is a system of ad hoc bodies, and regional direction through government bodies and advisory councils. We face government by anonymous nominated committees.
>
> (Hill, 1970, p. 160)

However, local government was still seen as the crucial part of the local political landscape of Britain and the 'threat' of quangos was dismissed as perhaps temporary and overstated; Hill (ibid., p. 42) was more concerned that the ignorance which the 'complex maze of officialdom' contributed to was inhibiting participation. The motives of those engaged in delivering quasi-government remained largely unquestioned and local government's position as primary provider appeared secure. With the benefit of hindsight, many of the views expressed in post-war textbooks of the permanence of local government's role may seem smug. For example, Jackson believed that whatever changes would occur, there was 'little doubt that the main structure of local government administration will remain...in the hands of popularly elected councils, sharing functions according to status and local needs under the general supervision of local government' (Jackson, 1963, p. 11; see also Warren and Richards, 1965, Chapter 1).

In the early years of Thatcher's 1979 government, bitter attacks were launched against the quango state (Holland, 1981). Perhaps as a reflection of this onslaught from a 'common enemy', defenders of local democracy saw the 'semi-independence' of quangos in a positive light (Hill, 1983, p. 124). Academic studies argued there was 'little justification for derogatory generalisations' about the conduct of quasi-government (Greenwood and Wilson, 1984, p. 174). The huge increase during the 1980s in the numbers of quangos and their further usurping of some of the traditional functions of local government was to change such perceptions for ever.

Post-war strains on the system

Although the post-war consensus increased both local government's budget and (arguably) its functions, this does not necessarily imply a benevolent view of local political institutions from central government actors. Much of local government's post-war expansion was connected to a rapidly growing state's devolution of administration, conferring little decision making power and more a 'marriage of convenience' than an administrative partnership; 'the national political consensus was that local government was more an agency administering welfare functions than an entrenched institution of the democratic polity' (John, 1997, p. 254). It is not surprising that national actors should feel this way as, in many ways, local authorities did function largely as agencies of central government. As long as resources were plentiful there was no problem with this, certainly not for local government professionals; there was plenty of room for discretion in most areas of service delivery. If the pre-war years were a golden age for local govern-ment, case studies (for example, Dearlove, 1973) indicate that the decades of the post-war consensus were also 'a golden age for local bureaucratic power' (Kingdom, 1991b, p. 3). Organised party politics (although growing) was still relatively rare, especially in the power-ful shire counties, affording considerable scope to professional and technical (that is, 'rational') solutions to local problems. For exam-ple, although a small political elite were involved in policy mak-ing with officers, neither Jones' (1969) study of Wolverhampton nor Bulpitt's (1967) analysis of parties in the North-West of England found evidence of party groups playing any significant role in policy formula-tion. Reorganisation in 1974 was to be a significant factor in changing this.

By the 1960s there was also a growing awareness that the existing structures of local government were inadequate. As Stoker points out, 'the ideological climate of the period was heavily infused with a commitment to efficiency, planning and technological progress' (1988, p. 12) and an essentially Victorian system of local government, complete with unelected Aldermen and powerful Town Clerks, appeared increasingly anachronistic. Harold Wilson's Labour government was elected in 1964 calling for, *inter alia*, the white-heat of the technological revolution to reshape both society and government (Comfort, 1993, p. 670). Just as in 1997 when New Labour's modern (or 'post modern', see Chapter 8) and dynamic image was contrasted with that of a tired and old fashioned government, 'modernisation' became a key concept in an increasingly prosperous Britain. There was also a developing reaction to the 'cradle to grave' control of the post-war bureaucratic state as a less deferential population started to demand more control over their lives. Local government, especially, was beginning to appear out-of-date and out-of-touch. The growth of pressure group politics and the need for institutions to react to calls for greater participation placed further demands on the essentially closed systems of local government. The professionalisation of local government, with local government professionals allegedly dominating amateur, often politically unorganised and over-deferential councillors (Kingdom, 1991b), contradicted calls for greater community involvement in decisions that affected the lives of ordinary citizens.

Whatever the strains on the system, and the belief by central elites that local government's role was to aid the achievement of national policy objectives (no change there, then), its place in the political spectrum was considered inviolate. Notwithstanding their occasional departures from the wishes of central government, local authorities appeared rational organisations for service delivery, being generally competent and giving important local electoral legitimacy to the state. As Bulpitt (1983, 1989) has noted, a 'Dual Polity' existed, in which national and local government operated in two essentially separate cultural compartments, with local government (by and large) left to get on with their own politics. For local authorities, post-war budgetary decisions had been an essentially incremental process (Rosenberg, 1989). However, the pressures on the capitalist economic system that followed a world-wide recession during 1973–74 were to place considerable strain on the viability of local government's relative freedom to gradually increase its budgets as the notion that spending could continue rising in most areas of government provision was challenged.

The global (macro-level) recession also coincided with two key moments in the history of the British state. On the meso-level, Britain entered the European Community in 1973, which was to have far reaching consequences for many areas of British life including local and regional politics (Benington, 1994). On the micro-level, an internal and external reorganisation designed to carry local government through to the millennium and beyond was instituted in 1974 by the Local Government Act (1972).

Principles underpinning the
1974 local government settlement

There are a number of reasons why it is important to examine the 'local government settlement' of 1974. For our purposes, perhaps the most important is that the rhetoric underlying the reforms (whatever the reality) promoted a vision of local democracy as somehow intrinsic and an essential part of the modern democratic state. Underpinning the original proposals for change was a fundamental belief in the value of local democracy as capable of providing more accessible, responsive and accountable government than national legislatures and politicians could ever deliver (but see Ashford, 1989), a belief that, despite challenges, still dominates the discourse. However, that belief remains unexpressed in any 'constitutional document' (such as there are in Britain) and appears more an article of faith than an expression of the view of central bureaucratic and political actors. For many reasons, not least the control a unitary state gives to national politicians, the concept of local democracy has never been embedded into the British constitution (John, 1997). Connected to this constitutional superiority of central government, local leaders have never gained the respect of national leaders (Bulpitt, 1983) and Whitehall has 'successfully concealed' the important role played by the local bureaucracy in implementing policy (Ashford, 1989, p. 77). Although central government was certainly more 'reverential' towards local government in earlier times than it is now, an extremely condescending attitude towards the importance of local democracy and to the calibre of people involved in local government is a major and long-term characteristic shown by central political and bureaucratic actors, as research has somewhat shockingly illustrated (Jones and Travers, 1994). When a quality newspaper dismisses local councillors as 'third-rate politicians' (Editorial, *The Independent*, 22 June, 1999) we can see that these unfair and inaccurate perceptions of the quality of local representatives have sunk deep into the psyche of the central establishment.

Whatever the opinions of central government towards the occasional tendency of local government to subvert central policy (Harold Wilson's Labour government was prevented from introducing a universal comprehensive secondary education system by the delaying tactics of some local councils clinging to the selective principles of grammar schools) any 'independent' review of local government was bound to treat the principle of local democracy with a significant degree of reverence whatever the constitutional position. So, there was an important core assumption underpinning the two Royal Commissions which were established in 1969 to review the structure of local government in England (chaired by Lord Redcliffe-Maud) and Scotland (chaired by Lord Wheatley) and the review body set up the same year to examine Northern Ireland; Wales was not considered important enough to merit any more than a ministerial White Paper. The assumption these bodies carried into their investigation into local government reorganisation was that 'there was something called local democracy which was a valuable part of the constitution' (Marr, 1996, p. 68). In contrast, Ashford disputes the commitment of the Royal Commissions, believing Redcliffe-Maud, like previous reformers, had little respect for 'local sensitivities or local democracy' (Ashford, 1989, p. 79). In this view, while the post-war relationship between central and local actors was less characterised by strife than more recently, at a time of an expanding state and comparatively little pressure on financial resources this is unsurprising – there was enough 'power' to go around for everyone. Whatever the reality, and with due regard to Ashford's reservations, the commitment to the principle of local democracy that characterised the reports of the various bodies is apparent.

New structural arrangements of 1974

The recommendation of the Redcliffe-Maud Report on Local Government in England (1969) was that a single tier of local government would be both more efficient and more democratic, with 'no doubt where responsibility lies [and] no confusion over which authority does what' (Redcliffe-Maud, 1969, Vol. 1, p. 68), although two tiers, already in place in London, were proposed for the large urban conurbations of Liverpool, Manchester and Birmingham. The 1966–70 Labour government broadly accepted the report and published a White Paper in 1970 but then lost power in the general election. Despite the report's recommendations, the Conservative government introduced a two-tier structure in England which reflected the views of the Wheatley Report (1969) on Scottish local government.

Most local government textbooks give the precise details of the structure of local government introduced in 1974; here, it is enough to note that in England and Wales a largely county-based two tier system was introduced. The new system gave the predominantly Tory dominated shire counties control of the big budgets of education and social services, although there was not intended to be a hierarchical relationship between the two tiers, each tier having separate responsibilities. Even where it made little sense the two tier structure in England was strictly adhered to so that, for example, the Isle of Wight was ruled by two district councils and one county council, a total of three councils and two tiers of local government for a population of around 100,000 people (Hampton, 1987, p. 37). In Scotland, reorganisation reduced the number of authorities and a two-tier system was introduced with widely differing sizes of authority in most of Scotland, while three island councils formed a separate single tier system. In Northern Ireland, there would also have been two tiers but the acceleration of the 'troubles' meant the introduction of direct rule from Whitehall and government by area boards and quangos at the upper level, while elected local government in the province was limited to 26 district councils with very restricted powers (see Wilson and Game, 1998, pp. 48–53).

The result of local government reform was a lack of overall consistency in the United Kingdom and a consequent continuance of citizen confusion about the roles and structure of the new system. There were other criticisms, including accusations of change for political reasons (Alexander, 1982; Byrne, 1994). The arguments on the merits of the different systems may have concealed a struggle for ideological supremacy which had implications for the structures adopted. What is undeniable is that an opportunity for clarity was missed; the final solution was 'a series of complex compromises' which merely provided the basis for further conflict (Hampton, 1987, p. 55).

The eventual structure adopted in 1974 might be seen as drawing back from a solution where the role and responsibility of local councils would have been more clearly defined and hence more apparent to the public. To be cynical for one moment, it could be suggested that it was not in the interest of a central political elite to clarify the nature and extent of local government. A single tier of local government, for example, would strengthen a rival's claims for democratic legitimacy vis-a-vis the centre. On the other hand, it is also unclear that local government has ever been more responsive and accountable than central government, such evidence as there is suggesting that for much of its formalised existence local government has been run by local elites whose connection to the electorate has been tenuous (Kingdom, 1991b).

The process of reorganisation involved a merging of urban authorities (usually strongly politicised) and rural authorities (with a 'non-partisan' tradition). Prior to reorganisation over half of all councillors were 'Independent' but pitched into more politically charged environments their reaction was inevitable; immediately following reorganisation in the elections of 1973/4 over 80 per cent of councillors in England and Wales adopted party labels and today, party politics dominates the overwhelming majority of local councils. Party politics had been spreading anyway, for other reasons. For example, during the 1960s the Liberals started to concentrate more of their energy in contesting local seats, attempting to build local power bases as a future springboard to success in national elections. This activity played a dominant role in ensuring the survival of the party and it also meant that the other main parties had to follow suit or risk their local power bases diminishing (Temple, 1996). Formerly Independent councillors for the most part campaigned on a Conservative party ticket (see Widdicombe, 1986, Research Vol. II, p. 37).

However, the institutional reformers had either ignored the spread of party politics or been rather 'sniffy' about it. The traditional 'Independents' of the shire counties deplored party politics while displaying overwhelmingly Conservative tendencies; on the bureaucratic side, party politics was often regarded as 'a rather seamy and disreputable underworld, best ignored by local government officers' (Brooke, 1982, p. 3, in Game and Leach, 1995). Perhaps as a consequence, Redcliffe-Maud, and the Bains Report on local management, were implicitly critical of the increasing party politicisation of local councils and displayed a failure to come to terms with the fact that power in local councils lay within party groups rather than in the formal committee structures (Game and Leach, 1995, p. 7). They also failed to see that their own reforms would inevitably accelerate the process of party politicisation.

The impact of the Bains Report on internal management

Following the 1974 reorganisation, the majority of new local authorities based their management structure on the recommendations of the

Bains Report (1972) into the management and structure of the new local authorities. Bains believed that a 'wider ranging corporate outlook' was necessary in local authorities (Bains, 1972, p. 6), and recognised that if this was to have any chance of occurring 'members and officers must recognise that neither can regard any area of the authority's work and administration as exclusively theirs' (Bains, 1972, p. 8). To this end, Bains made a number of recommendations which were intended to improve the overall management of councils. The most important of these were the creation of a *chief executive* to head the administrative structure, assisted by a *management team* of chief officers, and at the centre of the committee structure, a *policy and resources committee* to perform a coordinating function on the political side of the council. So, along with the changes to the external structure of local government, the recommendations of Bains introduced some fundamental changes internally which were to have repercussions for both officer-councillor and central–local relations.

Prior to reorganisation in 1974, the traditional pattern of administration was that of separate and often antagonistic departmental kingdoms within the authority. Each department would report to its committee, and there was little coordination between the different departments and committees. The needs of the council as a whole were often secondary to the perceived needs of the particular department, and 'departmentalism' reigned (Elcock, 1986, pp. 234–5). The only time committee decisions were examined in any sort of 'whole', was when the recommendations of the different committees were presented to the full council for consideration and formal approval. As Elcock points out:

> only then could committee decisions be examined to see whether they conflicted with decisions of another committee; whether the overall use of resources by committees met the priorities which the council's members wished to follow and whether the decisions formed part of a coherent plan for the authority's future activity…this traditional decision-making process was found wanting on all three counts.
>
> (Elcock, 1986, p. 235)

The result was a lack of coherence; difficulties with coordinating activities when the system encouraged fragmentation meant that most efforts at coordination were confounded by departmental rivalries and pressure of time. It was in order to counteract this lack of coordination that the Bains Report recommended the establishment of a chief executive officer in each local authority, as the head of the officer structure. The chief executive was to have no department to run (although many established large executive departments) and his or her main function was to coordinate the administration of the council and ensure a more coherent pattern to the plans of the authority. To this end, Bains also recommended the setting up of a management team of the senior chief officers, chaired by the chief executive, its main function being to decide on proposals to be submitted to the council or the policy and resources committee.

Both Redcliffe-Maud and Bains, inevitably given the importance of notions of 'accountability' to democratic theory, argued the need for elected members to be in control of the overall development and operation of services. In order to facilitate this, Bains (1972, p. 99) recommended the creation of a policy and resources committee at the very centre of the committee structure which would oversee the programme committees. Within a few years most local authorities had such a committee and it tended to function like the central government cabinet; the result was to create an internal network that more openly resembled central government. The overall result was not something Bains had intended. The management team gave the potential for extraordinary coordinating power to the chief executive, a post that was increasingly becoming an openly political appointment. A small elite of chief officers and senior councillors decided policy, senior party members and officers ensured committees delivered decisions based on that policy, and a compliant and largely powerless legislature (that is, the council chamber) became, in the great Walter Bagehot's terms, a 'dignified' (as opposed to an 'efficient') part of the local political system in much the same way as the House of Commons at central level. The rise of party politics and strict adherence to a party whip were to mean that, whatever the central constraint on their powers, local elites acted as if in control of a local state and would soon become willing to oppose the wishes of central government in a way rarely seen before.

Central–local relations: local councils as distinct political entities?

As Richards notes, our history has established that 'to a large extent our system of local government has been a system of local *self* government. There is a strong tradition that local communities should be able to decide how to deal with their own problems' (Richards, 1973, p. 83, emphasis in original). Although central supervision was widely (if often grudgingly) accepted, Richards argues that historically the relationship was not seen as one of principal-agent but as 'a balance of control and independence ... partnership and separation' (ibid.). There is no space here for an extended discussion of the important debate on the theoretical position of local government that has enlivened the debate on central–local relations; localist, dual-state, social relation and public choice approaches (to offer just four models) all have strengths and weaknesses and all offer considerable insights into the local political process. Stoker (1988) gives a first-class exposition of the various positions (see also Wilson and Game, 1998, pp. 115–25). What is clear is that most writers allow for at least some response by local elites to local preferences and 'characterise local politics as relatively open, plural and competitive' (Stoker, 1988, p. 241).

Whatever the belief of central government on the rightful place of local government in a unitary political system, the independent reviews and commissions into local government have tended to regard local authorities as distinct political entities, akin to a 'local state'. By using the phrase 'local state', it is not meant to argue, as Cockburn (1977) did when inventing the phrase, that the local state can be seen as a willing and active subordinate in the central state's role as an agent of capitalism. On the contrary, by the concept of a 'local state' it is implied that each local government area is essentially a semi-autonomous political system inside a national/supranational policy environment. Rather as globalisation sees the function and relative autonomy of the nation state within a global economic and political system, so this perspective recognises the external (and internal) restraints on local political actors but still sees them as having a measure of decision-making autonomy.

One critical report of the period of re-organisation noted how 'the whole myth behind local government is that it should be based on local democracy ... [while] ... in practice central government has a very firm grip on how it operates' (CIS/CDP, 1975, p. 25, cited in Dearlove, 1979, p. 216). As Dearlove argues, this is an inadequate perspective in the face of 'the complex and contradictory reality of local government' in so far as it relates to both class and state (1979, p. 217). While it is undeniable that the centre's legal power over local authorities is clearly demonstrated by the ways it has abolished and created new tiers of government, especially since the 1960s, the fact that the principle of local democracy remains intact is an indication that central government is not a free agent. Not only is a central political party inhibited by its own local activists, there are other powerful local and regional interests it would not be wise to annoy. In addition, central government has to take account of the polity's undoubted belief in local democracy and *cannot* abolish elected local authorities altogether and replace them with arms-length agencies and quangos. Recognising this, central elites have sought to minimise local governments' scope, especially over raising its own finances, and has always utilised the democratic argument when abolishing tiers of local government or changing its remit; what it cannot do is directly attack the very concept of local democracy, which necessarily limits the steps central government can take to keep overall control. Consequently, local government still has considerable responsibility for delivering services, and, more importantly, who is in power at local level still matters and makes a difference to the balance of service provision. Despite all the attacks on local government autonomy from central government, local government is still a significant part of the overall political system in Britain and control of local councils is still a considerable political prize. As Mellors notes:

> the units of government are large, the range of duties extensive and their budgets, although subject to considerable central interference, a major component of the nation's economy … despite all the constraints that are imposed on local government, control of a council gives a political party a valuable political foothold in the locality and an important opportunity to shape the community that it serves.
>
> (Mellors, 1989, pp. 73–4)

Local government is not just an instrument of central government. Despite increasing restrictions over local autonomy, central government is still unable to claim total control over local politics.

Unhappy with arguments that characterised local government's role as either one of agent or partner, Rhodes (1981) proposed a different perspective on the relationship between central and local government. Rhodes offered a resource-exchange model concentrating on a power dependency relationship; he argued the relationship is an organisational struggle with both sides fighting for the control of constitutional, financial, political, hierarchical and informational resources (Rhodes, 1981, pp. 30–1). Because the relationship is necessarily one of exchange and dependence, that is, central government needs local authorities to provide services and local authorities need central finance to provide those and other specifically local services, the relationship cannot continue indefinitely in the confrontational manner adopted by Thatcherism. Rhodes' model recognises that either central or local government may be more dominant at any particular time, recognises variations in the degrees of discretion and power, and acknowledges that the relationship has the potential to vary from outright conflict to cooperation or domination by one side. However, it is not, therefore, merely a variation on the 'partnership' model. Rhodes' model, when applied to the analysis of central–local relation, means that:

> local authorities are neither the agents of the centre nor partners of the centre, but are rather loci of power which is mobilised in relation to the power exerted by the central authority.
>
> (Rhodes, 1981, p. 24)

So, the idea of local government as merely an agent of central government or as compliant agents of capitalism is difficult to sustain. We must reject the orthodox Marxist view which sees the 'capitalist state' (including, of course, the institutions of local government) as 'an instrument of class domination' (Cockburn, 1977, p. 42), although it is undeniable that the development of local government from 1888 onwards in particular was closely connected with establishing the norms and values of a national (and clearly capitalist) ruling class/elite. Rather, I tend to share Saward's 'broadly neo-pluralist perspective' which sees the contemporary state as a complex entity lacking functional unity; partisan, depending on the institution or policy area, towards certain interests in society; possessing potential autonomy from broader social and economic interests and therefore able to act in the interests of state actors (Saward, 1997, pp. 16–17; see also Nordlinger, 1981). To a large extent, the 'local state' shares these characteristics and 'cannot be regarded as the simple instrument of either the central state or dominant [i.e., business] interests' (Dearlove, 1979, p. 221). In short, local policy preferences matter and local political elites make meaningful decisions which may conflict with the wishes of central elites. As I shall argue, the Thatcher reforms limited the ability for local discretion.

Local government and the constitution

To return briefly to our historical perspective, from the late Victorian era onward an unwritten and unspoken consensus had developed which left local government to deliver 'domestic services'. The creation of the National Health Service in 1948, in which central government assumed direct control over the provision of health care, was the first significant crack in this consensus. Andrew Marr's contention that the 1945–51 Labour government had 'no time for myopic municipal doubters' and openly followed a course of 'centrally-organised welfarism … and national economic management that left little room for local variation' (1996, p. 67) is arguable. However, notwithstanding the generally more consensual period of the 1950s and 1960s and the increased budgets of local governments, there is little argument that post-war central government has gradually increased its *share* of control over service provision (Jones and Travers, 1996, p. 89). There also appears to be a consensus that local government's position within the constitution fundamentally altered after 1979. Against this, Jones and Travers argue that while political authority was shared during the post-war consensus years, the dominant belief (over many years) has been that 'service provision or enabling is the pre-eminent role of local government' (ibid., p. 90). As others have maintained (notably Tant, 1993) it is the post-war consensus years that must be seen as the aberration in British political culture. In this view, and supporting Jones and Travers, the post-war conception of local government as being involved in a partnership with central government is similarly an aberration. So, the dominant centralist view of recent years that the concept of a unitary state means local government should not be entitled to act as a check or balance on the wishes of central government was not initiated by Thatcherism, but had a long tradition within British political culture. However, it needs to be made clear that until Thatcherism it existed side-by-side with an equally potent view of local government as possessing a degree of independence in order to meet particular local needs and to interpret central policy in a way that suited local circumstances.

The constitutional position of local government was largely ignored in the reports that central government commissioned in the post-war years. Despite the frequent accusations of 'unconstitutional' action against local autonomy by the Thatcher governments of the 1980s, the constitutional position of local government remained undiscussed or taken for granted. The unwritten nature of our constitution means that there can never be any guarantee of the status of local democracy and the constitution's much vaunted 'flexibility' enabled Margaret Thatcher's government to launch what amounted to all-out war on the actors and institutions of local government.

A 'myth' of responsive local democracy and political accountability has dominated the discourse before and since 1974. Notwithstanding the paucity of support for the proposal and the often clear evidence to the contrary, local elites, media and academic commentators, and many central actors (at least in public) bow to this picture of local and regional decision making. The challenges of the last quarter of the twentieth century have exposed the myth to much criticism, yet in defiance of its seeming fragility this perception clings on. Despite central government's attempts to minimise the role of local government, a largely compliant media's campaign to cast doubt upon the motives of all those engaged in local government, a series of political and financial scandals, and the declining electoral turnout at local elections, all of which should have contributed to a significant fall in its legitimacy, a positive conception of local democracy manages to survive as a totem of faith. This is partly due to the activity of a handful of local government academics who, whatever the flaws of day-to-day local government, cling to a belief in the essential rightness of the concept. Academics and local government activists who share the 'localist view', while explicitly arguing the pros of local democracy, also appreciate the flaws of the current system and try to 'avoid complacency' in their views of the calibre of individuals and institutions (Stoker, 1988, p. 220). In short, despite their understanding that everything is not for the best in the best of all possible local government worlds, their view could be expressed as – local democracy is a good thing and there should be more of it. It is easy to sneer at this, as Bulpitt (1993) has so eloquently done, and there are many criticisms of the standpoint, most notably in recent years from the New Right which sees political mechanisms for choice as inherently inferior to consumer choice in the market place (Pirie, 1981). Academics such as John Stewart, George Jones and Ken Young deserve great credit for their commitment to the principles of local democracy. Their beliefs underpinned one of the better government reports of the 1980s, the Widdecombe Report (1986). Their 'faith', with qualifications, is one this book unashamedly subscribes to. As Kingdom so stirringly puts it:

> local democracy is not something distinct from the democratic life of the nation – it is part of the wider system, as a limb is part of the body. If the local arm of the democratic state is amputated, the whole body politic is incapacitated. When the forces of centralism undermine local democracy, on the grounds of efficiency, cost saving or whatever, they attack the very soul of the polity.
>
> (Kingdom, 1991b, p. 6)

Local democracy, then, has a significance and strength that goes far beyond the bald constitutional contention that in a unitary state, central government not only has sovereignty but can also legislate local government out of existence. This is not the case; whatever the apathy often demonstrated by local populations, at 'the very soul of the polity' there is still more than a flickering adherence to the concept of local democracy and most people demonstrate a strong psychological attachment to their specifically local political areas (MORI, 1994).

Conclusion

An historical perspective indicates that local government has always been one of a number of actors engaged in delivering local 'public' services, although this century it has tended to be by far the most important local actor, and that its relationship with quangos has not always been as problematic as recent years would suggest. It is also clear that underpinning the reforms of the last century or so has been an abiding belief in the importance of a local democratic system to the British constitution. The various reports into the role and structure of local government took a benevolent view of local democracy and never seriously questioned the need for an elected local government in a unitary system. For the most part, the central state has accepted the existence of local government without engaging with the constitutional implications of the existence of a 'rival' democratically elected government system which may have conflicting preferences. It is also clear that the view of local government as a tool of either central government or of a dominant class cannot be upheld.

The system of local government in place after 1974 might have been flawed but there was a widespread belief that it would 'see us through until the next millennium' (Wilson and Game, 1998, p. 53). However, Margaret Thatcher had barely taken office before the criticism from ministers of local government as 'wasteful, profligate, irresponsible, unaccountable, luxurious and out of control' began (Newton and Karran, 1985, p. 116). Legislation designed to curb the power of local councils was not far behind. The stresses and strife created by central government's new mission to curtail or, as they would argue, enhance local democracy, is the focus of the following chapter.

3
Drowning, not Waving: Local Government under Attack

Introduction

It appears to be the conventional wisdom that, notwithstanding the more centralist role afforded to the state in the post-war consensus years, the years since 1979 in particular have been characterised by a gradual and significant reduction in the powers, resources and responsibilities of local government as alternative mechanisms for both policy making and service delivery have been created (for example, see Littlewood and While, 1997, p. 114). While it is acknowledged that the need for greater economic stringency had been recognised by the 1974–79 Labour government, it was Margaret Thatcher's Conservative government from 1979–90 that is seen as largely responsible for systematically (and at least partly successfully) challenging the 'traditional' role of local government as a multi-purpose, relatively independent, democratic and legitimate institution with the right to raise at least part of its own taxes.

This chapter outlines the ways in which the 'local state' model, with local councils seen as semi-autonomous bodies capable of a significant degree of decision-making independence from the concerns of both central government and 'dominant classes' (Dearlove, 1979, p. 244), came under pressure from a variety of sources in the 1980s and 1990s. Many of the challenges were posed by a central government which, unarguably, fundamentally challenged the validity and continued existence of a lower tier of democracy. I identify and discuss a number of challenges faced by local government (and local democracy) during the last quarter of the twentieth century, including: significant structural change to the local government system; the introduction of financial controls and mechanisms designed to curb local spending and discretion; government policy initiatives designed to introduce competition into the provision of services traditionally provided by local authorities; the quantum leap in the number and range of quangos and the creation of 'arm's-length' agencies; the impact of membership of The European Union; and the spread of ideas of participatory democracy founded in a belief of the importance of wider community involvement in local decision making. The cumulative effect of these developments on the nature of the central–local government relationship is outlined and the notion that successive changes have led to the 'hollowing-out' of the British state is criticised.

The impact of some of these changes in specific areas is discussed in greater detail in following chapters. This chapter takes a very broad overview of the changes and challenges to the local political arena. I offer an assessment of these challenges, concluding that the result has been a movement from local government to local governance; an adoption and acceptance of market-orientated methods by local political and bureaucratic elites; and the development of a more complex (and more cooperative) relationship between central and local government than is usually implied by recent studies of central–local relations. It is also time to acknowledge the positive nature of the often bloody central–local battles largely instituted by Margaret Thatcher's government. That said, a powerful argument can be made that the local governance structure is fragmented and incoherent and in need of a strong, democratically elected set of local institutions to ensure effective citizen representation and redress. Whether local government can fit that role is less clear.

Yet more structural change in local government

In 1969, Lord Redcliffe-Maud was highly critical of the then Byzantine local government system. His report to central government proposed a mainly unitary system. These recommendations were largely ignored and the result of reform was an almost equally confused system of local government and therefore an inevitable continuance of citizen confusion about the roles and structure of councils in the reformed system. While many observers were essentially positive about the changes, some concluded that the only certainty to arise from the 1974 reforms was that there would be further pressure for even more reform – but surely not for a while (Richards, 1973).

However, barely ten years after what was widely seen as a long-lasting and fundamental reform of the structure of local government, further significant changes were introduced. To the accompaniment of accusations of change for political reasons (Horton, 1990, p. 178), the Conservative government of the 1980s further complicated the structure of local government in England, with a single-tier structure being created in the metropolitan areas and in London. The Local Government Act (1985) abolished the Greater London Council (GLC) and the six metropolitan counties, all Labour controlled and thus hostile to implementing government policy without prevarication. Publicly unaccountable 'joint boards' were created to administer those services which were not re-allocated to the London boroughs and metropolitan districts. As always, for public consumption, the primary justification for the changes was that they would improve local democracy (Hampton, 1987, pp. 198–201). The struggle for political power is a more convincing explanation (see Dearlove, 1979).

In fact, the recent history of London's government provides an apposite commentary of the power of the core executive in Britain to ignore the wishes of local people. Briefly, in 1963 London's population jumped from just over 3 million to well over 8 million as the old 1888 boundaries were redrawn. The whole of Middlesex and parts of Kent, Essex and Surrey became part of Greater London. The bulk of functions were undertaken by new inner and outer London boroughs but the GLC was given overall responsibility for functions requiring coordination over the boroughs; that is, transport in particular but also, more contentiously, the capital's housing. Such coordinating control was soon translated into considerable political power and from 1979 the GLC assumed a role as a focus of legitimate (that is, elected) protest against Thatcherite policies, becoming a political embarrassment that resisted central directives with relish. Despite the overwhelming wishes of London's population, whom the opinion polls suggested resisted a campaign of press vilification largely directed against the leader of the GLC, 'Red Ken' Livingstone, in 1986 the GLC ceased to exist. No single event demonstrates so well the potentially enormous power of central government in a unitary state.

The result of the 1986 reforms was that local government in Britain now had an undeniably dual structure, with two tiers in England and Wales (counties and districts) and Scotland (regions and districts), and a single tier structure in the metropolitan districts, London boroughs and the island authorities in Scotland. The desire to reform the local tax system then took precedence over further structural change, although it was apparent that, for central government, large strategic authorities with responsibility for planning and regional coordination were unwanted, having the power-base to resist and subvert central directives. Although the consultation process had already begun, after the 1992 General Election and with local finance no longer a contentious issue, the Major government quickly and painlessly reformed the structure of local government. Despite some opposition, especially in Scotland, the Scottish and Welsh offices 'swiftly proposed, consulted on and implemented a one-tier system based on 20 large areas in Wales and 28 in Scotland' (John, 1997, p. 261). Strathclyde Regional Council, covering 48 per cent of Scotland's population, was among the casualties; previously the council and 19 district councils had 'ruled' most of Scotland. Following reorganisation, Strathclyde was run by 12 unitary councils, 7 joint boards (quasi-elected local government organisations, 'quelgos', made up of nominated councillors), 3 strategic planning committees and 3 new quangos and had also lost responsibility for major roads to the Scottish office. The result was an organisational mess, 'single-tier but hardly streamlined' (Wilson and Game, 1998, p. 65). As with the GLC, central government had once more demonstrated its powers over local elites, especially when there is little to lose electorally. Conservative support in Scotland and Wales was low and their electoral prospects were unlikely to change, whatever they did. The situation in England was much more politically charged for the Conservative government; unlike Scotland and Wales, it was deemed necessary to have a Commission which would, amongst other things, shield the government from potential criticism.

The Local Government Commission (1992), chaired by the former director-general of the Confederation of British Industry (CBI), Sir John Banham, was a major opportunity to rationalise and simplify English local government's structure, but the chance was missed. Banham initially recommended a predominantly single-tier system, although the rationale for deciding which area was to be single-tier and which two-tier was unclear. A combination of government concern at the creation of a largely single-tier system (although some ministers favoured this solution), combined with local opposition and the timidity of Banham's final recommendations, means the system in England is even less clear than it was before. After an exhaustive process of consultation Banham created 46 new unitary authorities but most of the existing counties were allowed to continue in a two-tier structure together with those districts not granted unitary status. So, following Banham, a number of 'city states' now have autonomy from their shire county, leading to some strange situations. For example, Stoke-on-Trent and Newcastle-under-Lyme are so joined together that even locals do not know the precise boundaries, yet Stoke now has control over its own education while Newcastle is under the aegis of the county council. Staffordshire's political structure now resembles a doughnut, with Stoke the hole in the middle as a unitary authority surrounded by the doughnut of a weakened two-tier system. Local preferences had real input into the process, but the generally preferred alternative by many actors of a North Staffordshire unitary authority was lost in a flurry of in-fighting and false calculation by local elites. The final solution was no-one's preferred outcome, with the possible exception of the county council, which retained control over as much as it could realistically have expected.

In Scotland and Wales, the merits of a unitary system were seen by ministers. By contrast, in England, what remains is a local government system in such a 'mess' (Game, 1997) that further reorganisation sometime in the future is again inevitable. This confused mess seems to characterise the final years of John Major's limping administration. As Wilson and Game (1998, p. 320) remark, the Major government's 'original vision of leaner, less costly unitary authorities throughout Britain has not materialised'. They argue it may even be that such efforts are now an 'irrelevant distraction' (ibid.) from the more important task of, for example, devising mechanisms for better accountability and community empowerment. However, this is to ignore the potential contribution of a clear structure of local government, within the fragmented world of local governance, towards creating a better informed, and hopefully more involved, local polity. There appears to be little hope of a forthcoming solution to the problem of fragmentation and incoherence in the structure of local government.

The situation is further complicated by the creation in 1999 of regional government in Scotland and Wales. A 129 member directly elected Scottish Parliament and a 60 member directly elected Welsh assembly (and typically, these bodies have differing remits and powers) now exist to further muddy the waters of both democratic accountability and central–local relations. In England, Regional Development Agencies with appointed members have been instituted, with the promise sometime in the far future of setting up directly-elected regional assemblies (Holliday, 1997). Finally, London now has not only a directly-elected Mayor but also a strategic authority (the return of a two-tier system in London!) which covers the area of the old Greater London Council and also has wider powers. So, the plethora of changes has only served to further confuse a public who still generally have only a limited and usually inaccurate knowledge of what a local authority does. A central government concerned about maintaining the *status quo* may have a vested interest in continuing the current structural confusion.

In addition to the control exercised by central government over the scope of local authority powers and structures, central intervention has also limited the financial autonomy of local government. In dramatic fashion, local tax was to become the focus of an unprecedented (in modern times) wave of citizen protest from all sections of the community in the late 1980s.

The introduction of financial controls and mechanisms designed to curb local spending and discretion

It is rare that local government takes centre stage in discussions of British politics. The fact that throughout the 1980s local politicians – Derek Hatton in Liverpool, David Blunkett in Sheffield, Shirley Porter and Ken Livingstone in London – became national figures demonstrates how important local government was during that decade. Local government was seen as one of the few bulwarks against the potential power available to a government with a minority of the popular vote but an effective parliamentary majority. Margaret Thatcher's government resented that alternative power base, unless controlled by 'one of us'. They were determined to stop what they saw as irresponsible spending by urban socialists protected from the consequences of their actions by a rating system that meant the cost of their policies was borne largely by people unlikely to vote for them anyway – middle class householders and local businesses.

Although Rhodes argues that central–local politics in the 1980s was characterised more by 'policy mess' than 'an era of centralisation' (1988, p. 8), most commentators agree that the level of central control has increased since 1979, when a Conservative government ideologically opposed to state intervention in the economic and social welfare spheres was elected with a pledge to 'roll back the frontiers of the state'. Local authorities, seen as responsible for a great deal of unnecessary spending, were an early target of Margaret Thatcher but the process of curtailing local spending preceded her government. A world-wide economic recession, exacerbated by the loss of Arab oil to the west following the Arab–Israeli war in 1973 and subsequent massive rise in oil prices, had already limited the ability of British governments to meet spending commitments. In 1976, following a £2.3 billion loan from the International Monetary Fund (IMF), the Labour government promised cuts in public spending and there began a shift from incremental growth to a centrally-inspired policy to cut back on local spending (Travers, 1986, pp. 192–4). The then Environment Secretary Anthony Crosland had already warned local government in 1975 that 'the party's over'[1] (in Jenkins, 1995, p. 43) implying that a perceived need to control local spending would have entailed similar central responses whichever party had been in power during the 1980s. That said, a Labour government with a disappearing majority was unlikely to take on seriously such a potentially powerful enemy as local government, and it was the Thatcher government which bit the bullet. During the 1980s, a number of Acts were passed (for example, legislation on 'rate-capping' and the introduction of the community charge or 'poll tax', followed by a power for central government to 'charge-cap') which lessened the ability of local authorities to set their own levels of income. The changes were accompanied by a carefully orchestrated barrage of tabloid and broadsheet criticism of the actions of 'irresponsible' local councils. The rewards of such service in the Thatcherite cause were to be knighthoods and peerages to supportive proprietors, editors and journalists (*Private Eye*, 7 December, 1990).

By far the most high profile of these changes was the introduction of the poll tax. Several challenges to central directives and the continuing increase of local spending at a faster rate than the government desired, although local spending actually fell in real terms (Jenkins, 1995, p. 44), convinced a generally unenthusiastic cabinet to support Margaret Thatcher, Kenneth Baker and William Waldegrave's idea to reform the local tax system (Butler *et al.*, 1994, pp. 70–87). The basic idea of the poll tax was that if every member of the electorate had to pay directly towards the cost of local government (and not just private householders and local businesses as under the traditional rating system) then high spending and predominantly Labour-controlled authorities would be punished electorally; essentially, and in a reversal of the traditional rubric, there should be 'no representation without taxation'. The irony is that the community charge was introduced in order that local voters would be able to 'punish' high taxing councils and 'reward' low taxers, but 'charge-capping' (limiting the amount councils could levy) nullified the justification (greater council accountability) for introducing the change.

As we have seen during the discussion on structural reform, on those increasingly frequent occasions that it reforms areas of local government, central government usually includes as one major justification for change that local democracy and local accountability will be strengthened and such claims were made for the poll tax. On the contrary, the poll tax is generally seen by most observers of local politics as part of a centralising process which, when allied to other legislation which ensured controls over capital expenditure, made it well-nigh impossible for local authorities to diverge significantly from the spending assessments made by central government and then enforced on councils. For example, the Local Government, Planning and Land Act 1980, the Local Government Finance Act 1982 and the Local Government and Housing Act 1989 all provided for extensive central control of local council expenditure (see Loughlin, 1996, pp. 44–7). Although Bulpitt (1989, pp. 68–9) argues such measures still left room for significant local autonomy, the legislation severely hampered local actors.

However, the poll tax topped them all. It was also 'without exaggeration … one of the most important policy mistakes in British government in the twentieth century' (Budge *et al.*, 1998, p. 460). It could be seen as an object (and abject) lesson in how not to introduce a new policy (that is, major change and no consultation) and it had unexpected consequences for the Conservative government, as the marches and riots that would eventually lead to its scrapping first helped to end the premiership of Margaret Thatcher (Butler *et al.*, 1994). Michael Heseltine's challenge to Thatcher's leadership had the abolition of the poll tax as a central plank and when John Major succeeded Thatcher as Prime Minister in 1990, Heseltine was given the task of devising a suitable replacement. The replacement of the poll tax by the 'council tax' (based like the rates on property values but with an individual element) in 1992 failed to alter a situation where close to 80 per cent of local authority funding is centrally provided, although that figure has been steadily falling as the central government transfers more of the burden of local spending onto the local tax (John, 1997, Table 13.1, p. 258). What is surprising (even allowing for the more generous system of rebates) is the way in which the new council tax quickly became so widely accepted and non-contentious, especially as it bears common characteristics with the community charge. Local government finance is now far less important politically, the new council tax is uncontroversial, and there have been few problems of collection.

Central government can now exercise a great deal of control over local spending through the centrally-determined standard spending assessments, the 'ring-fencing' of areas such as housing, and the business rate (formerly locally determined but now set nationally), and there is very little chance of New Labour making any serious reform of local taxation (John, 1997, pp. 258–9). Such control devalues the notion of local democracy still further. In addition, the introduction of new methods of delivering local services has further reduced the amount of public spending made by local government.

The introduction of competition

The Conservative government's main reason for introducing competition into the provision of local authority services is simple; a basic belief in the inherent superiority of markets (Walsh, 1989, p. 33). For the Thatcher government, competition meant greater efficiency and therefore lower costs, and it was determined to cut public spending and also fight inflation by, amongst other things, reducing local government spending. As the previous section showed, this was partly achieved by increasing central controls over finances, but for acolytes, by far the most direct way was to expose local services to the reality of market competition (Harrison, 1996, p. 127). The rhetorical attacks on local government that accompanied the reforms (see Newton and Karran, 1985, p. 116), however, were guaranteed to arouse concern within local councils and emphasised the struggle for political power that accompanied the government's genuine concern about greater efficiency. The introduction of competition would weaken the power of both local authorities and, just as importantly, the public sector trade unions. Union demands on behalf of their workers, both in terms of pay and in terms of increased government spending in certain policy areas, accompanied by a perceived predilection for industrial action, were seen by new right ideologues as largely responsible for spiralling public spending and hence inflation.

A leading Conservative proponent of new right ideas for local government, Nicholas Ridley, was convinced that 'inside every fat and bloated local authority there is a slim one struggling to get out' (Ridley, 1988, p. 26). At the most radical, Ridley envisaged the local authority as an 'enabling' authority meeting once a year to monitor performance, allocate contracts and then disband until the next round of contracts had to be awarded. The spirit of Ridley underpinned the government policy initiatives designed to introduce competition into the provision of local services. These initiatives have had a major and probably permanent impact on the scope of local authority service provision. In particular, Compulsory Competitive Tendering (CCT), seen by some as the most important influence this century on the operation of local authorities (see Byrne, 1994, p. 463), has successfully challenged the notion of the local authority as the major supplier of public services to the local community. Under CCT, a wide variety of services had to be put out for tender to private firms, although existing council workforces were allowed to bid competitively as Direct Labour Organisations (DLOs) and were often successful in winning contracts (Walsh, 1995). A number of Acts during the 1980s introduced CCT for building and maintenance, highway construction and maintenance, cleaning, vehicle maintenance, school meals, refuse collection, sports and leisure facilities management, and the Local Government Act 1992 extended CCT into the very heart of the local authority by making a whole host of council 'white collar' management activities subject to CCT (Wilson and Game, 1998, pp. 339–40).

For some, the changes introduced by greater competition are largely negative. For example, the deregulation of a number of services, such as bus transport, traditionally carried out by local authorities, has not only introduced other operators into the arena; the concentration of operators on profitable routes has led to the traditional council operators cutting or scrapping less profitable (but often socially desirable) routes previously subsidised by the popular services. The lack of subsidies meant rises in fare prices (ibid., p. 342), leading to declining passenger numbers and further falls in the number of services. There is evidence that in leisure services CCT can result in substantial increases in charges (Nichols and Taylor, 1995, p. 609). There are also arguments that competition has negative effects on work forces, as whether the local authority workers have won contracts or the private sector is awarded the contract, the end result is that wages fall and conditions of service worsen (Ascher, 1987; Walsh, 1995). For critics, CCT and other competitive initiatives have either failed to achieve their stated aims or achieved them only by reducing pay and conditions and by redundancies. Such savings will, it is argued, be in the short term only as private firms establish monopolies by rapid mergers of successful companies who then bid across a wider range of local services (Walsh, 1989).

Others are more positive about the changes, pointing out the 'considerable savings' made when councils services are exposed to market forces (Harrison, 1996, p. 128). Forsyth maintains that local ratepayers win because privatised services are cheaper and local businesses win because contracting-out offers a greater opportunity for 'enterprise development and profit' in the new activity (1982, p. 988). In further support, it is undeniable that public reaction to the new service delivery has been, if anything, positive about the quality of services delivered (Lynn, 1992). Admittedly, public knowledge of the impact of changes is largely limited to high profile services like refuse collection, which have few of the problems associated with more politically charged but publicly lower profile policy areas such as community care.

The movement from local authorities being both funder and provider of local services towards a distinction between the two roles has clearly been significant, not least in encouraging a 'contract culture' and a recognition that it is perfectly possible for a local authority to 'assume additional responsibilities for service provision without necessarily involving itself in the direct provision of that service and the detail of its administration' (Clarke and Stewart, 1994, p. 169). Also, and often forgotten in discussions about the introduction of market forces into local authorities, the imposition by central government of internal markets was crucial. Walsh believes the impact was at least as great as CCT because the network of internal trading organisations 'created an ethos of commercialism within the local authority' (Walsh, 1995, p. 28).

Whatever the balance of 'good' and 'bad' in the enforced introduction of competition, there is absolutely no doubt that the changes introduced market discipline within local authorities, often for the first time. Although CCT has been replaced by an ostensibly less centrally imposed regime whereby councils have to make sure they get 'best value' when 'buying' services, the principle of competition is here to stay. Even more importantly, the requirement that council services compete with the private sector has contributed to the gradual change of culture inside local authorities. Also, in general, academic discussions of how to improve local democracy have moved from deploring the nature of the changes to accepting that, not only are the changes generally here to stay, but that despite some weaknesses of the 'overall system', there are a number of strengths in the new competitive environment (Clarke and Stewart, 1994, pp. 166–9).

However, largely because of the often undeniably traumatic effects of new right influenced policies on individuals and communities, it has been difficult for some critics to ascribe any benefit to their operation. It is often implied that there is an immoral or 'sinister' core to the new right critique and the policies its adherents have adopted (Butcher *et al.*, 1990, p. 165). Such criticism is misleading, as new right philosophy is 'driven by a powerful moral vision of free market values' (Pattison, 1994, p. 547) which has at its core a sincere belief in individual responsibility. While antithetical with the dominant post-war view taken by central state politicians and bureaucrats, who were convinced in Douglas Jay's immortal words that 'the gentleman in Whitehall really does better what is good for the people, than the people know themselves' (in Comfort, 1993, p. 671), to ascribe undisputed moral superiority to Jay's perception of government's role is ludicrous. The new right view does not believe that the gentleman in Whitehall knows best. That said, it is impossible to deny the powerful centralising forces of Thatcherite policies, apparently antithetical to new right ideology (see below).

While the introduction of more competitive forces has gradually been accepted and even praised, academics have few kind words to say about the spread of the topic I now turn to – the explosion in numbers and range of unelected quangos and agencies that characterised the Thatcher years and have continued beyond her government. The following chapter discusses this growth in more detail but it is necessary to briefly address some issues here.

The growth of the 'quango state'

The wholesale introduction of measures designed to introduce competition was just one expression of a major change in central–local relations that took place during the 1980s. The forces of centralisation, as the government removed powers from local authorities and placed them into ministerial hands via the creation of arm's length agencies, lessened local control over service delivery and placed severe strains on central–local relationships during the Thatcher years. In the early 1980s, a Conservative government that had indicated its intentions to 'cull' quangos (Pliatzky, 1980; Holland, 1981) created hundreds of new quangos, not only by removing powers from local government but also by devolving central government functions while retaining ministerial control over appointments to the new bodies.

There is no doubt that the last two decades have seen a major change in the government of local communities as what Davis and Stewart (1993) characterise as a growth of 'government by appointment' has accelerated. Weir and Hall (1994) estimated that there were 5750 'executive quangos', who have a specific role and spend public money on that role; in addition, there were some 674 advisory committees. The New Labour government has failed to reduce that number. Why has there been such a growth of quangos? There are a number of reasons, but four may be paramount. Firstly, Conservative governments wanted to make sure that services were delivered in accordance with their policy so bypassed an often recalcitrant local government with the creation of bodies such as Urban Development Corporations (UDCs) and Housing Action Trusts (HATs); secondly, and connected to the first reason, the creation of more quangos was part of an attack on local government's power (Ling, 1998, pp. 133–6); thirdly, privatisation of public utilities required the creation of new regulatory agencies to ensure the new private monopolies did not abuse their position; and fourthly, there has been a large increase in the opting out of institutions in (especially) health and education (see also Budge *et al.*, 1998, p. 256). The creation of quangos to usurp the basic functions of local government, in direct contradiction to pledges to roll back the state, emphasised that this was a power battle first and a 'zeal for reform' second (Ling, 1998, p. 134).

Accompanying the growth in quangos, there has been an increasing agentification of government, with agencies set up to carry out 'functions for which ministers have made provision as a policy decision but which they have decided to deliver at arm's length' (Massey, 1995, p. 77). Examples range from the politically charged, such as the Child Support Agency, to the uncontentious, typified by the Vehicle Inspectorate. Their degree of independence varies according to their political importance, social role, the political context in which they operate and the ideology of their own senior managers (ibid.) but they remain under the ultimate control of ministers. Put simply, ministers make policy; agencies carry it out. The major criticism of agencies is the undeniable blurring of accountability that has occurred. Can policy and management be separated in the way the programme maintains? The introduction of private sector principles into what are still public services has also led to fears that the traditional ethos of public service has either almost disappeared or been fundamentally damaged (for example, Chapman, 1996). Also, public sector trade unions argue that the benefits of agency status have tended to go to management rather than to lower grade staff and the public (Radcliffe, 1993, p. 14). In other ways, the prognosis is more favourable; operationally the new agencies have generally been successful in meeting their performance targets (admittedly not an entirely satisfactory measure). Although Weir and Hall (1994) are sceptical of the efficiency of some quangos, there is some evidence that service to customers has improved since agency status (Radcliffe, 1993).

The main effect of the growth in quangos and agencies on local government has been to weaken its status as the major actor in the local governance system; that system has been extended and become a set of institutions and actors whose first allegiance is not necessarily to any conception of democratic accountability. This 'new magistracy' (Morris, 1981) of appointed or, at best, indirectly elected 'quangocrats', owe their primary allegiance to the people who appointed them and not to local populations. Some commentators have seen the changes as part of a trend they dub the rise of the 'regulatory state' (for example, Majone, 1994), where governments assign responsibility for overseeing the newly privatised companies and the new agencies of government to new regulatory bodies such as OFTEL and OFWAT, overseeing telephone and water services respectively. The potential consequences for democratic accountability are apparent, including lack of transparency, lack of redress and the threat of 'croneyism' in appointments to quangos, agencies and regulators (see also Loughlin and Scott, 1997).

The impact of membership of the European Union

As central government has attempted to restrict local government's activities and successfully limited their capital investment, so local actors have more actively sought the help of European funding. British local authorities are among the most effective lobbyists in Brussels (Barber and Millns, 1993). Cities including Birmingham and Glasgow have used big EU funding to change their image, a transformation that has helped to attract further investment. The impact of membership of the European Union has been much wider and deeper than the issue of receiving funds through this and other sources such as the European Social Fund (ESF), the European Regional Development Fund (ERDF) and the various community initiative schemes which attempt to tackle issues including race, poverty and unemployment across Europe. All such bids require evidence of multi-organisational support so the need to seek funding has been an important catalyst in the creation of regional (and cross-regional) networks.

There have also been consequences for local democracy. Membership of the EU (and all that goes with it) is 'fundamentally changing the economic, social and political context for local democracy' (Benington, 1994, p. 5). The levelling out of social policy with Britain's endorsement of the Social Chapter following New Labour's election is only the most high profile of the impact of European legislation. For example, tougher regulations on environmental issues have largely had to be faced by local councils. Economically, a number of issues, such as deregulation and the Single European Market (SEM) have brought a centralisation of economic decision making within multi-national companies, leading to a loss of democratic control over industry and employment. Benington (1994) fears that control over Europe's economy is already being concentrated within a small handful of powerful multinationals and that, unchecked, such economic trends will further disempower local government.

That said, there are more positive portents. The generally more participative and empowered citizenry of the rest of the EU has already meant that European money looks more favourably on projects which involve empowerment and community participation. Whether they want to or not, local authorities have to involve communities to be successful in gaining money. Interaction with European institutions and actors has forged new relationships outside of the rather parochial and centralist culture of British politics (Barber and Millns, 1993). One of the biggest impacts of the EU on local political elites has been raising awareness of concepts such as 'subsidiarity' and the general belief of European politicians in the need for local autonomy. Also, alongside this has come an increasing awareness of different forms of local government, for example, in Sweden and Denmark, in which participation is seen as a positive force rather than an inconvenience.

The EU's impact on local economic development, while significant, has barely been perceived by local populations and some commentators (Marr, 1996) and not all local authorities have acted positively towards a dialogue with the EU (Wilson and Game, 1998, p. 147). However, most increasingly recognise the importance of influencing European decision-making – and crucially they *can* influence both general and specific strategies from Europe, especially if they can form 'cross-regional networks' in specific policy areas, as many far-sighted councils are now doing (Benington, 1994, pp. 15–16). The EU has certainly been used by local authorities to bypass central government's capital constraints and, perhaps for this reason, there appears to be an increasing interest among local politicians in the concept of a Europe of the Regions.

The rise of political parties

As noted in the previous chapter, there has been a significant growth in the acceptance of party politics at local level, which may have been facilitated by the growing numbers of younger people entering local politics as a launchpad for individual national electoral success (Widdicombe, 1986, Table 2.4, p. 22). The Maud Committee found that approximately two-thirds of councillors believed that the work of the council could be carried out more efficiently without the existence of political parties (Maud, 1967, Vol. 2, Table 7.11). Twenty years later Widdicombe reported that the existence of party groups, and the disciplined approach whereby councillors of the same party vote with each other on almost every issue, was now 'widely accepted' in the authorities they surveyed (Widdicombe, 1986, Para. 2.43, p. 31). In addition, Sharpe and Newton (1984) found that 'virtually all the county boroughs … were run on fairly well-developed party lines for all major, and some minor, policies' (Sharpe and Newton, 1984, p. 215).

The political complexion of local councils clearly has an impact on central–local relations. In 1979, the Conservatives were the 'natural party' of local government, especially in the South-East and the shire counties; they controlled 244 councils against the 109 of Labour, their nearest rivals, and were a significant presence in many more. By the end of John Major's government in 1997 only 23 local councils remained under the control of the party (they reached a low of 13 in 1995) and they had been overtaken by the Liberal Democrats in terms of both councils controlled and numbers of councillors (Rallings and Thrasher, 1997a). This was a phenomenal turn-around which contributed to the more hostile relationship between central and local government during the 1980s especially. The generally suspicious central–local relationship could be destined to continue as the Conservatives gradually win back control of more and more seats during Labour's years of central control; by 1999 they had regained control of 74 councils. The removal of powers from local government undoubtedly acted as a catalyst for greater political discipline and the apparatus of party politics now dominates local government. It might also be that when other roles are weakened councillors are more ready to play a political role (Connolly, 1996).

The Bains Report (1972) clearly presented a model of decision making that moved local actors more towards an ideal of cabinet decision making. More recently, the 'Modernisation in Local Government' (DETR, 1998) paper indicated that the belief in the superiority of such a model continues to be held by central government. However, as the example of central government shows, such a model will tend to tighten even further the grip political parties have on local government; local elites, aided by the whipping system and a powerful hold over appointments to prominent positions, can control the local agenda. Such an approach clashes with the more consensual approach new structures and networks require. The growing number of hung councils (in 2000 over a third of all councils were hung) might militate against the trend for party elite control as such councils facilitate more collaborative and inclusive decision-making procedures (Temple, 1996).

Changing attitudes to community empowerment?

Outside of voting, the traditional attitude of local government towards wider participation was not to encourage it. Recent years have seen a necessary change, with many councils introducing mechanisms for public participation at committee meetings and setting up initiatives such as citizen's juries. Despite such developments, most of the senior councillors interviewed for this study are distinctly unenthusiastic about too much public involvement. On the record, they are supportive; off the record, they have a different attitude, feeling that more open councils have failed to inspire the electorate or combat apathy. Notwithstanding the attention given to 'community involvement' when seeking funds for urban regeneration, and the soothing noises councils make when discussing the involvement of the local population, effective community participation in decision making is both rare and unencouraged. All three major parties talk about 'community empowerment' but the suspicion remains that much of this is rhetoric. Central government initiatives are similarly flawed. For example, one study found that 'neither City Challenge nor SRB [Single Regeneration Budget] are designed to empower local communities to any significant extent but to keep local communities "on side" as far as possible'; key decisions were taken by government officials and community organisations cooperated with this for the pragmatic reason that this was the only way they would get their money (Colenutt and Cutten, 1994, pp. 237–8).

It appears we have a governance system where community involvement is essential but where the 'partnership' is either cosmetic or heavily weighted towards government and business. Even this unsatisfactory involvement is seen by some as more welcome than Michael Heseltine's Urban Development Corporations (UDCs), run by largely government appointed placemen from the private sector (Marr, 1996). Although agreeing that the process had been bloody and expensive, Jenkins (1995, pp. 161–2) found a 'new spirit of partnership' had developed between UDCs and local councillors based on mutual interests, but Marr argues 'solutions' were inflicted on communities and large amounts of money wasted without any effective accountability (Marr, 1996, p. 103). Community empowerment has been limited, to say the least, and huge amounts of public money were poured into projects which made big profits for private companies while offering little significant benefit to the affected communities (Colenutt and Cutten, 1994, p. 249). Such projects also demonstrate that economic growth requires more than just private sector investment (Ling, 1998, p. 205). However, these are still early days and 'just as quality regeneration takes time, so does community empowerment' (Colenutt and Cutten, 1994, p. 249).

Perhaps just as importantly, the rhetoric that accompanies such programmes has introduced the idea that wider participation is something that must be encouraged; community empowerment is generating a momentum of its own, part of a 'deep-seated trend in the development of the social and economic organisation of western democracies' (Hambleton, quoted in Byrne, 1994, p. 463). However unenthusiastic many local governance actors might be about this, local groups are gradually learning that they can, indeed are required to, have an effective input, especially as a new generation of councillors and officers dissatisfied with the current inadequate processes of representation begin to move into positions of power (Gyford, 1991).

Central–local relations

We can see that central government has a number of mechanisms available to ensure local government does not exceed its powers and that since 1979 it has not hesitated to use the full weight of the law, as well as introducing even more mechanisms for control. However, not all changes which on the surface might appear directive have been totally bad for central–local relations. Regional government offices were set up with a senior civil servant in control to administer and coordinate the distribution of central grants and broadly to police the system. In fact, government officers have tended to act as relatively benevolent overseers and have helped to contribute to improving the relations between central and local government. For example, former Labour leader of Stoke-on-Trent, the late Ted Smith, characterised his city's relationship with David Ritchie, Government Officer for the West Midlands (GOWM), as 'excellent'. Stoke's chief executive Brian Smith believes that if you demonstrate that you have embraced the need for cooperation with business and other interests then help will be forthcoming and the relationship will be a mutually beneficial one. Likewise, the Audit Commission, set up to scrutinise local authority finances, is obviously working for central government but it has also been supportive of local councils 'when it has judged them to reflect the preferences of the local population' and been 'outspokenly critical' of central government policy it has deemed inappropriate (Wilson and Game, 1998, p. 105). Central–local relations are more complex than the usual 'warring' portrayal allows, as Rhodes (1981; 1988) has shown; the potential for conflict has always been there but so is the capacity for cooperation.

Indeed, the post-war relationship between central and local government did not always run smooth and Attlee's government clearly had a centralist agenda. Harold Wilson also had problems with local activists, notably over the abolition of grammar schools, but despite their central social and economic agenda, post-war Labour governments generally left local councils to get on with delivering the services. Post-war Conservative governments were even less critical; as Marr points out, a measure of local autonomy was some rein on the growth of the centralised post-war state (Marr, 1996, p. 67). From the late 1960s onwards, the attitude began to change. For example, in 1972 eleven councillors from the Labour controlled Clay Cross urban district council were disqualified from holding public office, surcharged and threatened with imprisonment for refusing to implement the Conservative government's

Housing Finance Act 1972 which required all councils to charge a defined 'fair rent' for council housing (Byrne, 1994, p. 100). In the mid-1970s, demands to local government to cut their spending came from the Labour government. However, the relationship could still be characterised as one of a feeling of mutual dependency. All that was to change in 1979, when the 'live and let live' dual-polity type relationship of the 1960s and early 1970s (Bulpitt, 1983) was replaced by the 'do as I say' approach of a government determined to achieve its aims. Margaret Thatcher's government's attack on local government, strangely for a prime minister whose beloved father had enjoyed a distinguished local government career, was characterised by a vitriol unparalleled in the history of the modern British state. She 'detested' local government and there 'is no reference in her memoirs that is not pejorative'; she 'frequently shocked' her colleagues with her vehemence (Jenkins, 1995, p. 41). Allies (with a compliant and largely Conservative-supporting press to the forefront) were roped in to attack the actors and institutions involved in local service delivery. New Right ideology, which should have taken local self-determination to its heart, argued that local government was full of budget-maximising bureaucrats (Niskanen, 1973) and had been hijacked by interest groups. In order to roll back the state, local government had to be curtailed. Paradoxically, one of the measures to achieve this, the creation of agencies and quangos, was to increase the unelected state to unparalleled dimensions.

The Conservative governments from 1979–97 were not the first (nor the last) to seek to neuter local government, although Thatcher and Major's governments were certainly the most consistently hostile. Between 1979–97 there were over 200 Acts of Parliament affecting local government. For many reasons, not least the need to respect the views of their local councillors, national politicians have nearly always spoken 'soft words' about the value of local democracy (Marr, 1996, p. 68) but the idea that British central government values local democracy is not supported by the evidence (Jones and Travers, 1994). Local government, especially as the powerful shire counties tended to remain Conservative or 'Independent', was viewed in a generally benevolent fashion although this did not stop post-war governments contributing to the gradual removal of local discretion. In contrast, Margaret Thatcher had embraced an ideology in which centralisation was seen as anathema and small competing units of local government a 'good thing' (Summers, 1996, p. 206) yet her governments were seen (even by its local supporters) as fundamentally opposed to local decision making. Although Nicholas

Ridley (1988) emphatically rejected the charge of attacking local government, others were publicly hostile even to the concept of local
democracy (Tebbit, 1993).

This is not as contradictory as it may seem. As Marr points out,
everything in the British system ensures that even the most mildly
radical central government 'is likely to diminish local autonomy' (1996,
p. 70). 'Radical' governments do not want a pluralistic political system
where competing democratically elected institutions can challenge
their agenda. The unitary state, coupled with an electoral system which
with Britain's geographical distribution of party support tends to
bestow overall control of the legislature to a single political party, gives
any government the mechanisms to eliminate or reduce alternative
power bases. The radicalism of Thatcherite conservatism has so attacked
the capacity of local government that a 'massive centralisation of
power' has taken place since 1979 (Saward, 1997, p. 23), described by a
distinguished commentator as 'the Tory nationalisation of Britain'
(Jenkins, 1995).

The 'hollowing-out' of the state thesis

An important point needs to be made here. Such an assessment appears
to conflict with the popular notion that there has been a 'hollowing-out'
of the state. This contentious notion defies easy definition, but the
phrase suggests 'the state is being eroded or eaten away' (Rhodes, 1994,
p. 138). That is, while the 'core executive' of prime minister, cabinet
and senior civil service appears on the outside to have the same powers
and functions as before, it is actually a hollow vessel. The core executive
has been losing or conceding functions to actors in civil society, losing
the capacity to control other state actors, and conceding capacities to
'supra-state entities' such as the EU (Saward, 1997, p. 20). Saward convincingly questions these three basic assumptions, arguing, for example,
that if there has been a weakening of executive power due to globalisation, there is 'considerable empirical support' that core executives have
compensated by seeking to shore up their internal power (ibid., p. 34).
British governments, despite the appearance of devolving power to
agencies and quangos, have actually been diminishing the capacity of
local government and largely keeping a rein on the capacity of the new
bodies they have created.

Rhodes's (1994) important account of hollowing out argues that a loss
of accountability has been one *unintended* consequence of the Thatcherite
agenda. As Saward points out 'confused lines of accountability may

foster a concentration of power at the core' (1997, p. 20) and it may therefore be 'fruitful to explore the hollowing-out hypothesis by regarding core executive actors as rational maximisers of their own power' (ibid., p. 35). 'Rational maximisers' will regard confused lines of accountability as contributing beneficially to their capacity to control events, and the loss of accountability may therefore have been *intended* under the Thatcherite agenda. The rational actors of the core executive have carved out 'a more subtle and flexible domestic role ... agentification, privatisation and the "rise of the regulatory state"' point to a 'conscious reshaping of the state' to allow them to enhance their control of national policy making. Central actors profess to love democracy and accountability, but as Saward concludes, 'they may say otherwise but we must watch as well as listen' (ibid.). Whatever the intention, and whether one sees it as cock-up or conspiracy, the evidence is clear; the fragmentation of service provision has been a major contributor to ensuring that political accountability in modern Britain has never been weaker.

The triumph of Thatcherism?

The changes in the competitive environment initiated or encouraged by the Thatcher government in particular are now broadly accepted by local and central actors. Cairns (1996) has suggested that there has been a loss of public faith in local government as a democratic institution, which others argue is a reflection of the 'vicious circle' of government restructuring which has 'fractured the direct relationship between local authorities and citizens' (Littlewood and While, 1997, p. 115). However, for defenders of Margaret Thatcher's policies, such attacks are the inevitable consequence of introducing unpopular but essential reform and whatever the failures, 'her governments tried more boldly to extend choice within the community than any of their twentieth century predecessors' (Harrison, 1996, p. 131). For the more critical, cumulative change has weakened the role of local government from one in which 'the local authority as local government had a capacity for local choice – even if it did not always fully use it' (Clarke and Stewart, 1994, p. 167) to one where choice is severely constrained and it is merely another actor. Before the reforms of the 1980s, the key role in community government was played by the local council, now a complex system of community governance more accurately describes the reality. Clarke and Stewart say this may have been part of a world-wide trend of administrative reform, but in the United Kingdom the process has been especially traumatic because British local government has been marginalised in the process, whereas in most countries where reforms took place local government was strengthened (ibid., p. 166).

This is an unnecessarily pessimistic view of the situation. A more positive contention would be that local government's search for innovative working practices, and especially the acceptance of the need for partnerships involving all sections of the community (although generally the local community still gets only lip service paid to its needs), has given it the potential authority to act as the main agent of an otherwise apparently incoherent and *ad hoc* system of service delivery. This is allegedly what the New Labour government wants:

> It is in partnership with others – public agencies, private companies, community groups and voluntary organisations – that local government's future lies. Local authorities will still deliver some services but their distinctive leadership role will be to weave and knit together the contribution of the various local stakeholders … bringing cohesion and co-ordination to the current fragmented scene.
>
> (Blair, 1998b, p. 13)

Such sentiments from the prime minister supports the hope that the election in 1997 of a New Labour government has improved central–local relations, creating a more collaborative and consultative environment (Elcock, 1998: Clarence and Painter, 1998). In reality, that collaborative environment had already begun to be established as local authorities accepted the permanence of the changes, forgot their political differences, and forged new relationships with national politicians and civil servants. For the Government Officer of the West Midlands, his relationship with local politicians was at least pragmatic and 'warmer than that in most respects', a warmth returned by many of the local actors interviewed. Bill Austen, former Labour leader of Staffordshire County Council, had a high regard for the Conservative Minister of State, David Curry, as did other local politicians.

The new government is benefiting, as in so many other areas, from the hard and often unpopular groundwork done largely by Thatcher's government; there was low trust and fierce battles between central and local government during those years but that was inevitable. Just as Neil Kinnock's hard-fought internal reforms of the Labour party prepared the way for Tony Blair's relatively effortless 'modernisation' with the bloodless ditching of central ideological tenets like Clause Four, so the creation of a more competitive environment in local government, one of

Thatcher's legacies to him, has enabled Blair to more or less let the new local governance actors get on with it. The battles to allow market forces more influence have largely been won and there appears little prospect that local government will soon return to the openly hostile ideological battles it once had with central government, even as local political control swings back to Conservatives.

Conclusion

As Conservatives return to local power, they find an environment they could only have dreamed of when they lost control of their treasured local councils during the 1980s. There is no reason for them to pick a fight with a government that has brought on board much of their party's thinking. Overriding all of the changes is the undeniable operational triumph of what used to be called 'Thatcherite' ideology and is now more widely seen as a 'new realism' by most local actors.

The permanence of the forces 'unleashed' by developments designed to improve competition and efficiency is apparent, and while local government is now only one of a number of agencies involved in local service provision and policy making it still possesses the capacity to be the most important one. However, the proliferation of new agencies has led to a fragmented and largely centrally controlled local system in which local government still lacks the power to provide a necessary coordinating role (see Stewart and Davis, 1994). Yet, in terms of both public recognition and overall role, elected local government remains by far the most important local actor. If notions of local democracy are to remain important in our changing conception of the role of government, then only local government with its base of electoral legitimacy can fulfil that role. The formerly over-bureaucratised and elite-led local government system has been challenged by the emergence of new organisations involved in local service delivery and by the need to respond to the imperative of a more competitive environment. Still uncertain, local authorities have often been reluctant to take a dominant role in new 'collaborative networks' (Clarence and Painter, 1998, p. 18). If Tony Blair is serious in his vision of the leadership role of local authorities in partnerships then they must be empowered to take on that role.

4
New Partnerships and Output Politics

Introduction

We have seen that since the early 1970s central government has been unhappy with the service provided by local government. Margaret Thatcher was a severe critic of local government actions and it was no surprise that during her time as prime minister a number of measures were introduced to provide alternative sources of service delivery. This process was dramatic and hundreds of new agencies and quangos have been created. Removing power from local government has been hailed as part of a process of decentralisation, yet distinguished and far from hysterical observers of politics go so far as to argue that local democracy and accountability have been seriously challenged (Jenkins, 1995). Led by the powerful political force that was Margaret Thatcher, central government increased its control over many aspects of public life. That process has not been reversed by succeeding governments. Since New Labour's election, what does appear to have changed is the government's willingness to publish output targets and then report its progress (favourable or otherwise) towards their achievement, arguably giving a greater measure of legitimacy to its centralising tendencies.

This chapter begins by examining some of the changes in the British system of governance in the last quarter of the twentieth century. The creation of the new and extensive range of agencies, quangos and private companies which are now involved in the public policy process at sub-national level has introduced new key actors to local governance networks. After a brief outline of the 'policy network' approach, I address the question of how far such networks can be 'mapped' in any useful fashion. Without the safeguard of direct electoral accountability offered by local government, such networks may be unaccountable, unrepresentative and dominated by the political concerns of central government actors. New Labour's promotion of action zones promises greater community involvement in decision making and I assess the relevance of such claims. The argument that the policy process is now output driven and dominated by the concerns of central government is assessed by particular reference to Health Action Zones.

From government to governance

The long-held view that a public–private divide is, as far as community decision making goes, both ethically proper and desirable is one that still dominates much political discourse. Also, the proposition that legitimacy and accountability are best achieved via a formal representative process still prevails; certainly, the public and private sector elites interviewed for this book largely shared this view. The belief that decision making in the community interest should be both public and transparent is also deeply held. It is not only the belief in the desirability of such a process that still prevails, its continuing existence is often taken for granted by participants and observers. None of these beliefs stands up to empirical investigation when examining the local and regional political process in Britain. The political and structural changes of the late 1970s onwards have not adjusted the process of government – they have fundamentally changed its nature.

The changes during the last quarter of the twentieth century in the way Britain is governed have been influenced by a wide variety of social, economic and political forces, but two major developments of the 1980s have largely contributed to the current system of fragmented local governance; (1) the so-called 'managerial revolution' characterised most memorably by CCT and the 'Next Steps' programme, and (2) the spread of quasi-government which accompanied the Thatcherite reformist agenda of those years. The movement towards market-influenced solu- tions, emphasising what became known as New Public Management (NPM), has transformed the public sector (Hood, 1991; Rhodes, 1996). The driving force behind this agenda was new right ideology, which stressed (among other things) a need to reduce the size of the 'budget- maximising' state bureaucracy and a belief in the superior efficiency of the private sector. It could also be argued that a deep rooted dislike and distrust of local government drove some of the proponents of change. Although members of the Thatcher government reject this, as I have already noted there appears little doubt about the feelings of her and her closest acolytes (Jenkins, 1995, pp. 41–4).

What is undeniable is that during the years of Mrs Thatcher's premier-ship, local decision-making took a back seat to a broader vision of Britain. The strong centralising streak in Thatcherism failed to acknowledge the legitimacy of competing sources of democratic accountability. Given that local government was perceived by new right ideologists as 'bureaucratic, inflexible and tied to the interests of its own workforce and traditional clientele' it was no surprise that the Thatcher government decided 'to by-pass local government and use alternative agencies to tackle the problem' (Butcher *et al.*, 1990, p. 100). Thatcher's government could never allow the growing number of Labour controlled local authorities and hung councils (where the Liberal/SDP Alliance began exercising considerable power during the 1980s) a major role in policy-making and notions of 'community politics' could not be expected to flower in such circumstances. Those cases where local communities were given economic power (for example, in London where the GLC distributed yearly grants totalling £40 million to community organisations involved in housing co-operatives, the arts, women's groups, and ethnic projects) became a target for attacks from Conservative politicians and the largely right wing press (ibid., pp. 148–9).

The clashes with the GLC (see Chapter 3) were just one expression of a major change in central–local relations that took place during the 1980s. The forces of centralisation – as the government removed powers from local authorities and placed them into ministerial hands via the creation of arm's length agencies – lessened local control over service delivery and placed severe strains on central–local relationships during the Thatcher years. Her Conservative governments created hundreds of new quangos and agencies, not only by removing powers from local gov-ernment but also by devolving central government functions while retaining ministerial control over appointments to the new bodies. This process contributed to a fragmentation of government in our cities and regions. The decisions which have to be taken to ensure a coherent response to the challenges brought by rapid social and economic change brings can no longer be made by the single institution of 'local government'. So, at a time of often considerable societal anxiety and uncertainty, just when an integrated policy approach is most essential, the capacity to achieve the necessary cooperation is wanting, and when clear civic leadership is required the capacity of local government (or any one actor) to provide this is reduced (Davis, 1996, p. 5).

The removal of powers from local government and the consequent fragmentation of service provision, with a variety of agencies involved, was one of the driving forces in the creation (or more accurately, development) of the formal and informal networks or partnerships found in local governance (Rhodes, 1997b). Probably contrary to the intentions of the then Conservative government, which while centralising economic policy probably intervened in local politics more than any other government this century, its policies forced local authorities to improve their interactions with both the private sector and other governmental agencies. There may well have been 'a certain inevitability about new forms of joint working' (Clarence and Painter, 1998, p. 9) in that the loss of local elected power caused by Conservative policies meant that many local authorities were effectively 'driven into partnership' because severely limited resources ensured they would otherwise have been unable to achieve their operational goals (Bruce, 1993, p. 333). Any examination of the new local governance system would see that much public policy is now delivered to the people by an often complex network of actors from the public and quasi-public, private and quasi-private, and voluntary and community sectors.

Policy network theory: and some empirical problems

The term 'policy network' is used throughout both this chapter and the book. Policy network theorists have often fundamentally disagreed over the correct appellation and typology to describe the interactions of groups involved in policy formation and implementation (Wilks and Wright, 1987; Wright, 1988; Marsh and Rhodes, 1992; Dowding, 1994, 1995). This book does not adopt a policy network approach but in any examination of the interacting interests of local governance actors it is necessary to outline briefly the theoretical literature and the way in which I intend to use the term 'network', although this brief discussion fails to do justice to the ground-breaking work done in this area (see Dowding, 1995, for a [very] critical review).

To put it simply, Marsh and Rhodes (1992) classify policy networks as ranging along a continuum from policy communities at one end to issue networks at the other end, with policy network as a generic category encompassing these sub-categories; by contrast, Wilks and Wright (1987) and Wright (1988) regard policy communities as the generic category and networks as a subset. Dowding is critical of existing approaches and dismisses the debate between them, arguing:

> there is no 'right way' of producing an exact definition of 'policy network' because the term is merely a means of bringing together certain elements of the world that contain similar characteristics.
>
> (Dowding, 1994, p. 64)

The 'correct appellation' of policy networks and communities is characterised by Dowding as a 'naturalistic fallacy' (ibid., p. 60) whereby the 'various schema are defended as though the ontology of the world depends upon them' (1995, p. 140). Despite this, he is dismissive of Wright's suggestion that 'policy community identifies those actors … who share a common interest and that 'network' was best used to describe 'the linking process … within a policy community' (Wright, 1988, p. 606). Dowding announced that he would use the term policy network 'as a generic category' and policy communities and issue networks as subsets, a 'choice based upon convenience rather than a belief it is "correct"' (1995, p. 140). For precisely the same reason of convenience, and without implying a general agreement with any of the policy network approaches, I will use the term 'network' (rather than, say, 'community') to describe the groups of actors cooperating in any particular policy area.

In a seminal series of works, Rhodes (1981, 1988) argued that the 'sub-central government' of Britain was composed of a complex system of networks. Much of the literature on these networks has referred to them as a relatively fixed group of actors, a local governance equivalent of what Lowi's examination of US government policy-making networks called 'iron triangles' (Dowding, 1995). That may have been an accurate assessment when Rhodes first talked of these networks of influence, but John points out the irony that just as Rhodes identified the 'informal relationships between a range of central and local and public and private bodies … these networks seem to have been fractured by the reform-minded Thatcher administrations' (John, 1997, pp. 253–4). Identifying the new networks which have sought to repair the 'fracture' is therefore as problematic as any question of appellation.

The new local networks appear to be ephemeral and relatively open. The interest group 'map' at local level is probably 'less ordered' than at national level (see Jacobs, 1993, p. 18) and the closed networks 'discovered' by Rhodes have been challenged by the more pluralistic environment created by local government's response to the Thatcherite agenda of the 1980s. This is not to argue that all actors are equal or that major decision-making is not dominated by a few elite actors/institutions, merely that access to the networks is, of necessity, more open than before. Indeed, given their ephemeral nature, it is arguable that the new relationships of actors barely qualify for the description 'network' as traditionally applied. A senior 'quangocrat' , also an academic, spelled it out:

> you have to abandon a structural notion of what a network is … you
> can map groups of actors but this tells you almost nothing about

how decisions are made…it fails to inform you of the significance of most actors.

(interview, 1999)

As another quango member put it, 'most groups are relatively unimportant most of the time' and despite the widening groups of actors involved in 'policy making' it's the 'same organisations as always', the major distributors of funds, who hold 'real' power (interview, 1997). Unless you 'play the game' you don't get taken on board, if you're not on board you lack both funds and function, and without these you tend to lack influence in the new system of governance.

Dowding (1995, p. 150) has called for a more descriptive approach (bounded by a formalised theory) to the study of networks. Of course, this implies that such networks can usefully be empirically examined by outsiders rather as early anthropologists such as Margaret Mead scanned 'primitive' tribes in the belief that they could really understand these alien cultures; it is well to remember that 'when the anthropologist arrives, the gods depart'. Most local authorities develop both formal and informal 'patterns of consultation' with quangos which exceed the statutory requirements and it is 'the quality and intensity of the relationship which is important, not the formal statutory position' (Greer and Hoggett, 1996, p. 160). The networks are 'usually highly opaque' (ibid., p. 166) and attempting to chart anything other than the formal relationship is, to say the least, difficult. The community of actors involved in delivering health policy, for example, is much more complex, flexible and shifting, than much of the literature implies and there are so many permutations that with the possible exception of low-level implementation networks they are probably incapable of being penetrated by inquisitive social scientists. At the elite level they are certainly not capable of outside penetration. As one council leader put it, the elite network is informal and operates on 'highly personal' terms. For example, while there was someone' outside' his council who 'if there was a possibility of some big investment' he would call on the telephone and say 'what do you think of this?', he would not name that person on or off the record. His understandable attitude was 'I trust your discretion, but…' (interview, 1997); he clearly did *not* trust my discretion.

The arrival of new actors in the system

The changing of the boundaries of the British state has meant that divisions between public, private and voluntary sectors have become 'shifting and opaque' (Rhodes, 1997b, p. 35) and the range of actors involved in delivering public services has become more diverse. The increase in both 'the importance and number of appointed bodies exercising government powers' (Davis, 1996, p. 4) has meant the status of local government as the major actor in the local governance system has been weakened by centrally directed institutions whose first allegiance is to ministers and whose democratic accountability is confused, weak or non-existent. Once dominant, local authorities now maintain a precarious position as the most important local actor, although the perceived need to endow public–private partnerships and quango-led programmes with a sheen of legitimacy means that their electoral base provides authority to schemes which would otherwise be seen as dominated by private sector interests. This role should not be underestimated; shrewd local bureaucratic and political leaders can negotiate benefits for local populations which would otherwise be missing from such schemes. However, the competition for influence has increased as new actors enter the local policy arena.

CCT introduced the idea of competition into many local authorities and although in-house bids were predominantly successful private companies won many contracts. Arguably, this was not a major blow to the power of local authorities. They were still responsible for overseeing such services and for awarding the contracts, and in many cases, CCT had merely built on existing practices (Brooke, 1989) as notions of decentralisation and cost centres 'originated as local government experiments' (John, 1997, p. 255). However, what CCT did do was introduce a new range of private sector actors into the policy community. Companies whose relationship with local government had previously been either non-existent or peripheral (for example, as suppliers or competitors) were now intimately involved.

Quangos

There has been a major growth in the number of quangos. For example, in the West Midlands, in 1986, the number of appointees to quangos were less than one-third the number of elected councillors. By the mid-1990s there were twice as many of the 'new magistracy'; the number of elected representatives had declined and the number of appointees to quangos had increased five-fold (Davis, 1996, p. 2). What is clear is that 'there is now an appointed world of local governance sitting alongside elected local government' (ibid.) and the roles and boundaries of local governance organisations have become even more confused than they have historically been.

The number and type of responsibility taken from local authority control are too great to list completely here (see Weir and Hall, 1994); a few examples must suffice. Local councillors were removed from District Health Authorities (DHAs) and Family Health Service Authorities (FHSAs) and Health Service Trusts with appointed boards were created. Polytechnics (now 'new universities'), further education colleges and sixth form colleges were taken out of local authority control and self-appointed boards of governors subject to nationally appointed bodies (the funding councils) were given the responsibility. Housing Action Trusts (appointed bodies) were created to take over some responsibilities and Urban Development Corporations have taken control of much planning and development away from local authorities (see Stewart and Davis, 1994, p. 29; Skelcher and Davis, 1996, p. 9). One of the most contentious relationships has been that between local authorities and Training and Enterprise Councils (TECs), set up in 1989 to 'run government training and give business leadership to local enterprise policies' (Cole and John, 1996, p. 9). Directors and chief executives of TECs have made no secret of their disdain for elected local government and are often highly critical of the motives of councillors (Thomas, 1994; Haughton *et al.*, 1997; interviews, 1997). It is therefore no surprise that TECs have generally adopted an aggressive and business sector orientation towards training and development which has further challenged the role of local government.

A change of government has not halted the increase in the number of quangos, with Education Action Zones being set up to take 'failing' schools out of local authority control and Health Action Zones being set up to improve the health of communities with the worst health problems. These developments have also increased the involvement of private actors in the 'public' sector. Education Action Zones encourage public and private cooperation to assist educational provision in deprived areas. A mark of just how far such cooperation has spread is Lambeth Council's decision to broker such a deal with a private firm supplying educational services and to employ a private inspection and advisory service to assist in raising standards in the borough's primary schools (Rafferty, 1998). Effectively, the private sector is helping to run schools in the public sector.

Agencies

As noted, one major trend of the 1980s and 1990s has been for an increasing agentification of government (Massey, 1995). The 'Next Steps' programme was proposed by the Prime Minister's Efficiency Unit at

Number Ten, chaired by Sir Robin Ibbs. The Ibbs Report (1988) recommended radical reforms in line with the dominant new right ideology of Thatcherism. The most important was that' policy' should be separated from 'management'. Government ministers would continue to make policy decisions but the management of those decisions should be undertaken by decentralised and relatively autonomous 'executive agencies' working to specific budgets and performance targets (Greer, 1994). To facilitate this, a number of 'semi-autonomous' agencies were created which were devoted to particular functions. In some cases, as in social services, a number of very large agencies were created, including the Benefits Agency (the largest executive agency) and the Contributions Agency; in addition, a new (and almost immediately controversial) social services agency was created, the Child Support Agency (CSA). Other government departments became even more fragmented, with the Inland Revenue broken down into twenty separate sub-agencies. There are now hundreds of such agencies administering central government policy throughout the UK and these executive agencies have quickly become powerful players in regional governance.

Indirectly elected boards

Joint boards and committees made up of elected councillors nominated by local authorities provide some local services. As Leach notes, these occupy 'an intermediate position' somewhere in between 'the direct accountability of local authorities and the opaque accountability process of appointed bodies' (1996, p. 74). While they *may* offer a greater measure of accountability than appointed bodies (and, arguably, executive agencies) the lack of scrutiny they receive means they are an unsatisfactory mechanism for delivering local services. They also, along with the existence of the quango-state, expose the myth of unitary local government. Even if we discount quangos and agencies, unitary authorities in Britain are effectively part of a two-tier system of government in which they are the lower tier to an indirectly-elected upper tier delivering and controlling services such as waste disposal, fire services and passenger transport.

Regional bodies

The creation in 1999 of regional chambers and regional development agencies in England as part of a stated devolutionary process towards 'home rule' have further increased the number of appointed boards involved in local governance. For example, the West Midlands Regional Chamber (an appointed forum) will work together with the West

Midlands Regional Development Agency (RDA), which is made up of 13 government-appointed members, including Professor Christine King, Vice-Chancellor of Staffordshire University, to encourage economic renewal in the West Midlands. These bodies enhance the position of business actors in the local governance system. The Director-General of the Institute of Directors says 'to be effective the RDAs must be business-led … it is essential that central government gives the RDAs sufficient freedom and coherence to succeed' (Letters to the Editor, *The Independent*, 19 May, 1999). As it is the government's wish that RDAs *will* be business-led, and given the role RDAs will play in economic renewal and helping to shape the future governance of the regions, their lack of accountability and uncertain status in relation to existing local government institutions cannot fail to raise concern.

The ubiquitous 'quango'

Before examining some general problems associated with the new actors mentioned above, the problems of nomenclature and definition of quangos, agencies and other appointed bodies need addressing. Whether any particular 'non departmental public body' (NDPB) is a 'quango' or an 'agency' is often unclear to even the seasoned observer. One crucial distinction between agencies and quangos is that executive agencies have Policy Framework Documents, formal written statements of the policies they are to pursue, which also detail their formal process of accountability and which are reviewed every three years or so. However, overall the differences between NDPBs are minor. Executive agencies certainly resemble the traditional perception of what a quango is more than they resemble local or central government departments (Budge *et al.*, 1998, p. 256).

Problems of definition are important because how an organisation sees itself will affect its interactions with its 'clients' and other organisations. For Haughton, Peck and Strange (1997, p. 91), 'TECs represent an unusual institutional form … perhaps best described as quasi-partnerships'. The state classifies TECs as 'non-profit making private sector companies … working under contract to the Employment Department Group' (Marr, 1996, p. 78). Marr argues this is 'creative verbal accounting' (ibid.), whereas it is simply untrue. Not a single TEC has recruited members by open advertisement (ibid., p. 91); recruitment is solely by government patronage and TECs are funded and effectively controlled by the Department for Education and Employment. Despite this, their perception of themselves as 'private sector' companies dictates a certain operational style. Other organisations are also difficult to define.

For example, 'Business Link Staffordshire' is supported financially by a wide range of public bodies and private sector organisations, ranging from the local Chambers of Commerce, Staffordshire Development Agency, the Staffordshire TEC and local councils. Business Link Staffordshire is an independent company, with a board made up of both representatives of local authorities and (like the TECs) with a majority from private sector business managers. It also seconds staff from local authorities. Just what is its status? Ostensibly private, it could not (indeed, *would not*) exist without the encouragement and financial aid of the state.

For some observers it now makes more sense to look at organisational differences in terms of other variables (such as decision making structures and size) than the particular sector an organisation is in (see Lawton and Rose, 1991, p. 6). It is unarguable that these bodies are variously constituted and central government would see UDCs, TECs, police authorities, self-governing schools and Health Action Trusts being as different from each other as they are from local councils; they all have 'their own systems of accountability and audit' (Wilson and Game, 1998, pp. 141–2). As far as local government is concerned the distinction is academic. They share in common 'the fact that they are effectively agents for central government carrying out government policies' (ibid.).

Although the term 'quango' arguably lacks utility as either a descriptor or as 'a starting point for an analysis of their role and influence' (Massey, 1997, p. 21) it is that most often used to describe non-elected public bodies. One of the recommendations of the Pliatsky Report (1980) into quangos was that 'NDPB' should be adopted but despite the use of NDPB by the Conservative governments, 'quango' has been remarkably resilient. Skelcher and Davis's important study (1996) of the characteristics and attitudes of quango members looked at eight types of 'NDPB', including 'limited companies' such as the Career Services Pathfinders and the TECs. Skelcher and Davis treated them all as 'quangos' and the sheer ubiquity of the term mean it is likely to prevail. Therefore, I will use the term 'quango', except when inappropriate.

Jobs for the boys?

The lack of representativeness and accountability of quangos and the secretive nature of their appointments procedures cannot fail to raise serious concerns. As Davis notes 'there can be no justifiable reason for applying different standards to different public services simply because the bodies which provide them are constituted in different forms'

(Davis, 1996, p. 3). Quangos need at least the same safeguards as elected local government. Quango members (like local councillors) tend to be 'male, middle-aged, middle-class and white'. Only 3 per cent are black or Asian, only a quarter are women and quango members under the age of 30 are almost non-existent. Almost a third don't live in the area over which they have decision-making capabilities (Skelcher and Davis, 1996, p. 12). The head of one educational establishment noted the excessive influence and representation of 'the great and the good' on NHS Trust Boards, on Regional Health Authorities (RHAs), as governors of educational institutions, and in non-executive board positions of companies, with the 'same names' appearing time and again (interview, 1997). The appointment processes to such bodies remain shrouded in secrecy and establishing even the most mundane details concerning membership can be difficult. We do know that personal and party political patronage appears to have dominated the selection process (Stewart and Davis, 1994, pp. 30–1). Posts are rarely advertised and there is no process of external scrutiny of a system where appointees are largely responsible for appointing other people.

New Labour's leaders appear determined to maintain this partisan and secretive process, raising concern that such bodies will continue to subvert the local democratic process; appointments of their supporters to NHS bodies since New Labour's election victory have dramatically increased (*The Independent*, 19 August, 1999). Supporting this, appointments to some quangos in North Staffordshire and Cheshire since New Labour gained power in 1997 could seem primarily concerned to bring in members sympathetic to the aims of the new government. A Labour county councillor and a Labour district councillor, both senior figures in their local parties, stated (independently of each other) that they were quite sure their political leanings were a reason for their appointments to public bodies, although they both stressed they had other important qualifications. This may be so, but they were sounded out in secrecy and appointed without any public consideration of their suitability for the posts. Neither of them seemed concerned at the lack of scrutiny of such appointments, or doubted their own suitability for the positions, viewing them as the beginning of a process to redress the balance of 18 years of Conservative domination. Off the record, one quango member admitted he had already been 'discreetly' sounded out to take over the senior role in his quango when the chairman retired (interviews, 1997). Quangos are public bodies spending taxpayers money and such appointment procedures are therefore indefensible.

A major criticism of Next Steps is the decline (or at the very least, blurring) of accountability that has followed the changes. Can policy and management be separated in the way the programme maintains? The contractual conditions and arrangements under which agencies were placed were designed to, as closely as possible, create a quasi-market situation and impose the disciplines of the market (Budge *et al.*, 1998, p. 252). Cost targets often meant redundancies, and executive agencies were soon given more discretion on methods of recruitment and pay levels, taking them potentially further away from the formal accountability expectations, ethics and management styles of their former government departments. A clear example of the dangers is provided by the CSA. The agency was assigned to track down errant fathers (largely) and extract maintenance payments from them, which both emphasised the popular Thatcherite conception of individual responsibility and offered the promise of reduced state spending to dependent mothers and fathers. The CSA soon realised that establishing the whereabouts of non-paying absent partners and then ensuring they would pay was an expensive and time-consuming process. It was easier to meet its targets (and earn its bonuses) by dramatically raising the amount being paid by those who had already accepted responsibility. The resulting unfairness and widespread distress caused by the CSA's actions provide a graphic illustration of one potential downside of introducing market forces when implementing legislation. Attempts to assign responsibility for widespread public disquiet saw ministers refusing to accept it was a problem of policy and redirecting criticism towards the agency itself, especially its chief executive Ros Heppelwhite, who took the brunt of the criticism. However, blaming the CSA for the action they took is inappropriate. In the new policy environment, it took the steps it needed to in order not to be penalised and those who framed and drafted the legislation and conditions of contract should have been culpable. Claims that policy and implementation can be separated need to be treated with considerable caution.

The claim that quangos are less 'politicised' than local government also needs to be treated with caution. It is not only the interests which are excluded by the way appointments are made (as we have seen, one 'good chap' appoints another 'good chap') it is also the case that 'the articulation of independence can conceal a real set of political interests whose existence is clouded by the lack of openness and local accountability of the membership' (Skelcher and Davis, 1996, p. 20) of such locally appointed bodies. In the main, one set of interests appears to predominate, which given the composition and appointments procedure is only to be expected; for example, the TECs are quite clearly dominated by a business ethic which has often regarded public service interests with suspicion (Haughton *et al.*, 1997). However, party political influence is also clearly present in quangos, both in the appointments procedures and in the way they must achieve centrally set output targets. The autonomy of quangos will vary according to '(a) their political importance; (b) their social role; (c) the prevailing political context in which they operate; (d) the ideology of their senior managers' (Massey, 1995, p. 77). The more important they are, then the less likely they will be allowed discretion. When the policy areas are those where high profile targets have been set, like health and education, the likelihood of significant local discretion may be minimal, a point examined below.

Local policy community

At the elite level, the networks of influence are almost completely informal, although the relationship may be formalised (and importantly, legitimised) by the creation of, for example, a 'Community Forum' such as Stoke-on-Trent's 'City Partnership Forum' in which elite interests dominate. While such approaches can widen the participants, this process tends to occur only after the process of fundamental decision-making has taken place. The City Partnership Forum was set up to create a city in which 'the skills … of the people of Stoke-on-Trent are harnessed and directed towards securing the highest levels of prosperity; the community as a whole is able to enjoy the benefits of a high quality of life' and which would 'work in partnership involving all sectors of the community' (Forum document, 28 January, 1997). However, just one of the 62 listed representatives at a meeting of the Forum I was invited to was from what could be even remotely described as representing a community group (the Chief Executive of Cobridge Community Renewal). In what was an extremely high level group of people (including chief executives from Staffordshire's leading companies, both Keele and Staffordshire University vice-chancellors, multi-millionaire entrepreneurs, local government leaders, and a range of key people from quangos, church and the voluntary sector) it was clear that the process was elite driven. A total of 26 people were from the business community, and there were 11 local government officers, 3 central government officers, 2 senior local politicians, 8 quango/agency members, together with a smattering of trade union, church, charitable and voluntary representatives. 52 were men and 10 were women, predominantly white and middle aged, yet the meeting congratulated itself on the representativeness of its members. The idea that members of the electorate might be involved, or that the involvement of voluntary organisations might extend beyond the Director of the Council for Voluntary Services or senior churchmen seemed unconsidered. Also, most actors remain peripheral, if important for funding purposes; the discussions were dominated by the concerns of business. That there were only 2 local politicians there, the leader and deputy leader, yet 11 senior local government officers, could also be an indication of the tight grip kept on the political input into such forums by political and bureaucratic elites.

Community groups come into such projects and forums, if at all, only after the general direction of schemes has been 'decided'. If they are involved in the early stages their lack of professional planning, economic and business expertise tends to mean their input is an 'add-on' to professional solutions which dominate the discourse. For example, although there was some community consultation in the 'Stoke Approach' project to regenerate the heart of the city, improvements have been based on 'sound financial and commercial advice…commissioned from consultants'. Over a year into the project 'community forums' in each of the five Stoke Approach areas were still not established. The forums will 'have a powerful voice in how the project will tackle the improvements and regeneration of the area' (*City News*, June 1999), but by the time they are set up the direction of the project has been established by other interests.

This is not to disparage the real achievements of Stoke Approach, which has certainly had a positive effect on the quality of lives of residents, but the needs of industry and traditional public service providers appeared predominant in the crucial early stages. Organisations like the Joseph Rowntree Foundation have noted that *equal* partnership for local residents is an important ingredient for success in public–private partnerships (*Findings in Focus*, May 1999, p. 4) and that means *open* forums need to be established as early as possible, rather than a consultative process (for example, questionnaire based citizen's panel responses) from which leaders can extract the 'sense'. That said, local communities are becoming more pro-active in moves to regenerate their neighbourhoods. Empowerment is a powerful weapon in ensuring that partnerships between the voluntary, statutory, private and community agencies achieve their aims; these issues are examined more fully in the following chapter.

New Labour, new collaborative partnerships: life in the action zones

Action zones are based on Tony Blair's belief that partnerships spanning public, private, community and voluntary organisations will provide local government with the opportunity to use their 'distinctive leadership role' to 'weave and knit together' the contributions of 'local stakeholders' (1998b, p. 13). Arguably, the creation of Education Action Zones (EAZ) and Health Action Zones (HAZ), as well as giving local authorities the chance 'to develop a central role within networks that will place them at the heart of local governance' (Clarence and Painter, 1998, p. 16) also suggests (as noted in Chapter 3) that a 'more collaborative public discourse is emerging under New Labour' (ibid., p. 13). However, the partnerships much favoured by New Labour are not the same thing as 'networks', at least in the sense the term is adopted by policy network analysis (Clarence and Painter, 1999, p. 1). Partnership agencies have been artificially created at the insistence of external funders. Partnerships are a distinct form of governance with a 'life cycle' encompassing characteristics of markets, hierarchies and networks which can create stresses within quangos conflicting with the necessity for more collaborative ways of working (Lowndes and Skelcher, 1998, pp. 326–7). By contrast, actors in networks have tended to evolve patterns of need and cooperation. It may even be that networks could be seen as examples of local control over policy, while the new central emphasis on formal partnerships is yet another way of maintaining central control in the new policy environment. On the other hand, it could be argued that with New Labour's arrival in governance, the policy agenda has become (even if only superficially) more positive towards the idea of multi-agency partnerships with local authorities as key actors (Blair, 1998b). Also, these new partnerships build on the extensive range of formal and informal networks that have risen to help local actors achieve their aims in the new environment.

As I have already argued, most such networks are essentially part of an elite driven policy process. North Staffordshire's 'health and well-being improvement programme' illustrates the point. Driven by the health authority, it is produced with the help of 'partner agencies' all of which are statutory organisations or professional groups of one sort or another (North Staffordshire Health Authority, 1999, p. 1). Not a single representative of the wider community was there to even challenge the presumptions of these experts on exactly what 'local health needs' were. An 'understanding of health and health care needs of a population is fundamental' (ibid., p. 3) said the report and yet the timescale for drawing up the programme 'has led to limited public involvement' (ibid., p. 2). Despite the claims for public partnership, community involvement was minimal in establishing the aims of the programme. The same criticism that the policy agenda was elite driven (this time in response to central government's wishes) could be levelled against action zones.

HAZs provide a good example of an output driven policy environment. Successful bids have to be (a) competitive and (b) measurable by 'out-turn delivery'. The aims are specific outputs with numbers against them, another example of the move from a concern with processes to a concentration on output politics. There is undoubtedly a policy network involved in bidding for and then implementing the measures designed to produce the aims of the HAZ. However, those aims are professionally set by professional health care managers and clinical professionals who assess the probable aims of central government and then propose what is realistically attainable; that is, what will be acceptable to central government. Hughes argues that 'the views and experience of local people [are] regarded as of equal value to evidence obtained through more traditional means' (Hughes, 1998, p. 44). This may be so, but those views are only taken into consideration after a strategy has been decided. A member of the health authority put the process this way – 'if you underbid, you lose… [but] if you overbid it is a disaster if you win because you then can't deliver your out-turn promises' (interview, 1999). For him, this meant the bidding process was characterised by 'realism and pragmatism' and people could not build on the 'basis of ideology or justice or fairness or wish list but on what can realistically be achieved' (ibid.). It is in the professionals interest to set 'achievable deliveries'; to be blunt, the public and private interest is not marching side by side in this process.

Also, the health authority member felt that elite domination was both inevitable and desirable, which prompts the thought that too many interests involved in setting bids would mean an overlong process of 'partisan mutual adjustment' (Braybrooke and Lindblom, 1963) for local actors. The process of looking for partners, according to the health authority member, follows the production of 'policy driven aims'. He argued the team looked for partners who would answer 'yes' to the question 'are you willing to help and support us?' in achieving these aims. The process of drawing in those partners was haphazard; 'I' ve been in meetings… quite far down the line when someone says "you really should have invited so-and-so" and then someone says "okay, write to them, put them on the circulation list"'. So, the network might include a number of actors essential to delivering a part of the aims but whose interest is specific to just one small part of a project. The entire process is 'essentially RHA led'. The major issues, including important issues of implementation, are 'fudged'. Key questions such as, 'is there a mechanism for allowing money coming in through the Health Authority route to be spent via the social services route?' remain unanswered (interview, 1999).

The end justifies the means? Or a new and radical environment?

The rubric, 'the end justifies the means' implies a government unconcerned with ethical questions and this would be both unfair and to underestimate the electoral backlash which malpractice might cause. But it is the aims that are important to New Labour. The methods are up to the collection of organisations delivering the improvements in health care. At the most charitable, the government is effectively trusting service providers to deliver improvements and believes they will do this 'ethically'. The candour of the health authority member I spoke to was extraordinary, explaining his wish to remain anonymous, but he did not think the nature of the process was anything other than inevitable, given what he described as New Labour's wish to create real coordination; 'nobody's ever done it before… listed all the players… [the government says] you get the money if you deliver joined-up government'. When asked who is accountable he notes the difficulty of answering this question – there is a 'lead official in the health authority… [but] the integration of the gaps between organisations… is extraordinarily difficult and there are varying degrees and types of public accountability' in the network, further complicating the issue (interview, 1999). In the end, it could be plausibly argued that nobody involved in *delivering* the services is accountable, but central government is, as either a minister is forced to resign or the government's chances of re-election are harmed if its well publicised outputs fail to be achieved. Unsurprisingly then, quango chiefs are under enormous pressure to achieve policy aims and that pressure passes down the line to those delivering services.

At one level, the creation of new agencies and new partnerships at local level would seem to indicate a more pluralistic policy environment, a contribution to the 'hollowing out of the state' outlined (and disputed) in the previous chapter. The belief that the Blair government 'is anxious to restore community responsibility and devolve power' (Elcock, 1998, p. 34) is widely held (see Plamping *et al.*, 1998, p. 4). However, it may be more correct to argue that what appears to be the devolution of responsibility is just the opposite. The creation of complex implementation networks or partnerships could then be seen, not as a loss of control by central government but as a change in the method of securing central control 'as the centre sheds costly and time-consuming implementation tasks to concentrate on core functions of policy determination, monitoring and evaluation' (Taylor, 1997, p. 442).

Responding to the criticism that radical policy change was not possible in the incremental and output-orientated policy process now dominating the discourse, a prominent local Labour politician (speaking off the record) noted the way in which New Labour had introduced radical change while preserving the more market influenced changes of the previous government. In health care provision, the internal market (with hospitals competing against each other to provide health care) had been ended by New Labour. The creation of HAZs had altered the focus of managerial activity 'making the object of care…the driver and making a serious attack on the producer driven nature of highly professionalised activities such as clinical medicine'. These changes were 'highly radical' and happening quickly in:

> the biggest civilian employer of the western world, the health service… [they] alter fundamentally the conditions of service, the conditions of work, the work expectancy and career expectancy and the rewards of some of the most powerfully organised professions in the UK…this policy environment is radical by any standards.
>
> (interview, 1999).

Importantly this was not radical ideological change, but 'radical cultural/managerial change' (ibid.). For him, the radical nature of the changes has to do with the focus of power and not with particular proposals. An organisation previously 'over-professionalised and producer driven…being run for the benefits of the people who worked in them' were being redirected towards meeting the goal of a healthier population' (ibid.).

The belief that such changes are beneficial to the public is unchallenged. However, quite why producer driven changes will have the public interest at heart is unclear. If action zones are to be truly radical they will have 'to find new ways of working that are not based on traditional power structures' (Plamping *et al.*, 1998, p. 5). Actors from outside the 'usual suspects' need to be engaged along more traditional players (ibid., p. 12) but there appears to be little enthusiasm amongst current players for such moves. Other changes point up this dilemma even more clearly. Introduced by the New Labour government in April 1999, Primary Care Groups (PCG), designed to deliver health care to communities of around 100 000 people, are an example of the devolution of budgets in the health service. The majority of a Health Authority's budget connected to buying health from producers has been given to those dealing face-to-face with health problems at a domestic level, that is, General Practitioners (GPs). Newcastle-under-Lyme in Stafford-shire is a typical PCG. The town has a population of just over 100 000 and a PCG run by a team of thirteen; 7 GPs, 2 nursing representatives, a health authority representative and someone from social services. There is one lay person, and an appointed chief executive. While not disputing the public service interest most members of the medical profession evidence, the PCG team is producer dominated and direct community involvement is negligible.

From process to outputs

There are tensions inherent in the policy, and these lie in the way Labour has presented action zones:

> as an opportunity for local authorities and other stakeholders to develop new and different ways of working and to implement novel ideas for difficult problems. This has been increasingly tempered by both the implicit and explicit requirement from central government that the initiatives…meet key pre-election promises.
>
> (Painter and Clarence, 1999, p. 15)

Meeting their 'targets' has become a central concern of quangos. The movement away from a concern with processes towards a stress on outputs means that quangos such as health authorities are increasingly expected to deliver measurable improvements in their services. Education and health action zones are largely output driven. Central government is prepared to allow some flexibility to local actors in implementation provided they fulfil the targets, although the high profile, highly prescriptive and relatively short-term nature of education targets means EAZs probably have less flexibility than HAZs (ibid., pp. 16–17).

At national level, New Labour's five pledges to the electorate before the 1997 General Election established, along with some rhetoric about strengthening the economy, four specific performance targets – for example, a promise to 'cut class sizes to 30 or under for 5, 6 and 7 year olds' and to half the time from arrest to sentencing for young offenders (Labour's 1997 election manifesto). Since their victory, more specific promises have appeared in many areas of government. This process, of course, preceded New Labour. Executive agencies have annual business plans and three to five yearly corporate plans which tie them in to delivering certain minimum standards of service (Greer, 1994, p. 60). Even earlier, the post-war Conservative opposition promised to build 300 000 new homes per year if elected, a target it achieved partly by lowering housing standards from 1951 onwards. Governments have, however, mostly shied away from posting too many such hostages to fortune. Performance targets, league tables and customer charters, were often criticised by Labour when in opposition, as were the activities of regulators.

However, since its election, New Labour has introduced a 'new generation' of such monitoring and inspection agencies, including an Ofsted-like health inspectorate and a new local government inspectorate to oversee the implementation of 'best value' (see Painter and Clarence, 1999, p. 10). So, the New Labour government could be characterised by the same emphasis on nationally set targets as the previous government – the cynic might argue *plus ça change* but there is a significant difference. The Conservatives' 1992 *Health of the Nation* White Paper set a total of 27 health 'targets' but with the emphasis on achieving changes in sexual behaviour and eating, drinking and smoking habits they were widely criticised for being 'unrealisable' (BBC News *Online*, 19 May 1998). Likewise, Citizen's Charter commitments have tended towards the bland and unverifiable such as promises to deliver 'high quality services'. Specific promises are normally confined to the commonplace (if important) such as letter and telephone response times (Staffordshire County Council Charter, October 1993).

There appears to be a fundamental shift in government's acceptance of the need for the public to be given measurable output targets. Blair's commitment to output measurement clearly goes beyond both the 1992 White Paper's 'sound bite' and Staffordshire's prosaic promises. Although sound bites are everywhere in Tony Blair's party, in amongst the generalisations about 'improving standards', the targets set by New Labour tend towards the high profile and measurable. 'Improving standards' is almost incapable of being verified – cut hospital waiting lists by 100 000 is measurable. Blair' s frustrations at the slow change of pace in the public sector and the consequent delay in delivering service targets led to outbursts against outdated practices inhibiting New Labour's policy reforms. It is hard to avoid the thought that these outbursts were timed to prepare the way for the admittance in New Labour's second 'annual progress report' (another innovation) that it had 'so far' failed to achieve two of its four specific special election pledges, including cutting

NHS waiting lists. More positively, the report claimed that 90 of 177 election promises had already been met, although the Conservatives said Labour had only achieved 45. The Liberal Democrats dismissed Blair's promotion of the report as 'public relations gloss' but this overlooks its significance (*The Guardian*, 27 July 1999). Government is setting central targets and 'forcing' local service providers to work towards them, but by Blair's actions he appears to be signalling that central government is also taking responsibility for failure as well as success. Although that does not preclude them spreading the blame around a bit, the recognition that it is New Labour that will be judged if these targets are not met gives some authority to central direction. Macintyre (1999) believes Blair's annual report is an honest if somewhat limited attempt to make government more accountable to taxpayers. Since Blair, the spending departments are given clear targets against which the success or failure of ministers is judged; the formerly great Departments of State are now arguably little more than agencies of central government (or perhaps more accurately, agencies of the prime minister). Public Service Agreements 'are designed to measure each minister's output against his or her budget [and] the Treasury apparently has a matrix of 525 departmental objectives'. Unlike Macintyre's generally benevolent view of the process, for Jenkins, these are 'the madcap scorecards' by which ministers now get judged in Blair's 'joined-up dictatorship' (Jenkins, 1999, p. 24).

There is a local downside to nationally set targets; they can act as a restraint on local actors, limiting the scope for innovative action. Nothing must be allowed to get in the way of achieving such high profile targets, as government threats of privatisation towards quangos (such as the CSA) unable to achieve their targets indicates. As a Labour councillor, firmly in the Blairite camp, eloquently put it in the currently fashionable jargon of New Labour-speak:

> if the 1980s taught us anything it was that the Thatcher administrations demonstrated that to get solutions which were faster, more targeted, more effective, wherever you stand politically, you drove it by driving the policy environment from the top and letting the micro-level find local solutions to the aggregate out-turn demanded of them.
>
> (interview, 1999)

For some, there may an uncomfortable echo of the Thatcher government, which trumpeted its weakening of local government's power over other local actors while simultaneously (and silently) strengthening its own grip over those actors (Pollitt *et al.*, 1998, p. 179).

The move to outputs has gone beyond the setting of executive/ departmental targets designed for local agencies to achieve and has entered new constitutional territory. Following critical reports of Wormwood Scrubs prison by Sir David Ramsbotham, the Chief Inspector of Prisons, the prisons minister (Lord Williams) and Martin Narey, Director-General of the agency set up to run prisons, the Prison Service, both said they would resign if the west London jail was not' turned around' within 12 months (*The Guardian*, 26 June, 1999). Such ministerial behaviour is unprecedented in Britain. Ministers and quangocrats have traditionally resigned (if at all) for failures of correct process (or far more often) as a result of personal sexual and financial scandals. Now, a possible precedent has been set that ministers and quango heads who fail to achieve specified outputs will be expected to resign.

At one level, measurable outputs would seem to offer the 'consumer' of public services an easily identifiable target by which to decide whether an agency or government department is performing up to scratch. One problem with outputs is that targets become the sole aim and other important aspects of policy become secondary to their achievement. The Child Support Agency is set a financial target; the wider and much more important ideological output for a new right government of encouraging individual responsibility is lost. In schools, there is a danger that achieving the 'average' or above in test results becomes the goal of all teachers, especially with the threat of performance-related pay hanging over their heads; the more important but unquantifiable goal of encouraging each pupil to achieve their potential becomes secondary and education becomes a narrowly focused activity.

The other major problem of output dominated politics is how to hold politicians to account. If there are clear lines of accountability upwards from local agencies to ministers then it is possible to argue that democratic accountability is maintained, although one might prefer that accountability be more directly connected to the local population. There is concern that accountability for outputs will not be as 'tight' as that for process, but if the specifications are detailed enough and the 'sanctions for non-performance' severe enough (Deleon, 1998, p. 543) such concern could be misplaced (see also Painter and Clarence, 1999). There is also a fear that if the continental experience is replicated in Britain, agencies will become 'increasingly independent with their own distinct cultures and a marked reluctance to accept central guidelines' (Rhodes, 1996, p. 662). If so, the lack of 'downward' accountability would become more serious. However, Blair's high profile association with Labour's 'annual progress report' does at least mean that voters have something other than rhetoric and the 'feel-good' factor by which to judge the government's overall performance at a general election, and arguably answers some of the concerns about accountability. However, an independent body measuring the government's performances against such output targets – the National Audit Office already performs a similar function for Parliament – might be better than relying on the government to assess its own performance.

Conclusion

The movement from government to governance has introduced new actors into local governance networks. The networks have become more complex and local government's role in them less obviously powerful. Where once local authorities dominated the local policy process they now have to adopt more subtle tactics to achieve their ends. What is clear is that despite the insistent rhetoric of community empowerment which has accompanied the creation of quangos, most 'networks' are producer driven and community involvement in decision making is still minimal. The new partnerships such as Health Action Zones, which appear to offer an ideal forum for community involvement in an important area are not only producer/professional dominated, they may also be dancing to a tune composed by central government. Effectively, an HAZ could be seen as a local agency, albeit one more closely connected to the needs of a relatively small community than previous agencies.

Following New Labour's election victory of 1997 there were signs that a more collaborative discourse was emerging and that the new governance system could provide local authorities with an important role in co-ordinating and legitimising networks. However, the output politics which predominate New Labour thinking seems to require strong central control of policy and limited local discretion or effective community involvement. Tony Blair can defend this by pointing out the indisputable fact that the electorate will hold him responsible if local actors fail to deliver the targets.

Perhaps the most far-reaching consequences refer to constitutional questions which Next Steps introduced. The rationale for the traditional government department has been 'undermined' and the status of Whitehall departments and agencies is ambiguous. The Cabinet Secretary may maintain that agencies are 'very much a part of the departments to which they belong' and argue that such reforms are a managerial reform rather than a 'constitutional innovation' (Wilson, 1999) but the greater flexibility demanded by the agencies has meant that traditional lines of accountability back to ministers have become convoluted or fractured. The traditional civil service characteristics of impartiality, anonymity, and unquestioned commitment to the public interest, may be an inaccurate description of much of the processes of bureaucratic government. However, whether myth or reality, they have been embedded in civil service culture (and part of the myth of British democracy) since the days of the Northcote–Trevelyan Report of 1854, and have been seen as fatally weakened by the introduction of agencies (O' Toole, 1993). The removal of many functions from the clear control of directly elected actors has caused concern about ethics and accountability in the new system. The following chapters will specifically address the concerns about community participation, damage to the public sector ethos, and problems of accountability that have been raised by the new system of governance.

5
The Apathetic Community?

Introduction

Given that one of this book's requirements for a more democratic and responsive local governance system is wider community involvement in not only holding public and semi-public organisations accountable, but also to be more closely involved in agenda setting and decision making, I spend some time in this chapter examining the concepts of both community and participation. To be representative, local governance has to involve empowered communities and they must be well informed and motivated. Much of the evidence suggests the opposite but this may be misleading. For example, low levels of local electoral turnout are often cited as evidence of community apathy towards local politics but they might just as easily be held up as demonstrations of public awareness of the futility of turning out to vote. How do local people feel about the communities they live in and how do they identify with their area? Will an attachment to a community lead to greater participation in local politics? Such questions need to be addressed if effective solutions to the crisis of local accountability are to be found.

A key reason for the current enthusiasm for greater community involvement is rooted in the need for local governance actors to demonstrate to funders (especially the European Union and SRB bids) that there is widespread involvement in projects from all potential interests, and the relevance of such involvement in decision-making is assessed. Apathetic local populations are often cited as a good reason for a failure to involve them in policy making but apathy can be challenged by earlier involvement in community projects and more localised decision-making structures. Such measures are a prerequisite for greater interest and involvement. New methods of communication such as on-line community networks can also challenge apathy. In addition, the media have a part to play. The continuing success of local newspapers and local radio stations in increasing readers and listeners demonstrates an important truth, that people do care about their local community and are interested in reading and hearing about it. The way to encourage greater involvement and to harness the concern and energy that the growing number of community projects and self-help groups demonstrate is to devolve decision making to the lowest possible level and trust the people. I am aware that I am committing the sin here of treating community or civic society as a way of 'making government work better, rather than less' (Etzioni, 1997, p. 142). Given one of the arguments of this book is the need to improve citizen participation in government, that sin is difficult to avoid, although I accept Etzioni's point (ibid.) that many of society's 'needed remedies' could be better supplied by individual action and cooperation rather than state intervention.

Supporters of community government can have a rather rosy view of the past, as with Stewart's belief that 'the strength of urban government in the latter part of the nineteenth century was an expression of the community governing itself' (1989, p. 240). This fond picture of a local democratic system working 'under the censorship of local opinion' (see Dearlove, 1979, pp. 28–30), overlooks the composition of that governing community, which was even less representative of the population than it is today. In addition, the merits of wider community participation were scarcely an issue. Local government's somewhat smug sense of self-satisfaction that all was well with the local democratic system may well have been sustained by the general lack of interest and involvement in local politics, but the post-war years were (eventually) to produce a somewhat less compliant and more questioning mass electorate than previously. It was also a time when the British local government system was first subjected to a rigorous critical examination.

The 1960s and 1970s were an era when the merits of greater public participation in decision-making, especially at local level, were widely promulgated – helped by an enthusiastic media, participation became a 'vogue word' (Higgins and Richardson, 1976, p. 3). In 1969, the Skeffington Report on public participation in planning reported positively on the importance of maximum participation by both individuals and groups in the planning process, and made a number of radical proposals. Also in the late 1960s, the Seebohm Committee which reported on personal social services similarly expressed a belief in the greatest possible involvement of the public. In these and other cases, proposals for extensive local community participation have, to say the least, failed to be implemented fully. There have been improvements in the scope of public involvement but how far this has succeeded in enabling new interests to influence decision-making is another question.

What is a community?

Before examining the effectiveness of community participation the questions 'what do we mean by community?' and 'what do we mean by participation?' need to be addressed. These are less easy to answer than might first be imagined. The notion of 'community' is problematic in that it is such a vague term, incapable of any universally acceptable definition (Butcher, 1993). Broadly, there are two conceptions; it refers to either a territorial community (which can range from a street, to a nation, or to a collection of nations such as the European Community) or to a group of people who share a characteristic or interest unrelated to physical proximity – for example, the 'academic community'. However, beyond these definitions is a third dimension, encompassing elements of both, what could be termed 'attachment communities' where people, irrespective of their widely differing interests, share a common sense of identity with other people living in the same area (see Hollis *et al.*, 1992, pp. 281–4). Whatever its lack of precision, this is generally the sense in which the term is used when referring to notions such as 'community government' or 'community action'. For example, Smith and Anderson (1972, p. 303) take 'community action' to mean 'collective action by people who live near each other who experience either common or similar problems'. This simple definition of community should suffice for our purposes. What is unarguable is that, no matter how imprecise the term community is, its use as a call to arms against unpopular decisions can make it a powerful force in mobilising local opinion.

The idea of 'community' is often seen as unproblematically 'good' but as Colenutt and Cutten (1994) rightly note, communities can be excluding units, self-defining and essentially negative. Local empowerment can also lead to unanticipated consequences, as happened when British National Party (BNP) candidates were elected on a 'housing for the local community' ticket in Tower Hamlets, which had devolved considerable powers and money to neighbourhood committees. Although they failed to gain control of the committee, the prospect of racists controlling funds in a multi-ethnic community raised howls of protest but if we believe in local democracy we have to respect local electoral decisions (no matter how much we might abhor them). What the BNP's success does illustrate is the danger of low levels of electoral turnout allowing such well-motivated parties to gain power.

It may be that the community of most local government areas is too large. There is evidence that the public finds district and county councils remote from the wishes of ordinary people and unwilling to consult them or even listen to their genuine concerns (Morris and Brigham, 1993). Even when there is consultation, surveys reveal a suspicion that the outcome has been pre-determined (Byrne, 1994, p. 330) and studies have found a 'high degree of dissatisfaction with public consultation of service' (Morris and Brigham, 1993, p. 10). The Audit Commission has long argued for wider public consultation, arguing that the public are also experts in their own needs and should therefore be consulted as any other expert group would (Steele, 1992). The public believe that 'responding to local people's wishes' is the single most important factor which should be taken into account by decision makers when contemplating change in the local government system (MORI, 1994). However, 'the problem is that most residents do not make their wishes known ... only 20 per cent are active in any kind of local group' (Audit Commission, 1997, p. 27). These members of a local community have no problem being heard, but 'mechanisms for listening to the most vocal citizens will not give councillors a full picture of the concerns of local communities' (ibid.). There is clearly a perceived need to extend the scope of participation to counter the tendency of a limited number of 'established activists' controlling the agenda (Clark, 1998, p. 23).

What is participation?

We also need to address (albeit briefly) what is meant by 'participation'. Any definition of 'participation' is subject to debate, and will influence the conclusions of any examination of the topic. Do we mean some form of direct democracy, for example, or are the consultative processes largely favoured by local government at present the realistic limit of 'community participation'? The Skeffington Report defined participation as 'the act of sharing in the formulation of policies and proposals' (1969, p. 1). This is a definition that is potentially capable of encompassing all political acts, including voting, joining a voluntary organisation, holding elected office, and 'unconventional' action such as rioting, although Skeffington did not consider illegal action an acceptable form of local participation. Most studies of local and national participation have not considered violent protest and unlawful acts, although at least one study included an assessment of them (Parry *et al.*, 1992, pp. 16–19). In support of defining such acts as 'political participation', it is undeniable that the poll tax riots contributed to the demise of that unpopular tax, and certainly arguable that those occasionally violent demonstrations contributed to removing an apparently well-established Prime Minister from office (thereby contributing to more changes in policy). Given that the previously noted decline in deference has both weakened the appeal of voting and legitimised many forms of protest once deemed unacceptable, all forms of political action – including direct action – should be considered when assessing the scope of political participation.

The widening of participation is not just of parochial concern. The United Nations Conference on Environment and Development held in Rio de Janeiro in June 1992 (popularly known as 'Earth Summit: Rio 92') saw a partnership between local government, business, voluntary organisations and the local community as essential to the success of conserving and managing resources on the global scale. The Earth Summit made a number of well-publicised suggestions for reconciling development with the environmental concerns of an increasingly aware population. 'Agenda 21' was probably the most significant output, with detailed programmes for sustainable development 'based on principles of participation, inclusion and sustainability' (Littlewood and While, 1997, p. 111). It would be impossible to deliver most of the aims of Agenda 21 without the cooperation of local government (Levett, 1993) but in an increasingly inter-connected world 'localised community politics is not enough on its own to achieve the necessary wider coordination between interests at local, city-wide, national and international levels' (Jacobs, 1992, p. 255). Participation in local politics can and should have much wider repercussions, although it has to be admitted that central government has so far been reticent in providing the economic support necessary for effective local coordination (Littlewood and While, 1997, p. 121).

Why is community involvement important?

Instinctively, community participation is seen by democrats as, in Sellar and Yeatman's (1930) famous phrase, a 'good thing'. Greater participation and consultation is increasingly regarded as an essential element in legitimising local decision making. Most people in public life will respond positively to the general idea of community participation in local government but public commitment by elected representatives to greater participation is no guarantee of any real commitment to widen the decision making process. Whilst for the public the process of participation might mean full involvement in decision making, elite decision makers may see participation as a legitimating device for decisions they actually take themselves; as the previous chapter showed, decision-making within Health Action Zones provides an extreme example of such a process. 'Community participation', however they choose to define or limit the concept, is publicly supported by most local politicians but the idea of giving formal decision-making power on a wide range of issues to small local communities does not have wide support.

For example, while local authorities are developing new roles for voluntary groups, the scope of such involvement is often strictly limited, with public involvement kept within strictly defined boundaries. Local authorities and their representatives stress their commitment to devolving power to local communities and 'tempering' traditional representative forms of local democracy with a more participatory process, but they still tend to be defensive of their overall role. As the President of the Society of Local Authority Chief Executives (SOLACE) put it:

> Participation by people at local level monitoring service delivery; devolution of decision making, within defined limits, to area committees; extensive consultation and close working with particular communities – these are highly desirable options. Nevertheless, they cannot substitute for the representative democratic process when decisions are required on resource allocation between competing needs, when planning applications have to be determined amidst profound local controversy or when regulatory action is required in sensitive local circumstances. These are the proper roles for local government and it is appropriate for them to be discharged by democratically elected representatives. They are distinctively about choices and balances, reflecting local circumstances, making locally influenced judgements.
>
> (Gordon, 1997, p. 12)

Such views were reflected in my interviews with councillors. Yes, they say, community involvement is fine, but within clearly defined limits and subject to the overall control of democratically elected representatives. The notion that those representatives might be at community level remains unconsidered or summarily dismissed by most. For example, a Staffordshire Labour leader believes that 'community involvement is often ill-informed and driven by activists' and sees community involvement as a process that has to wait until the overall direction of action has been decided (interview, 1999), a not untypical view (especially in private) of how far participation should extend (see also below).

Such arm's length involvement, against the rhetoric of wider empowerment, inevitably leads to public disenchantment with the decision-
making procedures.

Throughout this book, the value of community involvement in local
decision making is supported and the centralising forces that have
undoubtedly been dominant over recent years, despite some often unintended positive consequences, are generally deplored. The overwhelming majority of non-partisan and informed opinion supports the broad
principle of 'local democracy' and even relatively dispassionate academics become passionate when they view the disdain with which that
principle has been viewed by an often ill-informed media and by central
politicians and civil servants (see Wilson and Game, Chapter 1, 1998;
Jones and Travers, 1994). Why should we care? After all, we are constantly told, to cite just a few apparently widely held beliefs, that local
town halls and county councils are filled with low calibre officers and
'loony' politicians, that corruption is endemic, that local politics is bor-
ing and unimportant, and that local people don't care about getting
involved and have no commitment to the ideal and structures of local
democracy. Even if all this was the case – and the evidence either suggests
otherwise or is ambiguous – there are good reasons for caring.

Local democracy is important for reasons that go far beyond the
(important) principle that local people should have some say in decisions
that directly affect them and their community. Local democracy plays
a crucial role in 'enhancing and developing democracy' at all levels
(Phillips, 1996, p. 36). It encourages and rewards participation, reaf-
firming and promoting the value of a more participatory democracy to
a population that grows more distrusting and cynical of the motives of
elected politicians every day. That distrust will not be changed by more
distant, less transparent and less accountable decision making by *national*
politicians. Involvement with grassroots politics (pavement politics, if
you like) is an essential antidote to the poisonous cynicism that threat-
ens to engulf our political culture. However, public distrust will also not
be changed by more distant, less transparent and less accountable decision making *at the local and regional level.*

There are sound democratic reasons, but the major argument most
likely to sway a pragmatic New Labour government is that community
involvement is a crucial factor in increasing the effectiveness of the sorts
of projects (for example, urban regeneration) which tend to present
the most public face of the partnerships governance engenders. While
there are inevitably costs to community involvement the benefits are
also considerable. As well as local service partnerships providing better

community health services and environmental improvements (Gregory, 1998), less crime, less vandalism, more positive attitudes to government and a greater sense of belonging have all been identified as positive outcomes from effective community involvement in local decision-making (Butcher, 1998).

Community participation: can it become a reality?

Despite the attention given to 'community involvement' when seeking funds for urban regeneration, and the soothing noises councils make when discussing the involvement of the local population, effective community participation in decision making is both rare and discouraged. All three major parties talk about 'community empowerment' but the suspicion remains that much of this is rhetoric. Much politics is now carried out through the public–private partnerships discussed in the previous chapter, in which the participation of 'ordinary' people is either not always welcome or subject to strict limitations. For example, as previously noted:

> Both City Challenge and SRB are accompanied by detailed guidelines and performance criteria (and limited resources) with all the major decisions made by government officials. Indeed, local regeneration strategies are often effectively designed around the wishes of officials and ministers. Community involvement in these initiatives is thus carefully circumscribed. Clearly, neither City Challenge nor SRB are designed to empower local communities to any significant extent but to keep local communities 'on side' as far as possible. Most community organisations take the pragmatic view that if they do not cooperate they will not get the money.
>
> (Colenutt and Cutten, 1994, pp. 237–8)

As a quango member said, managers 'can't actually go out to the public until they know the limits of the achievable … they've got to know what the consequences [of a potential decision] are' before they can bring partners in from the community and consult the public (interview, 1999). So, we have a governance system where community involvement is essential for both funding and public relations but where the 'partnership' is either cosmetic or heavily weighted towards government. That said, there has been a gradual improvement in community involvement since the heyday of Urban Development Corporations (UDCs), run by largely government appointed placemen from the private sector, where 'solutions' were inflicted on communities and large amounts of money wasted without any effective accountability (Marr, 1996, p. 103). However, the process is still led by established interests who might still prefer a freer rein. In the case of the bidding process for Health Action Zones:

> a health authority doesn't volunteer to get lots of people on board, because it doesn't come naturally to its managers to do that. It does it because otherwise you don't win the bid.
>
> (interview with health authority member, 1999)

In most areas of the country, community empowerment has been limited, to say the least, and huge amounts of public money are still being poured into projects which make big profits for private companies while offering little significant benefit to the affected communities (Colenutt and Cutten, 1994, p. 249). However, these are still early days and 'just as quality regeneration takes time, so does community empowerment' (ibid.) Despite the unsatisfactory nature of the process, community organisations generally express a welcome to the underlying idea of partnership. Certainly, Stoke-on-Trent's SRB bids included community groups (albeit heavily outnumbered by political, quango and business representatives) who were happy to be involved in the process.

There are a number of reasons for the shift from the initial essentially 'authoritarian' UDC model, in which central government decisions were imposed on local communities, to the more consensual 'partnership' model. These include policy failure, declining legitimacy, community activism, and perhaps paramount, the demands of regeneration bids that community groups be represented in any bid for money. Answering the problem of declining legitimacy, community involvement enabled private sector interests (especially) to adopt a public interest perspective in their profit making and public sector actors could trumpet successful bids as examples of their commitment to a wider decision-making process. Brian Smith, chief executive of Stoke-on-Trent's unitary authority, despite noting that 'more and more we do set up meetings, forums, regular groupings with … residents', warns that:

> it's a little bit piece meal at the moment, its not been developed that well, and one of the problems is actually identifying who are the representatives of the communities. Sometime it's possible to find one small group who are more valuable than others and they almost take it as a proxy then to vote for the whole community, which they are not.
>
> (interview, 1997)

It appears the concern with 'activists' is widespread. When the public don't get involved, it is deplored as evidence of apathy. When they do, their motives are suspect and they are apparently widely regarded as unrepresentative of the communities they speak for (Audit Commission, 1997; Clark, 1998).

Public attitudes to local democracy: a vision of apathy?

Among the practitioner community there is a strong faith in the value of local democracy and a feeling that central government (of whatever political persuasion) is fundamentally opposed to it because local government's legitimacy posed a difficult challenge when there were disagreements. Perhaps unsurprisingly, over four-fifths of local politicians thought local government understood the needs of the community 'very' or 'fairly well'. Local government officials were even more confident, over 90 per cent of them registering a positive view of local government's understanding of the needs of its area (Parry *et al.*, pp. 403–5, Table 18.7). Also, there appears to be, especially among elected representatives, a belief that the public respects them, judges them on their performance in office, and is keenly attached to their local political institutions. The officers and senior politicians I spoke to in Staffordshire (and over the years, countrywide) are generally upbeat about their public image. This optimistic view of the way they are regarded by the public is not always supported by the evidence; at best, it appears that the public have 'ambiguous attitudes to local democratic institutions and their performance' (John, 1997, p. 273). In North Staffordshire, only just over a half of the public (55 per cent) are satisfied with the performance of their local authorities (author's 1995 survey). There appears to be a 'popular indifference' to local institutions (John, 1997, p. 272). To be fair, many officers and councillors are just as disenchanted as the public with the ineffective representative process, which probably reflects a wider disenchantment with the way we are governed (ibid., p. 269).

Most politicians were aware of the way many people voted on national issues in local elections, and while in private they were prepared to admit the number was greater than voted for them personally, they still probably over-estimated their personal vote. On the record, they maintained the privately admitted fiction that they had a large personal vote. If the public are truly voting on local issues, one would hope that they had an awareness of not only local issues but also the duties and responsibilities of elected local representatives. However, the evidence suggests the opposite is a more accurate reflection of the local electorate. Over the years, surveys have tended to indicate that the public is largely ignorant of council procedures and duties (Gyford, 1991, p. 99). The Widdicombe Report (1986) found that less than one-third of respondents could name any of their councillors and that barely a half could correctly identify their county or regional council. The depth of public ignorance was a shock to many in local government, although Widdicombe did find that public knowledge was increasing. While some studies have painted a less distressing picture for proponents of local democracy, nearly one-third of people are still unable to name their district council and even fewer are aware of the political party in control. Although the electorate demonstrated a fairly broad knowledge of the services provided by local government, 'interest in local politics was not high' (ibid., p. 14). Opinion polls generally demonstrate that the public has little knowledge over which tier of government or which organisation actually provides the local services they consume (Morris and Brigham, 1993).

Such public ignorance about local institutions undoubtedly contributes to a sense of declining legitimacy. Perhaps the allegations of an inefficient and self-serving local system are too deep to be countered merely by academic argument. Empirical evidence could help, but unfortunately for 'defenders of the faith', levels of involvement in local politics are similarly depressing for the believers in community participation. That there is a declining interest in local politics as presently constituted is demonstrated by the rapidly decreasing levels of turn out for local elections. Quite apart from the low levels of electoral turnout, which seldom rise above 40 per cent and in some wards fail to reach double figures (Rallings and Thrasher, 1997a), regular political participation (for example, party canvassing, pressure group activity) is confined to a small section of the population, although all sections of the population demonstrate a propensity for action when their own interests are threatened. High turnouts appear to be related to specifically local political events (Rallings *et al.*, 1996, p. 77). Given this, and also that electoral turnout at the county level has been declining long-term while in the more local districts it has remained buoyant (ibid.) there is a case for arguing greater responsibility for 'lower' levels of government. However, given such a general ignorance of local politics, and the apparent lack of interest shown by the public, it is not surprising that central government has been able to emasculate local government over the past decades without a great deal of concern being expressed outside of the practitioner community.

Anecdotal evidence suggest more concern with the little things of life than with issues seen as remote and beyond influencing. Sean Dooley, the editor of Stoke's evening paper *The Sentinel*, remembers the time the paper ran an award winning series on Stoke-on-Trent's poor housing which earned the author the award of Regional Journalist of the Year. There was a great stir in the council, local politicians and officers were furious, yet the editor received only five letters from readers. Six weeks later, the paper 'ran half a page on dog shit [on city pavements] and we got fifty-five letters' (interview, 1997). Such a 'primary environmental concern' about dog mess appears to be widespread (Macnaghten *et al.*, 1995, p. 83) so issues that immediately affect the public seem to stir up local feeling more than issues which they feel they have little control over.

Who matters? Local attitudes to institutions and individuals

Who does this apparently disenchanted, disempowered and uninterested public feel has power, and which are the institutions they see as having most influence over their lives? There is some interesting conjectural evidence that, consciously or not, local populations recognise the importance of bodies other than local government institutions in the local governance system. When the people of North Staffordshire were asked which organisations had most influence on life in the area, their political institutions were not paramount (see Table 5.1). Universities, colleges and schools, and local financial and business organisations were seen as more influential on North Staffordshire life than the formal structures of government. The answers could be

Table 5.1 'In your opinion, what sort of local organisations have most influence on life in North Staffordshire?' (you may name up to two; *n* = 353).

Type of organisation	Number citing
1. Education	119
2. Business/Finance	93
3. Political	87
4. Entertainment	66
5. Medical	56
6. Media	55
7. Police	50
8. Religious	14
9. None of these	8
10. Other	4

reflecting the battering which local politics has taken over the last two decades. If central government and the media continually minimise the importance of local government it should be no surprise that the public fails to appreciate the impact of local institutions on their daily lives. When the more personal question of 'what sort of local organisations have most influence in your life?' is asked, the insignificance of formal involvement with politics in people's lives becomes apparent. As Table 5.2 shows, it's less important than almost everything else. Lives tend to revolve around leisure, school or college, health and work. Religious organisations may not be perceived as powerful influences on the general life of the community but their impact on most individuals is greater than that of political institutions. Most people's interaction with both politicians and police officers is minimal.

However, there is a discrepancy between the sort of local institutions seen as powerful and the individuals the public identify as powerful. While political institutions are seen as having less influence on life in Staffordshire than educational or business organisations, Table 5.3 illustrates that their local MP dominates when the public has to cite powerful individuals. What this could indicate is the higher public profile political individuals have; it may simply be easier to name them or say 'my MP' rather than struggling to name a powerful businessperson. Given the focus on national politics it is unsurprising that local people see their MP as so important. It might also illustrate one of the weaknesses of opinion polls, in that people feel they have to give an answer and give one quickly. Given that the impact of most MPs on the life of

Table 5.2 'What sort of local organisations have most influence on YOUR life?' (you may name up to two; $n = 353$)

Type of organisation	Number citing
1. Entertainment	112
2. Education	101
3. Medical	71
4. Business/Finance	55
5. Religious	44
6. Media	42
7. Political	39
8. Police	24
9. None of these	18
10. Other	11

Note: Polled in North Staffordshire, December 1994.

Table 5.3   'Please name specific individuals (or positions) who are powerful in North Staffordshire' (you may name up to five; $n=353$) (Figure in brackets = number of citations. Respondents were unprompted.)

1. Local Members of Parliament (170)	16. Members of European Parliament (4)
2. Chief Constable (55)	Church leaders (4)
3. The Mayor (49)	18. Health authority leaders (3)
4. Leader of District Council (39)	Headmasters/schools (3)
5. Business leaders (37)	Heads of public utilities (3)
6. District councillors (33)	County councillors (3)
7. Lord (Jack) Ashley* (28)	22. Lord Lieutenant (2)
8. Local government officers (18)	Local Labour party (2)
9. Judiciary (11)	Central government (2)
10. Sir Stanley Matthews** (9)	25. Local Conservative party (1)
Doctors (9)	Trade union leaders (1)
Press/journalists (9)	Freemasons (1)
13. Lou Macari*** (5)	Senior citizens organisations (1)
Senior academics (5)	Community leaders (1)
Leader of county council (5)	Rotarians (1)

Notes: Polled in North Staffordshire, December 1994.
* Former local MP, now Chancellor of Staffordshire University.
** World renowned former footballer, Stoke's most famous son.
*** The then manager of Stoke City football club.

the constituencies they 'represent' is (unlike American representatives) generally negligible in policy terms, this is a further indication of the lack of awareness of just who has power in local communities.

When local people were asked to name specific individuals who were powerful in North Staffordshire the most cited local politician was 'The Mayor' a position that in local government is purely an honorary and relatively powerless post. The leader of the district council received 39 nominations against the leader of the county council's 5 nominations, and district councillors 33 citations against just 3 for county councillors, which might indicate support for the proposition that people identify most strongly with their immediate locality (see the MORI poll on community identity, Table 5.4).

The wide range of people cited (see Table 5.3, above) provides some indication that the public recognises local power exists outside of the formal structures of government. That the Chief Constable is the most powerful single person cited could also indicate an astute awareness of the potential power such individuals possess. The very few people who regard MEPs as important may be an important factor in the extremely low turnout recorded in elections to the European parliament (1999). Why bother to vote for candidates in elections which don't appear to

Table 5.4   Sense of community identity in Staffordshire

Staffordshire survey (%)	Very strongly (%)	Very/fairly strongly (%)
This neighbourhood/village	45	80
This town or the nearest town	30	67
City/District/Borough	28	65
County	23	60

Source: MORI, 1994.
Note: The question asked was '*How strongly do you feel that you belong to each of the following areas?*'

have an important impact on your life? Table 5.3 lists all responses, in order to demonstrate some of the perceptions local people have of power in the community.

It would be wrong to claim too much for such evidence but, to be pessimistic, while official investigations into local democracy have consistently highlighted the need for better participatory methods and greater information for the public, the evidence appears to indicate that the majority of the public are just not interested and do not regard local politics as all that important, especially to their own lives. The number of people who thought The Mayor was a powerful individual, and the low numbers of people recognising the importance of local government officers or quango members (barely cited), does not indicate an informed population. This is not surprising given the current deficiencies of local governance.

Combating apathy

After a series of in-depth reports on many aspects of local politics, the Commission for Local Democracy concluded that:

> the present system of local government in Britain is seriously inadequate to meet the requirements of a mature democracy. It obscures and distorts what should be open and lively political activity for the majority of citizens and it fails to supply clear lines of public accountability...the basis of local administration is secretive in itself and confusing for the bulk of local people. From that confusion arises apathy and cynicism towards local democracy.
>
> (Commission for Local Democracy, 1995, pp. 16–17)

Despite the evidence of apathy and an undeniable general disinclination towards activism, Nevin and Shiner (1995) take the desire by communities to be involved in decision making as given. While they admit necessary cultural changes 'may be difficult to achieve' (1995, p. 319) the problems they believe need overcoming if community empowerment is to succeed do not appear to include tackling community apathy. However, if it is the case that local communities are uninterested in local political involvement then the frequent calls for community participation in decision making could be based on unrealistic expectations. An examination of SRB bids found that 'exercises that demand relatively little effort, such as public meetings … are relatively well supported' but more regular and formal requirements of participation fail to generate the same level of interest (Butcher, 1998, p. 1049). That said, if community involvement in such programmes is as limited as some have suggested (Colenutt and Cutten, 1994) then the lack of interest is hardly surprising.

Often, suggestions for improving interest and involvement rely on creating new institutional frameworks (Nevin and Shiner, 1995, 1996) which by themselves do not tackle the 'barriers to maintaining widespread participation' (Butcher, 1998, p. 1049). Many of the new frameworks proposed are also unrealistic, requiring as they do fundamental reorganisations which the actors involved are unlikely to agree upon, especially when one recurring feature involves the most powerful single actor (central government, which has the power to restructure or abolish most of the actors involved) seceding significant measures of control. So, it is difficult to disagree with Parry *et al.*, who argue that:

> those who would see community as the ground on which a more participatory Britain can be built need first to convince their fellow citizens of its relevance to modern life and then of its value as a stimulus to common action.
>
> (Parry *et al.*, 1992, p. 344)

Of course, it could be pointed out that a more local level of government is needed before feelings of local identity and community can be engendered in urban and suburban communities and lead to greater levels of participation (Rallings *et al.*, 1994). It has been argued that there is little community identity for units of local government above the parish level (Young *et al.*, 1996). Would smaller units of local government increase involvement?

Sense of identity and participation in local politics

There is already a network of parish/town/community councils and supporters of community councils are positive about their potential as 'enablers' for local people (Griffiths and Lawton, 1992). Sceptics could point to the low levels of public involvement in such councils as evidence against the proposition. However, in England and Wales, such councils are not universal (having a predominantly rural presence) and have very little power and no specific duties; Scottish community councils have even less power. The governmental significance of such councils is therefore limited (Wilson and Game, 1998, p. 37) and it would be unrealistic to expect widespread community participation. Anyway, research by MORI suggests a more complex picture of community identity. MORI carried out a number of polls assessing community identity on behalf of district and county councils preparing evidence for the Banham Commission, which reported in 1997. As it is the area where my own research into elite and public attitudes was carried out, I will utilise MORI's findings in Staffordshire as a general indicator of community identity.[1] Given that Parry *et al.* (1992) found little difference by locality in the frequency with which citizens participate, the views of the Staffordshire public should not be too far divorced from those of the rest of England, although it must be pointed out that citizen attachment to the shire county was high in Staffordshire compared to many other counties (Rallings *et al.*, 1994, p. 14).

Table 5.4, above, details some of those findings and clearly indicates that people feel a greater sense of community to their immediate neighbourhood than to their town. The larger the area, the less the feeling of 'belonging'. However, even such a large geographical area as the shire county still evokes a quite powerful sense of community identity, supporting the findings of other researchers of 'multiple loyalties' to villages, towns and counties as well as attachment to their immediate locality (Jones, 1988, p. 9). Such multiple loyalties could obviously present problems when deciding the size and boundaries of a more 'community-based' system of local government.

MORI also found a clear correlation between a sense of belonging to a community and factors such as age, class and length of residence. As many previous studies have also found (for example, Quantin, 1989), MORI identified a general tendency for a sense of community identity to strengthen with age and length of residence, factors which may of course be related. In addition, there are indications of a relationship between social class and sense of identity, with C2s and DEs (largely skilled and unskilled manual workers) more likely to feel a sense of belonging with their neighbourhood, village or nearest town than AB and C1 social classes (largely professional, managerial and clerical workers).[2] This could be explained by greater mobility among the professional classes which could inhibit a strong sense of community from developing. It also needs pointing out that Parry *et al.* (1992) found that notions of 'community' appear to have less meaning for those living in urban areas.

While it is true that the empirical evidence for the belief that strong attachment to a community will lead to enhanced political participation is ambiguous (Quantin, 1989) it has historically been supposed that 'feelings of attachment and identity with the locality, its population and its values... will encourage action to support and defend its interests and values' (Parry *et al.*, 1992, p. 300). How important to a healthy local democracy is a public sense of community and identity with the geographical and administrative area? Do such feelings translate into a better informed and more highly motivated local population? The 'traditional orthodoxy' of studies of local democracy is convinced, and it has often been noted that a knowledge of local problems and an interest in their resolution, as well as increasing local participation, has beneficial effects at both individual and societal level (Butcher, 1993), although as usual Bulpitt (1972) offers a critique of the traditional orthodoxy. However, while many observers do believe there is 'ample evidence' that a sense of community demonstrates a positive *attitude* to the local political environment (Parry *et al.*, 1992, pp. 338–9) the evidence is less encouraging for those equating such a sense of local identity and community spirit with high *participation* in local politics and voluntary activity. Paradoxically, voluntary and political activism is strongly associated with the middle class, the group who supposedly feel less community sense while the 'working class', with a greater sense of community, are less active.

Despite this, proponents of 'community government' remain in no doubt, and are convinced that local authorities 'should be closer both geographically and organisationally to their citizens, who can be more readily involved in the choices necessary for change' (Stewart, 1989, p. 245). Unfortunately for such optimists, when the evidence is examined, the proposition that the level of participation is enhanced in localities characterised by a sense of 'solidarity and common identity' (Parry and Moyser, 1989, p. 190) has often failed empirically. To be blunt, the relationship is highly debatable. Studies have tended to find that 'attachment to the area in which one lives and the recognition of it as a community does not translate into local participation', even within a traditional 'solidaristic mining village' (ibid.) That said, it is clear local populations do form deep attachments to the areas they live and work in and whether or not they directly participate in local politics they are usually strongly opposed to change in the structure and boundaries of their political institutions. For some, community participation is flawed because it rests on an idealised notion of community (or of the working class?). It is argued that 'local communities' contain many social groups with diverse interests and resources and the battle by multiple interests for control of resources in communities works against the least advantaged (also usually least organised) classes in society (Duffy and Hutchinson, 1997). As a general rule, this is difficult to deny, but interests based on 'locality' clearly exist (Butcher, 1998, p. 1048). That said, it is probable that local community organisations have a better chance of becoming established 'where it is perceived there is a chance to achieve or influence things' (ibid., pp. 1049–50) and the correlation between non-participation and social class (Rallings *et al.*, 1994, p. 31) means the least advantaged classes are less likely to feel they can change things. But all classes of people now appear to have little faith or trust in their governing institutions (Macnaghten *et al.*, 1995).

Nimbyism as a positive force?

From what we have seen, it would not be too much to claim that citizens are largely unaware of the structures, services and personalities of local government. The overall picture is of a public attitude of 'ignorance and indifference tinged with suspicion' (Hampton, 1987, p. 126) towards local government. Respected observers of British local government find a 'lack of esteem…and even hostility towards councillors' (Byrne, 1994, p. 321). Few members of the public bother to get engaged in local politics of any description, except on those occasions in which 'nimbyism' (the syndrome that recognises developments such as roads, hospitals and prisons must be built somewhere but 'not in my back yard') generates involvement. Even in disadvantaged areas, residents feel a strong commitment to their local community regardless of factors such as age, gender and ethnicity (Forrest and Kearns, 1999) and they will collectively mobilise to defend their specific local interests.

There is an important point to be made here. Nimbyism is constantly criticised as evidence of an essentially apathetic and selfish population, most memorably (and undeniably humorously) when the late Nicholas Ridley (then Conservative Environment minister) was caught on camera in mid-hypocrisy by a BBC interviewer. While castigating the rest of us for nimbyism, the interviewer pointed out that Ridley was then engaged in opposing a development in *his* own 'back-yard', upon which Ridley stormed out of the interview in a temper. It is undeniable that nimbyism has selfish characteristics, but perhaps the tendency is telling us an essential truth. In Britain, supporters of local democracy usually insist that local authorities should be as close to the consumers of services as possible. There is wide support for the belief that such a closeness would reflect the parochial nature of most Britons' concerns. In 1969, the Redcliffe-Maud Royal Commission on local government in England found that most people identified with a clearly definable locality known as their 'home area' (Redcliffe-Maud, 1969, p. 99); 25 years later little had changed (MORI, 1994). By the standards of British local government units, such home areas tended to be very small, neighbourhoods rather than cities and this is not a recent historical phenomenon. Our immediate concern has *always* been especially localised and we tend to think disproportionately in terms of needs or problems that affect ourselves, our family or our immediate neighbourhood (Mabileau *et al.*, pp. 253–4). It appears that at least for the British citizenry, the fundamental concept of 'community' is closely linked to immediate territory (see also Macnaghten *et al.*, 1995, p. 82), but we are not unique in this. American research has indicated that:

> people first participate locally in their communities and neighbourhoods on concerns and issues that effect them personally. Then they see themselves as closer to the political process though they never use those words. They 'feel' more ownership and have a greater stake in the process of community building.
>
> (Troxel, 1997, p. 105)

The message is apparent that 'ordinary people' will be much more likely to get involved in politics when the decisions being taken quite clearly affect their interests and quality of life. A natural conclusion is that decision making structures need to reflect this. Structures and innovations which recognise the importance of personal factors to political motivation are essential. 'Reinventing government', as Osborne and Gaebler (1992) put it, is an attempt to revolutionise the whole structure of government but that process also requires a reinvention or 'radical renewal' of citizenship (Troxel, 1997, p. 103). That reinvention must start at the personal level to invigorate a polity disaffected and disillusioned with conventional politics.

Lack of trust: the role of the media

What needs to be rebuilt is *trust*. The people of Britain appear to have lost faith in established institutions and the people who inhabit them.

They distrust the information provided by local government and hold 'intensely sceptical attitudes towards official institutions' (Macnaghten *et al.*, 1995, p. 83). Re-engaging trust in public life will require institutions 'responding to the citizenry…finding and publicising new examples of public stewardship [and] collaborating across traditional boundaries…of party, class, geography or perceived interests' (Troxel, 1997, p. 108). Trust is an essential factor of all social and political relationships (Axelrod, 1984). As an integral part of 'social capital', rebuilding trust is also important to New Labour's Third Way project and Tony Blair makes frequent allusions to this (see King and Wickham-Jones, 1999). Trust is 'the lubricant' that drives community involvement and 'effective local government leadership will embrace and encourage citizen involvement and input rather than be threatened by it' (Roulier, 1997, p. 190). As Ranson and Stewart point out, these concepts are inextricably bound together:

> participation is needed to complement representation if the evolution of a more elaborate system of community governance is to be developed. Such a system would encourage public choices which were more responsive to the community as a whole…while, at the same time, holding services more accountable to the public…the basis for trust can only be established through such transformations.
> (Ranson and Stewart, 1998, p. 265)

One problem for re-establishing trust between 'ruler and ruled' is that trust tends to be based on 'myths, images, reputations and other symbolic constructions…much of the struggle for legitimacy is concerned with constructing, appropriating or rewriting appropriate myths, images, language and history' (Newman, 1998, p. 48). In other words, trust is manufactured 'through the construction or manipulation of images' (ibid.). In modern societies the mass media are essential carriers of such messages and their attitude towards elected politicians in particular cannot have helped the brand image of our representatives. So, negative public attitudes about local government may be reflecting the priorities of a media that concentrate on sensationalism and fail to report the good things local government does. Even most local newspapers, traditionally less critical of elites than the British national press, tend to give local politics a low priority, although the proliferation of alternative local media may have somewhat rectified this (Gyford, 1991, pp. 34–5). It appears unlikely that the largely negative press and television coverage of local affairs, and the way the national media treats local elections almost exclusively as an opinion poll on the popularity of the government, will have failed to colour the public's perception of the propriety and importance of local government. Therefore, low levels of commitment to, and involvement in, local politics are only to be expected.

Many people in public life feel angry about the way local media treats them and, as they see it, trivialises local political issues. The former leader of Stoke-on-Trent council, the late Ted Smith, saw the local newspaper (*The Sentinel*) as spending more time running the city down than building it up and maintained it was also engaged in a 'vitriolic' personal campaign against him. Ted Smith also maintained that the BBC local radio station, Radio Stoke, was 'turned against its own community' after it had criticised the council for 'junkets' around Europe (interview, 1997). Off the record, other local politicians and businessmen were also critical of *The Sentinel* in particular, feeling it tended to present a negative picture of local business and politics; 'scurrilous rag' was one of the more printable comments. Sean Dooley, the editor of *The Sentinel*, responds that 'we don't criticise for criticism's sake, and we don't criticise willy-nilly, everything we do we like to feel is constructive'. Dooley also emphasised the paper's independence from powerful vested interests and saw the paper as being 'there for the community'. When the local further education college were campaigning for a third campus which would have reduced the size of central parkland *The Sentinel* took the community's side despite the fact that the college was then the paper's biggest advertiser. For Dooley, as for newspapermen and women everywhere, the media are one of the public's few effective weapons against poor government (interview, 1997).

The argument that people are not interested in local affairs is not supported by the growing number of readers of local newspapers and the rise in the audience for local television news. In the second half of 1998, over two-thirds of the country's 370 regional newspapers increased their year-on-year sales, with some recording double figure percentage increases; the *East Kent Mercury* increased sales by nearly a quarter after appointing 17 community correspondents in response to readers' requests for more news about their particular community. Independent Television Commission research shows that whereas national news was once preferred to local news, since 1995 the audience preference has changed (Marks, 1999). Such interest indicates that, if empowered, and if adequately informed, local communities may not be as apathetic as some allege. A more positive media portrayal of local government might also help, and public bodies of all types are increasingly using marketing techniques to try and improve their public image. However, given that 'significant gaps between image and reality are hard to sustain... [such tactics] will not succeed unless they are accompanied by a transformation of the institutions themselves' (Newman, 1998, pp. 48–9).

Painting a false picture?

On a more general level, it must be considered whether the picture of local government often presented by academia and the media is a true reflection of the current state of affairs. Some academic research has painted a rather different picture of public attitudes to local government than is normally shown (see Rallings *et al.*, 1994, p. 10). Also, the Widdicombe Report (1986) found that 72 per cent of respondents were generally satisfied with the performance of their local authority. Supporting Widdicombe, Parry and others studying political participation have found high levels of satisfaction all round among people who have actually contacted their local authority, a public content which 'appears to imply a certain vote of confidence in the system' (Parry *et al.*, p. 283). Parry *et al.* discovered that 'participants displayed remarkable degrees of contentment with the outcomes of their dealings with local authorities' which ought 'to provide grounds for satisfaction to those who believe in local government as a basic element in a democracy'. The study also found that two-thirds of respondents believed their local authority understood 'the issues, needs and problems of their particular area' either 'very well' or 'fairly well' (ibid., p. 403).

More negatively, it has to be noted that respondents were less convinced that this general understanding of their problems actually led to effective solutions, but the positive public attitude was summed up by a conservative attitude towards changing the structure of local government. Respect for local government in Britain was only very marginally less than respect for the 'overall system of parliamentary government' and there does not appear to be any widespread discontent with the operation of local politics (but see Rallings *et al.*, 1994, pp. 10–11). Studies also tend to find high levels of satisfaction with district and county council services. Although there is concern and frequently discontent about the maintenance of local roads and pavements, overall, more than three-quarters of people are satisfied with the services provided by their local council; refuse collection and the provision of public libraries get impressively high satisfaction ratings of 86 and

92 per cent respectively (Lynn, 1992, pp. 70–8). The public's satisfaction with their service refuse collection could be seen as an endorsement of the new environment in which local government operates and may be an indication of the success of CCT. The positive picture found by Lynn reflects very well on local government's responses to the trials of the 1980s. However, it appears that local authorities may be failing to get across to the wider public – those people who are disinclined to complain or whose only contact may be council tax bills or hostile media coverage – the general improvement in access and approachability I have noted above. This is despite the increase in public relations activity, especially in terms of printed information such as free council newspapers.

So, while there is no cause for complacency, local politicians may have responded to public concerns about accountability and consultation rather better than their critics at central government level or in the media have ever acknowledged. Surveys suggest considerable improvements over the last 20 years or so, improvements which may of course reflect the introduction of competition. As I point out in the following chapter, one of the impacts of the private sector on local councils is an increasing tendency to treat the citizen as a customer/consumer. Councils are now more conscious of a perceived need to develop a 'consumer-oriented culture', encompassing among other things politeness and access to information, if they are to regain and keep public confidence.

Improving community participation

As we have seen, the evidence on local attitudes towards local democracy and towards higher participation is ambiguous. What can be said is that, while the negative picture painted by opponents of local democracy and those against increasing participation is far from an accurate reflection, the image of communities bursting to join in which some academics present is also inaccurate. However, when the public do call for change it tends to be in the direction of more say in local affairs (Parry *et al.*, 1992, p. 411) and they approve of the publication of information, such as performance indicators, that will enable them to make more considered judgements on their local council (Morris and Brigham, 1993, p. 11). A major problem is that local and central government actors are not rushing towards community empowerment, perhaps reflecting, to be charitable, a concern that the principles of fairness and equity may be compromised by local provision of nationally-funded services. While admitting the need for effective pre-planning and coordinated national and local frameworks for strategic development, Nevin and Shiner (1995, p. 314) argue for a lead role for local communities in 'the planning and implementation of urban regeneration schemes that do not have city-wide or regional implications', and where such implications exist, that local communities should have an *equal* role 'within local partnerships that may be led by local authorities'. Unfortunately:

> while there has been considerable talk of the need for community participation and involvement in wider processes of public decision making... to date there has been little evidence of such participation... from ordinary individuals.
>
> (Macnaghten *et al.*, 1995, p. 9)

Pessimistically, there are major cultural changes which need to be effected before a community-led approach can be effective; at present, despite the rhetoric there is no strong commitment to community empowerment (Nevin and Shiner, 1995, p. 318). One notable strategy was the handing back of financial control to local interest groups carried out by Ken Livingstone's ill-fated Greater London Council (GLC); as I noted earlier, in 1983–84 the GLC 'handed over a total of £40 million in grants to voluntary organisations in a programme of active and coherent support with a clearly identified set of overall objectives' (Habeebullah and Slater, 1993, p. 145). The GLC's relationship with the voluntary sector and its communities was notable in that it allowed a large measure of self-determination. As we saw in Chapter 3, central government's response to such largesse was to abolish the GLC.

The process of community involvement cannot be taken for granted and there is no magic formula for generating it, but studies indicate that successful involvement needs people to feel 'that the issue matters and that they can do something about it' (Duke *et al.*, 1996, p. 107). Consultation with community groups should not be tacked on but should be a first stage, 'an integral part of the action research process' (ibid., p. 108). The strategy adopted from this preliminary consultation should be a draft only, and be followed by intensive community consultation. From that process, 'partners' should be selected and mobilised and only then should an action plan be constructed. Implementation needs to be an 'organic process' of constant feedback and learning (ibid., pp. 108–10). There is plenty of evidence from detailed studies of local projects that communities want 'to be in control of deciding priorities which professionals would then pursue on their behalf'

(Joseph Rowntree Foundation, 1999). As we have seen, the process is generally the other way around.

The negative view of local government presented by its critics might be a misrepresentation of the actual situation. The growth in central control, the removal of many functions from effective procedures of accountability, a sceptical media and attacks on the desirability and propriety of local democracy, have almost certainly had a negative effect on public attitudes. Despite this, local government is still valued as an essential element of British democracy, and members of the public who have contacted their council or engaged in local participation are generally positive about the experience. In general, the public attitude towards local government is no less respectful than their attitude to our overall system of government, admittedly not necessarily that positive a finding given that the public now have more trust in many private sector companies than they do in their public sector institutions (Newman, 1998, p. 49). The public are also generally opposed to any radical change in the structure of local government.

However, it has to be admitted that despite the far from universal efforts of local authorities to involve their population there is still a great deal of cynicism about local government in Britain. For supporters of local democracy, the best remedy for such negative attitudes is more community involvement in local decision-making. As the Department of Environment noted during a friendlier time for central–local relations, perhaps public participation can provide a link between councils and citizens, helping to 'overcome the apathy and 'we–they' cynicism which can affect people's attitudes to local government' (in Boaden *et al.*, 1982, p. 98).

The vagueness of the term 'community' causes problems for its utilisation as a basis for action but all local politicians pay at least lip-service to the need for community involvement. Participation has grown with the post-1960s decline in deference towards our rulers, and is now seen as an essential element of local democracy. That said, the Liberal Democrats perception of community participation, based on the devolution of decision-making power, is radically different to Conservative interpretations which stress individual and voluntaristic solutions to local needs. Much of the philosophy of New Labour's Third Way has built upon the more participative processes of the local governance system (see Chapter 8) but the feeling remains that little attention is paid to effective community participation. In addition, as Mayo (1994, pp. 195–6) found, although there has been a great deal of 'official support for community participation and community development from international agencies and local government organisations', reductions in grant aid and a 'policy of disinvestment' prompt questions about the seriousness with which official sources treat community participation.

The response of the major political parties to the perception that local government has been failing to involve its population or meet its needs has been uncertain, and that uncertainty has not been helped by the constant changes to the rules by central government. When local responses have been positive and devolutionary, as with the Labour party in Greater London, central government has taken the ultimate step and abolished that stratum of local government. The attempt by Labour district councillors in Walsall to devolve responsibility to community structures was received with great alarm by New Labour, who clamped down on such 'socialist' developments. The Liberal Democrats have occasionally been innovatory and clearly have a vested interest in operating in this way; the 'bottom-up' route to power requires such tactics. However, even from Liberal Democrats there is some disenchantment with the effectiveness and take-up of attempts to draw people into the decision-making process (Temple, 1996).

Conclusion

What is clear is that community participation and interest in local issues goes beyond the traditional ways of involving the local citizen. Britain is becoming a more complex and fragmented society, and there is a feeling that the current mechanisms for involving the public are failing to cope with increased interest in local politics and the increasing diversity of local interests. As Marr has pointed out:

> there is growing and irrefutable evidence of the rise of a new kind of community politics in Britain … this local activity fails to follow the conventions that stimulate the national media – the political parties are only vaguely involved … it is unglamorous … it is confusing. The array of self-help groups, community schools, neighbourhood schemes, voluntary organisations and devolved local authorities that have started to criss-cross housing estates, boroughs and villages are beyond the imagination of Westminster.
>
> (Marr, 1996, p. 100)

Bringing in that community spirit and desire to participate, which is there if only both central and local authorities are prepared to devolve responsibilities and, crucially, money to neighbourhood communities, is essential if the anti-democratic tendencies of the new governance networks are to be balanced by a more participatory democracy at the grass-roots. However slowly and uncertainly, a more participatory politics is emerging. For example, Brian Smith maintains that Stoke's Citizen Panel, 650 people representative of the whole city, have had a significant input into the city's corporate plan (*City News*, June 1999), and decentralisation of council offices has also resulted in closer community links. He applauds such developments but notes some problems:

> In our Single Regeneration Budget Scheme where we've had to…been delighted to, but we've had to do it…get proper formal community involvement on our Single Regeneration Boards, so in Cobridge, Bentilee and Berry Hill…we actually have formal, community representatives, formal representatives sitting at the table… having an equal vote to the Chief Executive of the City Council for example, and that's good and it's happening. The representatives aren't always representative and, of course, they require a lot of training and support because sitting around a table with people like Chief Executives of the City Council who've spent a life time working in that sort of environment, who knows the ropes, who knows how to handle a meeting, and how to, frankly, get what he wants. And these people don't particularly. So, I think, watching, participating in those processes, I think it's good in theory but needs more support and training than, than sometimes is given recognition for. But I think it's a one way step, a one way process and more and more of that's going to happen.
>
> (interview, 1997)

Encouragingly, despite reservations, Brian Smith can foresee a time when elected neighbourhood committees are a realistic proposition. District councils have largely shied away from devolving power to local committees/forums/councils, and where they have done have imposed severe limitations on autonomy. Fears that such 'very local committees' will shy away from hard decisions in favour of protecting their own backyard may be accurate or they may be unfounded. Unless we try it we will never know. More crucially, despite the importance attached to community empowerment by New Labour's Third Way, the Blair government's concentration on achieving its output targets clashes with the basic idea of small local communities setting their own priorities.

6
The New Public *Service* Ethos

Introduction

There has been a great deal of research into the effects which the political, organisational and cultural changes already noted have had on the practices and structures of the public sector. Arguing predominantly from an anti-Thatcherite and broadly pro-public service perspective, much of the research has argued, amongst other things, that the introduction of private sector motivations and practices has weakened the core ethos of public service within the public sector. In addition there is, and has been for some years, a general unease in what (for want of anything more precise) might be called 'the public mind' about the conduct of public life in the UK. This sense of moral malaise is real and reflects a change in public perception which is the consequence of some of the unanticipated (at least by the ordinary citizen) outcomes of the important, and broadly publicly supported (if only in retrospect!) 'Thatcherite' reforms of the 1980's.

This chapter examines the concept of a public sector ethos as it is manifested at regional level. I argue that the increased interaction of the public and private sectors in recent years has had a more complex effect than is usually acknowledged. While the demands of the market have clearly imposed strains on the conventional view of the public sector, the increasing involvement of private sector organisations in public projects has also had a reciprocal effect on private sector companies. As a consequence of this interaction, a new ethos of public service is emerging which more accurately reflects organisational behaviour than the (largely misperceived) public sector ethos which it is replacing. This synthesis of public and private ethics, manifest in both the public and the private organisations engaged in the new governance of Britain, reflects a fundamental shift from a concern with process to a concern with outputs, and offers an insight of general importance into the way in which what might broadly be characterised as 'New Public Management' (NPM) impacts upon the delivery of public services.

Below, I first examine the concept of a distinct public sector ethos. Next, the trend towards private sector solutions and NPM is explored, with particular reference to the allegations that such developments have contributed to a decline in the traditional ethos of the public sector. Thirdly, and drawing on both previously published sources and the opinions of senior Staffordshire decision-makers, the empirical evidence for changes of attitude in both public and private sectors is outlined. Finally, it is suggested that a synthesis of private and public ethics is occurring and that it now makes sense to talk of a new 'public service ethos' which is colonising both public and private organisations engaged in the new system of governance.

What is the public sector ethos?

Definitions of the 'public sector ethos' reflect both the vagueness and the ambiguity of the concept. The terms 'public *sector* ethos' and 'public *service* ethos' appear to be used interchangeably in the literature; for example, Poole *et al.* (1995) talk of a public *sector* ethos while Pratchett and Wingfield (1996) use public *service* ethos when clearly describing the same concept. Given that this chapter intends to propose there has been a public sector–private sector synthesis, and that the term *public service ethos* can be used to characterise the new attitudes in both public and private sector organisations, the term 'public sector ethos' will be used to describe the exclusively public sector values and ethics, except where quoting or where inappropriate. The traditional ethos is characterised by O'Toole as:

> first, and most important, it is about the setting aside of personal interests … working altruistically for the public good. Secondly, … it is about working with *others*, collegially and anonymously, to promote that public good. Thirdly, it is about integrity in dealing with the many and diverse problems which need solving if the public good is to be promoted.
>
> (O'Toole, 1993, p. 3, his emphasis)

This characterisation, as with other 'vague and ambiguous statements of traditional bureaucracy', has contributed to 'fostering a myth that there has always been a set of values and beliefs that characterises those employed in the public sector' (Pratchett and Wingfield, 1994, fn24, p. 11)

Myth or not, it is undeniable that many people do feel a sense of loss (ibid., p. 6). Privatisation, de-regulation, 'marketisation' in the areas of employment, health care, housing, education, transport and other sectors of social infrastructure together with the progressive contracting-out of some of the regulatory functions of local government and the passing of broad areas of publicly funded activity (such as training) to quango style bodies, represent the operational triumph of what, in the late eighties, became known as Thatcherism. The broad social gains of these changes, expressed in terms of the modernisation of both the quality and efficiency of some service delivery, are undoubted – although those 'broad social gains' were not distributed evenly in the population and probably represented, at the most charitable, no gain at all for the least advantaged sections of British society. They brought with them however, an unanticipated debate about the values that inform the conduct of public life.

Public concern, at least as reflected in the media, has centred on a number of 'high profile' issues (such as the consultancy and other related activities of some MP's, the salary levels of the senior staff in the privatised utilities, the appointment procedures and reward levels in the new quangocracy). Of probably more significance to the electorate, because of a greater penetration into the everyday experience of large numbers of citizens, is the general unease engendered in and around the 'caring professions' (medical, educational) about the ethics of the new marketisation, which has resulted in the hitherto unusual politicisation of (for example) the nursing profession and parent/teachers' organisations. It is plausible to suggest that the operational success of the new right critique of public bureaucracy has served to expose the fragility of a myth of public sector values that lies at the core of British public administration (a point explored below).

Inevitably, some have sought to assert the concrete reality of the ethos. Pratchett and Wingfield (1994, p. 9) identify a set of core values which they argue inform the behaviour of local bureaucrats:

(1) accountability;
(2) honesty and impartiality;
(3) serving the community;
(4) altruistic motivation;
(5) a sense of loyalty to community, profession and organisation.

Pratchett and Wingfield point out that not all public sector bodies manifest the ethos in the same way. For example, two distinctive features are unique to local government: its 'inherently local focus' and the fact that it is 'overtly politicised'. In addition, local authorities are about 'multiple purposes [and] multiple values' (Malde, 1994, p. 9). Pratchett and Wingfield's survey of local government officers found that there was no 'universal' ethos, clearly articulated and defined (Pratchett and Wingfield, 1994, p. 32). While there was a degree of consensus about the key values, there were considerable differences in interpretation of those values. That said, there were clearly certain values that local actors felt they should at least attempt to follow (Greenaway, 1995). The introduction of CCT and changing fashions in organisational management have been seen as major contributors to a change of emphasis within that set of values (Pratchett and Wingfield, 1994, p. 34; see also Radcliffe, 1996).

Challenges to the ethos

For defenders of the traditional concept of a public servant, the honesty, integrity, impartiality, passion for justice and absence of self-seeking they associate with public servants is contrasted with a venal and profit-driven private sector (see Malde, 1994; O'Toole, 1993). To be fair, such defenders are responding to an equally simplistic attack on the public sector in which the mantra 'private sector good, public sector bad' is chanted as if self-evidently true (Institute of Economic Affairs publications, *passim*). The mantra has so dominated political and academic thinking during the past two decades that any notion of the private sector having something to learn from the values and practices of the public sector has come to be seen as risible. During this period, opponents of market-led change feel the ethos of public service has been so 'tainted, debased, spoiled and perverted' that it has become a rarity (O'Toole, 1993, p. 1); it is alleged that morale is at 'an all time low' (Hoggett, 1996, p. 10).

So for critics, introducing some of the demands of the market into the public sector is largely responsible for the perceived loss of integrity. Implicit (and often clearly stated) in the belief of those who posit a decline on the public service ethos is the view that the private sector is somehow morally corrupt. The implications that 'BCCI and Robert Maxwell' (Malde, 1994, p. 9) are representative of the private sector or that honesty, integrity and commitment to the public interest are rare commodities in the City (Baume, 1991) are offensive to the majority of workers in the private sector. A commitment to making a profit for one's company does not preclude a commitment to one's workforce or local and national interests, and nor need it preclude an element of altruism in a personal or corporate ethos. A combination of 'local capital, local self-esteem and local public-mindedness' built commercial and political centres all over Britain (Marr, 1996, p. 62) and, despite Marr's often pessimistic view of local government today, such projects can still flourish. For example, in Leeds the private sector has been instrumental in promoting the city as a thriving economic centre (Cole and John, 1996, p. 10). In Stoke-on-Trent, a number of public–private initiatives have stimulated capital investment, resulting in highly successful developments which have helped rejuvenate the local economy; the Festival Park site in Hanley, combining leisure, retail, hotel, government agency and business premises on previously derelict land, has been one such public–private success story, helping to rejuvenate the local economy of North Staffordshire.

The former Cabinet Secretary Sir Robin Butler might be right in his belief that there are inescapable differences in aims, values and objectives between the two sectors (Butler, 1992, cited in Malde, 1994, p. 9), but this overlooks the blurring that has taken place over the previous two decades. It has been taken for granted that there is much the private sector can learn from the public sector, but is O'Toole (1993, pp. 4–5) right that private sector attitudes and practices are inappropriate in the public services? While he admits there is much room for improvement, O'Toole offers no suggestions for improving public sector management beyond that they should be run in 'the public interest'. For O'Toole, the dog-eat-dog ethos is 'inexorably' taking over the public service (ibid., p. 4).

Some of the defenders of the public sector ethos appear to have strange notions of what previously existed. Rather as sports fans look back to a golden age when all cricketers were Comptons, the quality and personal integrity of present day bureaucrats and politicians is nearly always compared unfavourably to those in the past (see Chapman, 1996, p. 15). The belief that integrity has markedly declined confuses the official rhetoric of previous ages with the often sordid reality; a severe code of official secrecy and media deference meant that politicians and officials were able to hide misdemeanours in a way that is largely unthinkable now. Given the increase in media access and scrutiny and the relaxation in society's attitudes towards sexual matters, the number of cases now publicised of 'politicians behaving badly' is unsurprising, unless we *really* expect our elected members to behave differently from the rest of the population.

Like their political counterparts, unelected public servants have not escaped this concern with declining standards. The growth of agencies at national and local level and the concern over 'politicisation' during the Thatcher years has stimulated the belief that the prevailing ethos of the civil service 'has moved away from one of public service towards one of private gain' (O'Toole, 1993, p. 5). It is undeniable that developments which have devolved managerial authority and attempted to promote entrepreneurial cultures and a commitment to privatisation have at the very least raised questions about the current accountability (Weir and Hall, 1994) and financial probity (Doig, 1995b, pp. 204–7) of such agencies. Such developments also raise concern about the position and motives of senior civil servants. However, the contention that there is a *'prima facie* case' of erosion of Whitehall's ethos of public service (Greenaway, 1995, p. 373) seems to overstate the position. There is very little hard evidence that standards of probity have declined. The majority of civil servants remain committed to the traditional Whitehall 'high standards'.

Local government also has believers in a golden age who feel that standards have declined (Marr, 1996, p. 99). The evidence is slim, with a few high profile cases largely contributing to public suspicion about the motives of local councillors and local government officers. That public suspicion has been fuelled by reports of 'loony left' councils and by central government propaganda questioning the motives of local councillors and professionals; the hostility and suspicion of central politicians and civil servants has contributed to both the decline in the confidence and self-esteem of those who work in local government and in the poor public perception of local democracy (Jones and Travers, 1994, pp. 15–16). There have certainly been external pressures on local ethical standards. As I have noted, one major development in central–local relations in the past two decades has been a move away from co-operation towards central direction, led by legislation designed to impose strict financial control on local authority spending. Central attempts to increase local government accountability have foundered on ill-conceived and contradictory legislation – on one hand the community charge and on the other hand, capping. However, the factor which most concerns defenders of a traditional public sector ethos is the intro-duction of measures (such as CCT) designed to introduce an element of competition into the provision of local government services. Some local officials do feel the concept of public service has been weakened by the growth in contracted-out services (Pratchett and Wingfield, 1994: 1996)

Whatever the reality, there is a widespread belief (both within the public sector and in academic circles) that the changes in the public sector introduced by recent governments are undermining an ethos that has long been a feature of British public administration. Despite noting that 'the public service ethic has not … always been uniformly applied or accepted', Doig (a long-time observer of standards in public life) felt that the problems arising were more than 'the teething troubles of change' (1995b, pp. 209–10).

New Public Management, old private values

As I have already noted, 'new-wave' management thinking from the private sector has permeated public-sector thinking. New Public Management (NPM) emphasises lean and purposeful administrative structures (Hood, 1991, p. 13). The conventional wisdom is that the bottom line for public officials has become the performance of their own cost centre to the detriment of traditional public service values (Hood, 1991). At their most extreme, critics have compared the introduction of 'rational' models of management as 'either an act of culpable ignorance … or an exercise in … ideological imperialism' (Pollitt, 1993, p. 144).

Moreover, it is clear that NPM is 'emphatically, not a uniquely British development' (Hood, 1991, p. 3). NPM's 'transformation of the public sector' (Rhodes, 1996, p. 655) and the shift towards privatisation and quasi-privatisation has had a world-wide impact. Not only that, but in a number of countries (for example, Australia, New Zealand, Holland, the United States, Japan) pressures arising from the implementation of a 'set of broadly similar administrative doctrines' (Hood, 1991, p. 2) have subsequently been noted on the public sector ethos and British concerns of a subsequent decline in standards are shared by observers in other countries. For example, Jacobs' study of Pittsburgh notes that public–private partnerships, for all their positive contributions to regional innovation, can 'dissipate … core organisational competencies commonly associated with government' such as high public service standards (1998, p. 333) while Bovens argues such developments have posed 'formidable challenges for … managerial integrity' in Holland (1996, p. 132). The wide reach of the fundamental changes in government has been recognised by the attempts of the Organisation for Economic Co-operation and Development (OECD) to draw up an 'ethics infrastructure' in an effort to promote ethical public behaviour in the new 'risk-taking' environment (McRae, 1997). While I focus on the UK experience, the almost universal increase of public–private interaction (although Christiansen, 1998, notes Denmark's rejection of such developments) suggests that the synthesis of public and private ethics and motivations I propose reflects a more general phenomenon. Certainly, similar networks of public and private actors sharing 'commercial risks and commit[ing] resources to achieve common aims' have produced new forms of collaboration which have 'blurred distinctions between the public and private sectors' in countries other than the UK (Jacobs, 1998, p. 330).

In Britain, Pratchett and Wingfield feel that the dual impact of CCT and the internal reforms introduced by NPM has meant a movement away 'from the traditional focus on procedural integrity to concentrate much more upon efficiency and performance measurement' (Pratchett and Wingfield, 1994, p. 34). This movement away from a concentration on procedural matters and towards greater concern with quality of output is a defining aspect of the new public service ethos. Indeed, despite reservations about the divisive potential of the changes, Pratchett and Wingfield see the ethos as 'evolving, rather than declining' and being augmented by new features:

> a greater dedication of officers to the provision of qualitatively better and more efficient services; a more innovative and flexible approach to the management of functions that comes from a competitive and entrepreneurial environment; and an acceptance of the need for objective measures of organisational and individual performance.
>
> (Pratchett and Wingfield, 1994, p. 34)

Some British actors however, refuse to recognise the permanence of some of the forces that Thatcherism released. For Malde:

> the grounds are ripe for the public servant to retreat back into the neutrality camp and to argue the virtues of the tradition of honesty, integrity, fairness and equity, as the vital principles of democratic governance which only public servants are uniquely placed to uphold. Blurring this with the notions of profit and 'market testing' or even 'politicised public servant' would risk the breaking down of the bedrock of democratic life.
>
> (1994, pp. 12–13)

Malde advocates direct action by public officials and maintains that as public servants and citizens 'they are entitled to have their views better reflected in government policy' (p. 13). This is an astonishing statement, especially coming from someone who is vigorously defending the traditional ethos of public service; as well as being antithetical to the traditional 'minister–mandarin relationship', it is in direct contradiction to the characteristics Malde identifies as essential to a public sector ethos – honesty, integrity, fairness and equity! As noted, it also fails to recognise the permanence of the changing nature of governance (see Kirkpatrick and Lucio, 1996, p. 7). However, what Malde's comments do reflect (perhaps unconsciously) is the increasing involvement of local government officers in policy making, especially when bridging the public–private divide. The integrity of our appointed officials is a valuable commodity in such negotiations.

There is an important point to be made here. As Pattison (1994) observes, it is the success of the moral vision of the market which has made ethical concerns more visible; prior to the new right critique the existence of an essentially altruistic public sector ethos was taken for granted. NPM assumed 'a culture of public service honesty as given' and devices instituted to ensure 'honesty and neutrality' (such as rules of procedure and restraints on discretion) were therefore removed without concern (Hood, 1991, p. 16). If there *has* been a decline in probity, the champions of the traditional public sector ethos have to face up to the possibility that it was kept in place for so long as much by rigid sanctions as by a saint-like devotion to abstract values.

The blurring of the boundary between state and civil society

Given the above, it is unsurprising that the concept of a unique public sector ethos has been most seriously challenged by the growth of agencies which straddle the boundary between the state and civil society. The blurring between the private and public sectors and the 'hybrid' organisations which can result, noted by Jacobs (1998, p. 330) in his examination of an American region, becomes apparent in Britain when one tries to classify local organisations. The difficulty of deciding the status of, for example, the new universities or TECs is not just a discussion for academic amusement. The debate about definitions, as the ethos of many TECs indicates (see chapter four), is an important one. For Davis, an acceptance of different definitions can lead to an:

> acceptance of different principles of standards … [and] … there can be no justifiable reason for applying different standards to different public services simply because the bodies which provide them are constituted in different forms.
>
> (1996, p. 3)

The new working practices of such bodies, where both public and private values co-exist, are clearly under pressure to evolve a new ethos to inform their working practices.

The blurring of the divide by new forms of local service provision and the creation of new bodies are not the only reasons for pressure on the ethos of public sector workers. Public and private co-operation on large-scale projects is increasingly being seen by local elites as essential for economic success. As Cole and John have discovered, local policy makers now try to influence:

> a wider set of processes which are thought to affect local economic prosperity. Whereas in the past only a few private sector actors really wanted local economic policy intervention, now there is a greater awareness of the need to market economic activity and more competition with European cities…the result is networks based on trust and exchange between public and private sectors.
>
> (Cole and John, 1996, p. 8)

The meeting of public and private ethics can be positive, then. As briefly noted earlier in this chapter, in Leeds:

> there has developed a culture of co-operation between public and private elites in the city which has its expression in public decisions whether it is for charitable causes or to join public–private partnerships.
>
> (Cole and John, 1996, p. 10)

This is not a case of Mammon calling the shots, but 'an accommodation between the city and business based on sharing many objectives' (ibid., p. 11). Staffordshire's successful bids for SRB money were founded on just such an accommodation. Developers seeking planning permission for development are required by some local authorities to provide a new community facility as part of the agreement (Heatley, 1990). Agreements like these may draw entrepreneurs into more co-operative working relationships with the public sector but add, of course, to the ethical uncertainty. Such working relationships have the capacity to go far beyond areas such as economic development. In health and education, for example, public and private actors now cooperate to provide what are still unarguably 'public' services. Given such developments, it does not appear far-fetched to suggest that the synthesis, fusion or accommodation, call it what you will, between the public sector ethos and the private sector ethos will continue to subtly alter the individual and organisational ethos of both sectors.

Towards a new public–private synthesis of values?

The ability of 'street level bureaucrats' to guide organisational policy is well documented (Lipsky, 1980). The ability of firms to co-ordinate and control is generally over-stated, organisational efficiency often taking precedence over central direction (McGuinness, 1991, p. 71); despite the growth of centralisation, this can apply as much to central government's attempts to control local government as it does to private sector organisations. For senior representatives of commerce and industry in Staffordshire, it is clear that the majority are aware of a whole range of influences impinging on their ability to meet their organisation's objectives. For the most part, senior private sector decision makers recognise the need to balance community and private interests. Similarly, an examination of private and public sector partnerships in Sheffield and Wakefield noted that both sides had become 'genuinely committed to the philosophy and practice' underpinning the partnership; such co-operation was combating 'one of the fundamental weaknesses of the British economy, the degree of separation between the private and public sectors' (in Bruce, 1993, p. 333).

It is perhaps uncontroversial to note that there is a consensus that the private sector ethos has 'invaded' the public sector, but given the blurring of the state–civil society divide and the growth of semi-private and semi-public organisations, it seems inconceivable that, as Cole and John's findings intimate (1996, p. 21), the process has not been happening the other way. That is, elements of the public sector ethos will have affected those private sector organisations with which it is in regular contact. For example, Richard Priestley, chief executive of the North Staffordshire Health Authority, feels the relationship of the health authority with its private sector partners is 'stimulating' and he feels the issues those partners have to face mean they may gain organisationally from an increased sense of 'social responsibility' (interview, 1997). Such gains may be especially felt at local level, where the consequences of commercial decisions impinge more obviously on the decision-maker's own community. Research supports the belief that there has been a growth in public and private sector local actors developing strategic policy based upon their common interests (Cole and John, 1996; Peck and Tickell, 1994; Heatley, 1990; Hutchinson, 1994) a growth paralleled in other countries (Jacobs, 1996, 1998). Not all observers are convinced that they represent 'some new found spirit of cooperation' (Peck and Tickell, 1994, p. 263) and it may be that one driving factor is the failure of local authorities to achieve their aims given more limited resources (Bruce, 1993, p. 333). However, many actors are convinced that such co-operation is largely positive and that the public–private commitment to partnership is genuine (Askew, 1991).

For example, one of the key players in Staffordshire decision making believes:

> It's not difficult to get [the business community] on side in a partnership, because identifying common purpose in the city isn't difficult … if I'm sitting on a board with four or five private sector key leaders from the business world here they've more and more become to understand the public sector ethos and vice versa.
>
> (interview with Brian Smith, 1997)

While Brian Smith recognised that some local business people still adopted a 'blinkered approach', the increasing number of joint projects had led to a much greater level of understanding and appreciation than he had ever believed possible; he felt that private companies had adopted elements of the public sector ethos and a 'community perception' could be seen. Most managing directors of local companies in Staffordshire saw their employees as their paramount personal obligation (whatever their formal obligations) and the majority also recognised a formal obligation to the public (more details are given in Chapter 7). Some went further – Brian Patterson, chief executive of Wedgwood, felt that:

> my job is to reconcile the needs of the key stakeholders, the investors, suppliers, customers, employees, local community [and] local authority … is there a clear order of priority? I guess there isn't, it's a continual balancing act trying to balance the needs of all these stakeholders with your ear to the market.
>
> (interview, 1997)

Such responses make it clear that, whatever the overriding needs of profit, a commitment to broader values is real, and informs private sector decision making. Many clearly had a deep attachment to their local communities. It was not only local companies who felt this attachment; managers of multinational companies felt personally obliged to play a part in the local community and some followed an organisational strategy of actively supporting local businesses.

For Bogdanor, any analogy drawn between management in the public and private sectors is highly flawed because there is no accountability or ethical code in the private sector that can be compared to the norms governing public sector workers and elected members (Bogdanor, 1994). I would argue, on the basis of my investigations, that while there may be no formal accountability to the public nor a common ethical code, managers and executives in the private sector clearly have a set of generalised ethical objectives, which they pursue in their daily life and against which they judge the operational activities of their organisations (see Table 7.2, Chapter 7).

Despite this, local bureaucrats often have negative views about business and business people, believing that public sector workers behaved with more honesty and integrity, and that those in the private sector are 'not always as honest as they might be' (in Pratchett and Wingfield, 1994, p. 27). However, there does not appear to be a general hostility to change in the public sector; Haughton *et al.* found that 'most local players are broadly sympathetic with the competitiveness initiative' (1997, p. 95). For Richard Priestley, 'very many aspects of the private sector now permeate our acts and our thoughts' and he found 'no conceptual difficulty in ensuring that the best and appropriate aspects of practice from the private sector are incorporated within the public contracts' negotiated by the North Staffordshire Health Authority. For Butcher (1993), such acceptance is a consequence of a number of complementary factors emanating from different points on the political spectrum. 'New-wave' management thinking from the private sector, as symbolised by Peters and Waterman's *In Search of Excellence* (1982), has permeated public-sector thinking because our society has become more pluralistic and more demanding and because new right ideas have been so successful across the political spectrum. Butcher (1993, p. 66) therefore suggests that this should lead to the interests of consumers becoming better represented.

However, it appears that some public sector organisations are much less responsive to the interests of consumers of public services than they are to those of their sponsoring organisations. Organisations in the (non-profit making) private sector are also weighted towards the interests of client groups and 'public sector policy makers'. That sector appears to have been at least partly colonised and captured by the public policy network, illustrating the blurring between private and public in this sector. To quote the remarks of the local head of one well known national pressure group:

> Our organisation seeks to serve the interests of [the particular group in society]. However, we are obliged to serve the interests of social

services and the area health authority. We also serve the interests of the [national organisation]. ... I feel most obliged to serve the interest of social services. Without their support, both financially and esteem [*sic*], we would not be able to serve our client group.

(questionnaire reply, 1996)

Likewise, the head of a registered charity offering advice to the public said that, while formally he served the 'community', he personally felt most obliged to serve the local politicians who were the main source of his organisation's operating funds. Profit making private sector organisations might also be partly 'colonised' in this way; when formulating policy or making operational decisions, some private sector organisations claim to take more consideration of the views of local government actors than they do of their own board (questionnaire replies).

Public–private cooperation and the problem of accountability

Such problems are the inevitable, if unintended, consequence of the changing boundaries of the state and the numbers of new bodies with governmental powers. Changes which were intended to shake up a perceived moribund local state political system have also demonstrated the importance of the traditional values held by such organisations, which were often undervalued during the Thatcher years. Public and private actors are now developing strategic policy together in all our regions. This cooperation is forging a new public *service* ethos rooted both in public notions of, for example, honesty, impartiality and community service and private notions of, for example, competition and consumer choice.

Undeniably, there has been real concern about the processes of accountability in agencies spanning the public–private divide, as noted by the Nolan Committee's report on standards in public life (Nolan, 1995, p. 24). The group Democratic Audit was more critical than Nolan, noting that the majority of such agencies are unaccountable; for example, less than half of them allow the public to examine members' interests (Weir and Hall, 1994). For Daly, accountability in the Health Service is now 'deeply flawed' (Daly, 1996, pp. 61–2). The following chapter will discuss such problems of public accountability in detail; here I briefly address the problem as it relates to the new ethos of public service.

It is important to note that the growth of agencies is not implicitly 'anti-democratic'. Marketisation has meant that public services have been made to take some notice of what the public really wants (Potter, 1988, p. 160). Rhodes notes that 'the exercise of citizenship is not equated with one activity (voting)' (1987, p. 67); as Potter points out, 'the voting slip cast in the ballot box cannot be used to signify consumers' preferences in any but the grossest fashion' (1988, p. 152). Such 'democratic accountability' amounts to little more than a request by public actors to 'trust our motives and ethics' rather than offering anything concrete and useful to the consumer of public services. The much maligned Citizen's Charter – revamped with measurable acceptable standards for delivery of services – could offer a greater measure of accountability than the charade of democratic accountability given by the current electoral system.

However, Ranson argues that 'a new moral and political order' built on 'individual rights and public accountability of government to consumer choice in the market place' (1990, p. 193) is fundamentally flawed. Hill agrees that attempts to marry consumer sovereignty and state regulatory power have been weakened by increasing centralisation. As Hill recognises, consumer and citizen should not be seen as 'antithetical concepts', and services 'need to be accountable to individuals and communities in both a political and a direct sense' (1994, p. 232). Underpinning this must be a new sense of public service, traversing the increasingly blurred barrier between the state and civil society. As this chapter indicates, there is evidence of a 'new sense of public service' manifest in private sector actors engaged in the delivery of 'public' services.

A paradox in public perception

There is an important paradox in the public perception of the impact of new right ideology on the delivery of public services and the changing role of the state. Most citizens never were active in the public sphere. They were consumers of the products of public and bureaucratised state institutions whose occupants at all levels broadly adhered to, and cultivated public trust in, formal public morality and the values of service. This community of value has not survived the changes of the 1980s, and like all communities it cannot be recalled into being by the popular demand of non-participants. It is, put bluntly, merely sentimental to mourn the passing of institutions in whose patriarchal good intentions the citizen felt he could trust, since from the Monarchy to the Water Company these are now colonised by possessive individuals like himself.

The evidence that the public is against the private provision of local services is in any case, unconvincing. As noted in Chapter 1, research indicates overwhelming public satisfaction with their refuse collection service, the most common service to have been privatised (Lynn, 1992, pp. 70–8); standards have 'improved significantly' in that area since CCT (Deakin and Walsh, 1996, p. 44). The belief that the public cares little about how services are provided, but is primarily concerned with the quality of service provided, may be a more accurate reflection of public attitudes to service provision. There has, for example, been a more positive attitude about local government in recent public surveys which suggest considerable improvement 'which may of course reflect the introduction of competition' and that 'local politicians may have responded to public concerns about accountability and consultation' rather better than their critics have ever acknowledged (Rallings *et al.*, 1994, p. 12).

The 'general popularity' of the changes of the Thatcher years is undisputed (Budge *et al.*, 1998, p. 658) as New Labour's acceptance of the new consensus and their subsequent electoral endorsement in 1997 indicates. However, that general popularity has not prevented a sense of public unease about the conduct of public life which has been fuelled by the large number of financial (and sexual) scandals which seemed to characterise the final years of John Major's Conservative government and have continued under Tony Blair and New Labour. So while the public prefer, for example, the service record of the privatised industries to their nationalised predecessors they continue to resent the salaries and profits now generated and the marketing techniques employed.

This paradox (welcome changes which improve service, deplore the ethics of the same changes) lies at the heart of the current debate about the public sector ethos. Clearly, a mismatch has arisen between the 'new ethics' (they are, of course, very ancient ones) of the social market place and a set of deep seated expectations in the political culture of the UK. This mis-match is probably best generally categorised in terms of de-institutionalisation. The values of public life, and the ethics of conduct governing the behaviour of public people in the UK, have never been reflected in the private behaviour of the citizenry. What was expected of the denizens of the public sector in all its incarnations (to some extent it still is) was a personal ethic of service to the commonweal. In their private behaviour public sector figures were called upon to symbolise and embody the formal (even ceremonial) morality of Church and State. If the private morality of the population in general might, from the 1960's onwards, undergo significant change, the moral expectations of the State – from the Monarchy to the gasman – might not. The State, in all its massive post-war extension, might be bumbling, antique, self-important, slow and laughably inefficient. Its integrity and its good intentions were never, however, in question.

The experience of an empowered and aggressively market-oriented finance industry (in the housing sector, pension sector, private investment/savings sector) has clearly shocked many citizens whose expectations were formed by the (highly bureaucratised) supportive integrity of the 'nanny state'. Many signally failed to appreciate that the market doctrine they endorsed electorally for application to public affairs, would impact significantly on the conduct of their private affairs. From the financial wreckage of the Gooda Walker syndicate at Lloyds to the more modest (but more widespread) scandal of oversold mortgage debt, the lesson is of the exploitation of individual trust in pursuit of private interest. The trust thus exploited was (and is) a product of the residual expectation that great institutions will reflect public (and institutionalised) morality and not the newly embraced morality of the market place.

In deconstructing broad swathes of the public institutions that delivered services in the UK, the edifice of public sector ethics was also deconstructed. The citizen was pleased to buy gas shares but appears to be dismayed by the discovery that the gasman is now in the business of profit and not in the business of social provision. With the de-institutionalisation of services comes the de-institutionalisation of morality. The well-understood distinction between how a citizen *did* behave and how a citizen *ought* to behave (that which allowed an 'Arthur Daley' to be an earnestly principled moral pillar when called upon for jury service) is eroded. The great institutions of State no longer symbolise and embody the ethical aspirations of the private person as citizen but are instead colonised by the private morality of private aspiration. The loss is to both the concept and public perception of 'citizenship' – the activities associated with citizenship can no longer be readily distinguished from those associated with the pursuit of private interest.

A new perspective: a synthesis of values

However complex the ethical issues, it is undeniable that the current meeting between private and public sector can be seen as positive. The beneficial impact of market imperatives has been too often overlooked or minimised by critics. As Summers points out:

> one of the most valuable benefits of opening up what have traditionally been local government domains to outside organisations – whether they be commercial organisations, quangos, charities, NHS

trusts or housing associations – is that there has been the opportunity to see how different means of decision-making perform; thus presenting alternatives to the traditional monolithic, hierarchical and departmentalised local authority model.

(Summers, 1996, p. 210)

To fear that such changes to 'existing attitudes, values and procedures may lead to mismanagement' (Doig, 1995a, pp. 109–10) is too pessimistic. Local government officers have often been recruited from outside the public sector, and it cannot be seriously argued that such appointments have led to a less honest local culture. The appointment of private sector managers to NHS boards does not appear to have led to a 'relaxation of ethical standards' (Sheaff and West, 1997, p. 202). In central government too, the appointment of 'outsiders' as Permanent Secretaries and the increase in open advertising for senior public service posts (Mountfield, 1997) indicate that the public sector ethos will continue to be enriched by other imperatives.

While the suggestion of a synthesis occurring between public and private values which has affected both sectors is rather bolder, there is support for the proposal. One examination of public and private sector managerial responses to Thatcherism found 'an emphasis…on the enterprise culture and on market values have impacted on managerial attitudes' and that 'there does appear to be some convergence between public and private sectors in these respects' (Poole *et al.*, 1997, p. 285) The authors also found that market values have led to a refocusing towards the views of consumers 'and this has progressively impacted upon managerial policies, actions and behaviour' (ibid., p. 285).

Of course, changes in the public sector ethos raise concerns about 'the demeanour of the whole state'; notwithstanding the attempts of the OECD to construct an 'ethics infrastructure', a new ethos which covered civil servants, ministers, local government and 'appointed managers' would be breaking 'new constitutional territory' for Britain (Greenaway, 1995, p. 373) and an ethos which attempted to encompass private sector actors would encounter even greater difficulty. The Audit Commission still seeks to 'identify a locus for the building, owning and policing of an ethical environment' (Doig, 1995a, p. 112) and Nolan appeared to offer a framework. The Nolan Committee's investigation of standards in public life proposed 'seven principles of public life' which have been seen by some as essential principles for holders of public office (Davis, 1996); briefly, those principles are 'selflessness, integrity, objectivity, accountability, openness, honesty and leadership'

(Nolan, 1995, p. 14). The principles, noble as they are, are too rooted in the traditional notions of a public sector ethos to be applicable to the new systems of governance emerging and they are also difficult to quantify. For example, the requirement that holders of public life need to be accountable and 'must submit themselves to whatever scrutiny is appropriate to their office' (ibid.) is clearly open to a great deal of dis-agreement as to what type and degree of scrutiny is 'appropriate'. There has been an 'increased pressure on public sector managers to adjust to a rapidly changing environment but without a series of supports at local level having necessarily emerged' (Poole *et al.*, 1997, p. 285). One such support must be the emergence of an ethical environment which reflects the new reality of widespread private sector involvement in the provision of public services.

The Chartered Institute of Public Finance and Accountancy (CIPFA), noting that developments such as more commercial styles of manage-ment were changing the culture of the public sector, identified three fundamental principles equally applicable to private and public sector organisations: (i) 'openness or the disclosure of information'; (ii) integrity or 'straightforward dealing and completeness'; and (iii) accountability or 'holding individuals responsible for their actions' (in Rhodes, 1996, p. 654). The nebulous nature of these 'three fundamental principles' hints at the difficulties of constructing an operationally viable new public *service* code.

From process to outputs: a shift in ethical focus

Changes in public service values are, as Pratchett and Wingfield put it: 'more than peripheral phenomena ... they strike to the very heart of the institutional transformation taking place in contemporary local gov-ernment' (1996, p. 655). The thesis, the public sector ethos, has been confronted by its antithesis in developments such as new public man-agement, but the belief that the effects of the resulting synthesis have been largely negative cannot survive empirical examination. That the effect has been one way can also not go unchallenged. While the evi-dence for a benevolent effect on the private sector offered here is largely anecdotal, the findings of empirical research also suggest the adoption of public sector ethics by private sector actors. A new ethical code – an ethos of public service applicable to both public and private sector actors and organisations involved in service provision – is seen by some as a desirable result. For example, Palfrey and Thomas (1996, pp. 282–4) argue that the starting point of such a code for the next century might be that policy makers and implementors follow:

(a) honesty;
(b) equity;
(c) impartiality;
(d) respect [for views of all participants in the process];
(e) [in the case of the professional evaluator] adherence to high levels of competence.

I wish to suggest, however, that listing the key elements of a code of conduct in this fashion is an inherently unsatisfactory way of characterising the culture of the policy and managerial community engaged in the business of service coordination and delivery.

As in the case of the work of the Nolan Committee, whose aspirational list of the characteristics of the good public servant increasingly informs codes of conduct and accountability across a wide spectrum of the public service (see DETR, 1998), such formulae provide a legalistic checklist but throw little light on the policy orientation or managerial 'mind set' of those engaged in the new governance. They define the ways in which shortcomings and malfeasance shall be identified – and presumably acted against. They do not describe the way in which such communities now define the nature of the public interest and identify the most appropriate means for its pursuit. In contrast, this study of the Staffordshire decision-making community has led me to characterise the newly emerging culture through a description of the way in which members of that community now conceptualise their task. This reconceptualisation lies at the heart of that synthesis of private and public sector values which might accurately be called the public *service* ethos.

Central to the new culture of governance referred to here is a shift in ethical focus from process to end product, and from a professionally self-referencing definition of efficiency and effectiveness to one defined in terms of outcomes. This shift in focus informs the range of solutions available for the resolution of public service delivery problems, the way in which priorities are identified and set, and the style in which solutions are presented and justified. Importantly, such a characterisation offers the possibility of a generic explanation of a range of phenomena associated with NPM including the concepts of 'enabling', 'customer service orientation', the demands for greater access and accountability in the conduct of public affairs, and the concern with 'market-led' solutions.

It also generates its own shortlist of managerial characteristics which proceed naturally from the shift in focus – but this list is of descriptors and not prescriptions. The list includes *pragmatism* (and by implication the eschewing of ideologically prescribed policy solutions); a concern with *quality* (as defined by the client/customer and not by the producer/professional); the need for *procedural transparency* (where transparency is understood as information about the decision-making process which is in a form accessible to the ordinary concerned citizen); the proposition that *consumer consultation* should lie at the heart of priority setting.

The public *service* ethos borrows from the private sector the notion of the discipline of the marketplace (with all that flows from that) and applies it to the 'pseudo-market' of the recipients of public services – who are, of course, without real market power. Moreover, the absence of a market-powerful primary customer for public and semi-public services is not compensated for via mechanisms such as the introduction of a 'quasi-market' of producer cartels (as, for example, in the NHS internal market). Rather it is achieved through the change in managerial culture described above which treats the users of public provision as *if* they were market-powerful. The term I use to refer to this, 'pseudo-market', is used advisedly, since I seek to distinguish between the market-like terminology currently fashionable among service deliverers but which reflects no real market relationship, and the term 'quasi-market' which already has a specific and different meaning in the literature (Le Grand and Bartlett, 1993, p. 10).

The move from public sector ethos to public service ethos might thus be understood as a move from seeing the public as a client/supplicant to one of seeing them as a consumer/purchaser. This change, where it has already occurred or is in process of occurring, manifests itself in a range of different ways. Local Authorities, for example, increasingly have Press and Public Relations departments, just as companies do. They operate expensive reception desks modelled on Bank or Building Society high street premises with staff in smart corporate costume. The function of these is chiefly to confirm the (artificial) status of their clients as customers and this confirmation is required as much by the organisation itself as it is to make a signal to the citizen.

Similarly, Housing Authorities in the 1980s and early 1990s, especially where they were Labour controlled, generally resisted the various changes in the policy environment that led to the privatisation of their housing stocks. Three of Staffordshire's nine housing authorities, all with Labour majorities, are undertaking the voluntary transfer of their entire housing stock out of direct control. While central government's housing finance regime is clearly the catalyst for this, it also represents a change of attitude away from one whose origins were largely ideological to one whose ethical foundation is the pragmatic question 'how can we get the most people housed in the manner and style which they prefer'. Interestingly, this 'outcome oriented' approach renders redundant some of the sorts of questions which had importance in the past. 'Will any private interest benefit from the use of a public sector asset?' is no longer a problem since the ethical consideration is now couched in terms of an optimum outcome for the customer/consumer group and not in terms of the motives of the actors engaged in service provision.

Conclusion

It is this outcome-orientated service ethos which is increasingly emerging as the managerial and decision-making style in local authorities and local and regional quangos. It is a style which at face value bears resemblance to some aspects of private sector values. The resemblance however, disguises a complex redefinition of what constitutes service to the public and involves a synthesis of a managerial culture with more traditional notions of good conduct.

The solution both to current concerns about the conduct of public affairs and to the paradox in public expectation referred to here cannot be by recourse to a lost code of public ethics. Rather, it must be to a mixture of formal regulation and clear lines of accountability, suitably informed by the new consensus currently being forged across traditional private/public divides by the practitioner community now involved in delivering public service in Britain. That consensus is still emerging, and as is inevitable in so large and disparate an area of national life, it is not doing so with either geographic or sectional uniformity. Nevertheless, the Staffordshire research leads me to believe that the delineation of that consensus, which I refer to as the new public *service* ethos, offers the most productive route to a general understanding of the impact of New Public Management and related developments on the ethos and motivation of regional and local practitioner communities.

7

A Crisis of Accountability

Introduction

A concern with accountability is a natural consequence of the spread of public–private partnerships. Although, as the previous chapter has shown, concern about the motives of private sector actors involved in the provision of public services may often be misplaced, the lack of direct public accountability for such private and non-elected public actors means such concern will not go away. The difficulty of ascribing responsibility in the new system of governance in Britain is the focus of attention in this chapter.

After a brief assessment of the concepts of accountability and responsibility, I examine the nature of accountability in the local governance system. Some aspects of service provision in the more market-orientated culture (for example, the tendering of services) still apply electoral accountability, albeit attenuated. But in quangos, agencies and privatised companies, the mechanisms of accountability are either unclear or unsatisfactory and many quango members demonstrate a lack of understanding about the importance of public accountability. Such flaws in accountability are partly responsible for the declining public trust in government. The chapter also notes that private sector perceptions of accountability are more complex than critics acknowledge. Throughout, I argue the preference for a directly elected base for legitimacy; if responsibility is to be less direct, it must be clearer and less equivocal than the current lines of accountability from quangos and agencies to central government ministers. It also needs to be less of a blunt instrument than the publication of output targets and annual progress reports by which we must judge the overall performance of the Blair government.

A fundamental problem

That there is a problem of accountability in the new system of governance is undoubted. However, that problem is not just, as is often alleged, because of the political and organisational changes introduced by central government during the 1980s and 1990s especially. Undoubtedly, private sector companies delivering services previously delivered from within the public sector, the growth of quangos, the increasing number of agencies following the Next Steps programme, and the growing number of informal public–private networks now making policy, have all contributed to the concern about declining accountability. Such political and organisational changes have also been accompanied by a growing willingness by the public to complain about the quality of services they receive.

The accountability problem, however, is more fundamental. For some time now, decreasing confidence in government generally has meant that 'the framework of constitutional myth and ritual in which accountability processes are embedded and from which they derive their legitimacy' has been an 'an object of scepticism and cynicism' (Metcalfe and Richards, 1990, p. 43). There are many reasons for this decline in public confidence, not all of them the 'fault' of public actors; social changes have contributed to a decline in deference towards established authority and a subsequent unwillingness to trust the motives of those engaged in public life. As Walter Bagehot once archly cautioned, rulers need to be careful not to 'let in daylight upon magic' (1963, p. 100). The close scrutiny public figures and institutions now receive from the remorseless media has demonstrated the fragility of some of our constitutional fantasies and failed to flatter the presumptions of our representatives.

Declining legitimacy and a failure of political accountability has encompassed both central and 'sub-central' government (for example, see Jones, 1977; Rhodes, 1988). For some time, the lack of clarity in the 'sub-central' system (with functions haphazardly distributed between different levels and bodies of government) has contributed to citizen confusion. The ineffective and essentially inactive mechanisms of accountability currently operating ensure that holding anyone to account for policy failures is rare. There is a clear failure of political accountability which cannot be replaced by legal and managerial forms of accountability, which should be supplementary to the central mechanism (that is, political accountability) of liberal democracy (Rhodes, 1988, p. 403).

Despite the undoubted declining trust in government (see Chapter 5) the growing public disregard for politicians and those in public life must not be overstated, especially when referring to local politics. The elected base of local government still gives its members considerable legitimacy in the eyes of the public and, as we have seen, public satisfaction with local government is, on the whole, greater than with central government, although given the unpopularity of the Conservative government in the early to mid-1990s we should not get too carried away with this finding. Private sector companies winning local government contracts still have to answer to democratically elected local representatives answerable through the ballot box if they fail to deliver acceptable standards of service. When compared to the failures of accountability to the local community which the proliferating numbers of quangos exhibit, the services under the control of local government, no matter how they are delivered, still appear to offer the public some reassurance that local democratic accountability has not been forgotten. The political accountability local councils demonstrate is essential to counterbalance the privacy of the new professional and managerial networks.

A failure (or refusal) by critics of local government here to appreciate the nature of the accountability problem has been one constant. Local government is not the only deliverer of local services, yet central government has identified the failure of accountability as resting with one institution (local government) and the remedy has consistently been seen as attempting to improve the financial accountability of local authorities to ratepayers. The institutional complexity of the local governance system has been ignored and local government has been made a scapegoat for problems it has little or no control over. Removing services from local government control and placing them under some sort of central (and often attenuated) ministerial control has been a post-war constant in the central–local government relationship. The result has been to obscure further the responsibility for service delivery.

Enforcing responsibility: the essence of accountability

There is no space here to enter in any great detail into the complex question of the many meanings of accountability; Lawton and Rose (1991, pp. 16–24) give an admirably clear and relatively succinct account of the concept. They identify five dimensions – political, managerial, legal, consumer and professional – to the concept of public sector accountability. With the arguable exception of 'political', which could be substituted with 'shareholder', all these dimensions also apply to private sector organisations. I am primarily concerned here with accountability as a method of achieving responsive and responsible governance.

It is apparent that there are a number of mechanisms by which this could be said to be achieved along these five dimensions. However, I would argue that political accountability through the ballot box is an essential ingredient of any system of accountability in the workings of the new and more differentiated system of governance, although the traditional mechanisms of representative democracy might need to be adapted (Rhodes, 1997, p. 22). For example, when private companies are helping to deliver public services they should be subject to (at the very least) indirect political accountability such as effective scrutiny by elected representatives.

As John Stuart Mill observed, 'responsibility is null when nobody knows who is responsible' (in Birch, 1964, p. 20). Therefore, accountability is the enforcement of responsibility (Simon, 1957) which requires the ability (ultimately) to punish those spending public money who have failed to deliver. Such a decision must be taken by either (preferably) the electorate directly (for example, by having elected members of health authorities) or under the direction of elected representatives (for example, councillors) who are themselves subject to the ultimate sanction of removal from office. In the case of private sector companies engaged in governance, the 'ultimate sanction' will be the loss of the contract(s) they hold. In many cases (for example, refuse collection) there is no reason why consumers themselves cannot vote directly on the decision to renew (if not award) a contract and in other cases they should at least be consulted on the quality of service they have received. Without the elected link to responsibility, the notion of political accountability is fundamentally flawed.

Of course, this is not to maintain that the mere existence of such a link is enough. An element of 'accountability' is seen as essential for all public organisations, whether directly elected or not, but the concept is rarely satisfactorily delineated and the terms 'accountability' and 'responsibility' are riddled with ambiguity (Pym, 1996). Indeed, in his evidence to the Scott inquiry into the sale of arms to Iraq in contravention of the government's embargo, the then Cabinet Secretary Sir Robin Butler sought to draw a distinction between 'accountability' and 'responsibility'. He argued that while a minister might be required to give an *account* to Parliament, *responsibility* should only be assumed when the minister has a direct and personal involvement. This is 'Sir Humphreyism' of the highest order; there is a distinction to be made between 'giving an account of' and 'being held to account for' which Sir Robin attempts to fudge. If accepted, his interpretation has clear constitutional implications for ministerial accountability (see Radcliffe, 1997, p. 9) although one might argue that whatever the myth of ministerial accountability Sir Robin merely outlined the way ministers actually behaved. The conceptual ambiguity is paralleled by the institutional ambiguity of precisely which body is responsible for which service at local and regional level. The existence of a variety of bodies carrying out 'public' services – the network of actors from local government (elected councillors and the bureaucracy), quangos, indirectly elected appointed boards ('quelgos'), 'arm's-length' government agencies, the private sector and voluntary organisations, direct control by central government governments, the involvement of the European Union – creates a web of quite staggering institutional intricacy. Each of these different types of institution (and there are, of course, organisationally different subsets within each broad category) has a different perception of accountability and hence a different interpretation of what is required to be accountable. Given that all are now engaged in governance this can contribute to a 'democratic deficit'. The link between the spending of taxpayers' money and directly elected representatives responsible for spending that money (and directly accountable through the ballot box) has either disappeared or become obscured.

Therefore, for many reasons, political accountability, 'the compass for which one has the authority to act and make decisions' (Pym, 1996, p. 50), needs to be made clear. Public confidence in local government (and by implication, the new system of local governance) will not be restored until public decision-makers and spenders of public money can be clearly seen to be called to account by the local electorate. That said, some people in local government remain unconvinced of the benefits of 'too much democracy' feeling that direct elections (for example) to quangos were not appropriate when specialist knowledge is an essential requirement of membership (interview with political leader, 1997). Others, including the leader of the Conservative group in the London borough of Waltham Forest, felt that 'we can go too far down this road – some functions are too important for democracy at a local level' (in Percy-Smith, 1996, pp. 40–4). However, overall the response to the Commission for Local Democracy's (1995) call for direct elections to health authorities and police authorities and an open appointments procedure to other bodies was broadly favourable (ibid.).

The issue here is also one of empowerment. The sort of accountability I propose can only operate if those held accountable have the power to influence events. The move to 'quangocracy' is also a move to local management and administration rather than 'government'. Elected health authority members (for example) would have to be able to challenge the implications of central policy rather than simply be agents of administration. The move to measurable outcomes (such as waiting list targets and primary and secondary educational attainment tests) also militates against local discretion, with actors forced to respond to nationally set outcome indicators. These targets can acquire a 'magnetic attraction' with regard to local interpretation of policy and wider policy questions can take a back-seat in the drive to meet the targets (interview with health authority member, 1999).

Accountability in local governance

Within these constraints, however, local actors can exercise some discretion in how they meet targets. As we have seen, British government, from health care to training and social services, now works primarily through a large number of interdependent policy communities which form implementation networks. Many of these networks are self-organising (that is, informal) making them potentially autonomous from central government. Offering a counter-balance to the centralising tendencies of New Labour, their dependency on these extensive networks of powerful local and regional actors delivering services means central government has to consider local wishes when setting output targets. Even then, the policy communities develop their own interpretation on policies and mould their environments in ways that suit the actors involved in the networks. The institutions comprising the network do not necessarily act to the primary benefit of either their target 'customers' or their sponsoring agencies, both of which organisations they are supposedly operating on behalf of at the point of delivery of the services. These networks cross geographical, professional, and departmental boundaries, and include actors from a wide variety of public and private organisations; the interests of fellow members of the network inevitably achieve a degree of importance which can transcend those of their target 'customers'.

So, as Rhodes and others have noted, the dilemma, 'who is accountable to whom for what?', is not an easy question to resolve at any level of the new governance and has led to a number of high profile crises of accountability. It may be the case that, as the chief executive of one health authority put it, 'it's easier to be accountable formally up the line, it's much more difficult … to fulfil the … local population accountability' (interview, 1997). If so, then direct accountability to the public will assume secondary importance. This might not be too much of a problem if ministers were clearly in control and hence 'punishable' for policy failures but the lines of upward accountability are often obscure and frequently difficult to enforce. Questions of accountability arising from serious problems in the Prison Service and the Child Support Agency have caused considerable problems for governments in recent years. The House of Commons' Public Accounts Committee noted a 'serious failure' by the NHS Management Executive to secure accountability of Wessex Regional Health Authority, an error which cost the taxpayer at least £20 million (Rhodes, 1998, p. 26). Despite such examples, while agreeing that patterns of downward accountability to service users and local communities is often 'non-existent', Greer and Hoggett believe that 'the system of upwards accountability is very strong' and that most quangos and agencies have 'relatively little autonomy' (1996, p. 158); ministers are firmly in charge. If this *is* the case, then defenders of central government can at least maintain that democratic accountability is still working well, especially in the case of 'national' services such as health, because national politicians have a tight grip on events. This argument can be criticised on three crucial grounds. Firstly, even when clear centrally-imposed targets are set, it overstates the ability of the centre to control local actors; secondly, it ignores the failure of Members of Parliament to scrutinise the executive; and thirdly, the argument consequently exaggerates the ability of electors to hold individual ministers or even governments to account for policy failures. It is undeniable that similar caveats could be applied to local elected representatives.

We must also be careful not to always couch 'accountability' in terms of 'allocation of blame for failure'; it is equally a way of allocating credit for success. A more positive interpretation would be to see 'representative accountability' as responsible for putting together the 'out-turn jigsaw' and delivering more joined-up government by interpreting and implementing the wishes and needs of the target population/community. This implies greater diversity in service delivery at local level which central government, although it must always be careful not to appear too directive when dealing with potentially powerful local actors, appears unwilling to allow. Given that one possible answer to the accountability deficit would be an incremental increase in the supervisory power of local authorities over local service delivery, the flaws in their systems of accountability need to be closely examined.

Local councils and accountability

Historically, the model of accountability which has been dominant in local government is one that emphasised the importance of political mechanisms. Local accountability has thus been dominated by the idea of corporate political accountability, through the ballot box, other than, for example, forms of accountability at the point of service delivery. This *may* have been acceptable when local government delivered or held to account most services, but those powers have been systematically eroded by all governments this century, and especially since 1945. We are close to (if we have not already arrived at) a system where local authorities have a formal responsibility 'out of all proportion to their ability actually to control services' (Loughlin, 1996, p. 48). Therefore, it is unsurprising that there have been strains on the institution of local government. The rationale on which local government is based in the United Kingdom – that it should be responsible for a wide range of functions, have a significant element of local discretion, have some financial autonomy from the centre, and perhaps most importantly, that its elected base gives it considerable political legitimacy to safeguard these characteristics – are increasingly questioned (see Loughlin, 1996, for an excellent discussion) with crucial implications for accountability.

The formal position on local government accountability, couched in terms of democratic custom and statute, is clear and relatively unambiguous. The elected members make policy and are held to account for the success and failure of those policies by regular elections. There is a growing feeling among critics of local government that the general accountability at local level of the elected representative is incapable of indicating the policy preferences of local voters in anything but the crudest way (Potter, 1988, p. 152). In addition, there are those who question the usefulness of local elections as mechanisms for holding decision-makers to account. It is not only that the low electoral turnout at local elections has continued to dog local government's claim to democratic legitimacy (Rallings *et al.*, 1996). Critics argue that councillors are an 'insulated local elite' who (in general) are neither called to account for their mistakes nor rewarded at the ballot box for a good performance in office. In this view, local electors usually vote on national issues and according to their perception of how well national party leaders are performing, an argument given considerable weight by the close correlation between local election results and national opinion polls (Rallings and Thrasher, 1997b). Although Miller (1988) found that a majority of people claimed to be more influenced by local than national issues when voting in local elections and Wilson and Game offer a trenchant defence of the 'local' nature of local elections (1998, pp. 197–213), the widespread decimation of Conservative councillors during their 18 years of national government supports the view that voters at local level are largely voting on national issues. The 1997 general election was held at the same time as local elections, and while there was a significant difference (as usual) in the propensity to vote for the Liberal Democrats – voters are far more inclined to vote for the party locally than in national elections – there was a close correlation between Labour and Conservative national and local share of the vote (Rallings and Thrasher, 1997a). If it is the case that local voters tend to vote on national issues, then the legitimacy that local government derives from accountability through the ballot box is suspect.

There are certainly grounds for doubting the effectiveness of traditional representative democracy at local level. Stoker (1996) argues it has become a mechanism by which decision-makers claim legitimacy rather than a mechanism by which citizens can hold local decision-makers to account. He cites three main problems with the accountability of the current representative system. Firstly, it is 'too crude' in that some important local governance agencies are not covered because they are not elected; secondly, the narrow spectrum of society from which office holders come means local governance is 'too exclusive'; and thirdly, accountability is 'too uncertain' because the checks on office holders are not strong enough and public influence on decision making is too limited (Stoker, 1996, p. 196). The difficulty faced by individual councillors fighting for the interests of their wards when facing up to powerful political leaders of the same party means accountability is unlikely to increase without fundamental changes to the system of representation. In many local authorities today, despite the spread of hung councils, one-party rule is the norm and electoral accountability is largely a myth, albeit a myth to which even practitioners sign up to. Whatever mistakes they make, it is unlikely that the dominant party will lose overall control. Perhaps introducing proportional representation would give local electors a reasonable chance of introducing some opposition in the council chamber and could also improve turnout. In addition to improving electoral accountability, this would also strengthen local government's claims for legitimacy.

Despite their claims to the contrary (Ridley, 1988), throughout the 1980s central government was openly hostile to the existence of a competing set of institutions claiming political legitimacy and sought actively to weaken those claims by every means possible. A compliant press helped to create the myth of a large number of 'loony left' councils, profligate, over-ideological and anti-democratic, helping to legitimise central government's attacks on the autonomy of local government. Cynically, as the power of local authorities was curbed their failure to 'deliver' what was required became increasingly highlighted. Paradoxically, it was the need to engage with a series of proposals with which some local authorities initially strongly disapproved, such as CCT and public–private partnerships, that enabled councils to seek other avenues by which to achieve their policy aims. Unfortunately, democratic accountability was not one of the mechanisms strengthened by the need to work with new networks of actors. The essentially secretive nature of most such networks has been a barrier to transparency in local decision-making.

The accelerating creation of such networks is in part a response to the excessive centralisation of past governments, contributing to the devaluation of the notion of local democracy. There is an important caveat which needs to be made here. It must not be thought that the local networks of public, quasi-public and private actors which now direct much of the policy of central government are subverting a process which would otherwise be essentially democratic, and hence electorally accountable. As I have already argued, the perception of those who look back to the past is generally hopelessly romantic. Even today, local government actors (along with many of their academic defenders) are too frequently characterised by a quite unjustified smugness about how wonderful local government is compared to those nasty undemocratic alternatives (see Bulpitt, 1993). Local government has to become more responsive to the requirements of local communities and, perhaps, more humble in its attitude to the people it exists to serve.

Compulsory competitive tendering: still democratic control

Compulsory competitive tendering (CCT) not only resulted in a loss of power for local councillors over the way services are delivered, it also led to the increasing 'centralisation of important aspects of strategic decision making and cost controls' (Radcliffe, 1996, p. 153), weakening the ability of the public to call decision-makers to account. There appears to be a consensus that many of the changes in governance have led to an increasing centralisation of power in ministers and Whitehall, and similar problems arising from such privatisation processes have been identified in other countries (Gilmour and Jensen, 1998). Given that the new right supposedly does not believe the gentleman in Whitehall knows best, such a contradiction was one of the less edifying aspects of the Thatcher and Major years. It does not appear that this centralisation of power led to a greater acceptance of responsibility by ministers (although Blair's annual report is some improvement) or a lessening in their expectations of how much more 'democratic' local government should be.

However, it must also be noted that local government retained significant controls over service standards through the awarding and subsequent monitoring of the contracts awarded under the CCT process, so despite the lack of day-to-day control it is arguable that CCT has not led to a significant weakening of the principle of local democratic accountability. Also, some of the direct control local councils lost through the introduction of CCT has been restored by the replacement of CCT with a 'best value' system introduced by the New Labour government, in which *every* local authority service has to satisfy three basic requirements of efficiency, quality and acceptability to the community (McNaughton and McNaughton, 1999, p. 32; see also Chapter 8).

Agencies, quangos, privatisation and accountability

The Next Steps programme also involved some devolution of accountability. Previously, the line of political accountability had been clear, if somewhat convoluted, in that elected government ministers were ultimately responsible to the national electorate for the way such services were delivered locally by an essentially national civil service. The major change was that managers of the Next Steps agencies were to be responsible for the day-to-day running of agencies; ministers were accountable for *policy* decisions which agencies were obliged to deliver upon. In actuality, such a distinction has proved untenable and has only succeeded in blurring the lines of accountability from agencies to ministers and hence to Parliament. The failure of ministers to take responsibility, for example, for serious errors in the prison service and the apparently endless rows over whether such errors were matters of operation or policy, has seriously weakened the credibility of such accountability. When, as sometimes happens, agencies are subsequently privatised (such as the Stationery Office) they no longer have even this unsatisfactory accountability to Parliament (Elcock, 1998).

Training and Enterprise Councils (TECs) vividly demonstrate some of the problems of assigning responsibility in the new systems of governance. Given the strategic importance of technical education and training programmes to regional economic developments, and the wide-ranging powers and big budgets enjoyed by the TECs, there is a need to ensure closer local control over their activities. To be blunt, however, many observers raise serious doubts about the nature of their accountability (Peck and Emmerich, 1993, p. 18). As I discuss below,

TEC officers are not only fundamentally opposed to local democratic control, they also strongly disagree with negative assessments of TEC accountability.

Like Next Steps agencies, quangos are also not accountable to local elected representatives. The ineffectiveness of parliamentary scrutiny (and hence, political accountability) has been much criticised but for some observers this poses no problems (Hunt, 1995); the fact that 'national' services such as health are under the control of ministers accountable to Parliament ensures that the proper democratic account-ability is currently being exercised and this is certainly Tony Blair's view. Judge argues that writers on policy communities underplay the role of 'the broader framework of representative government' (1993, p. 124) and sees Parliament as playing an important role as the core of the legitimising framework of government. However, despite the role it still plays in legitimating the current inadequate structures of accountability, Parliament's role in the policy process is peripheral and its theoretical control over a whole range of quangos is now largely a fiction. Rhodes argues Judge underestimates the weakening of accountability that has taken place and that the erosion of the myth of parliamentary sover-eignty is accelerating as the gap between theory and actuality becomes more apparent to the electorate. So, 'key tenets' at the core of the Westminster model of representation and accountability are not work-ing properly (see Rhodes, 1997b, pp. 21–2). That there are problems of accountability throughout the British state is unsurprising. Doubts about political accountability go right to what is traditionally seen as the heart of British government, the accountability of our central executive to the supposedly sovereign body of Parliament (Weir and Beetham, 1998). If there is no effective responsibility towards Parliament then the chain of accountability which unites the whole of our politi-cal system is broken. Such problems of accountability have been made more apparent by the changes in the way Britain is governed and have contributed to the declining public faith in the efficacy of Parliament (Sumners, 1996).

If the political accountability of quangos upward to ministers is unsatisfactory, there is a great deal of concern that the responsiveness of, for example, health authorities to local requirements and local pub-lic opinion is, to say the least, flawed (Daly, 1996, p. 620). Some mem-bers of health authorities believed that their natural concern for the health of their 'neighbours' was sufficient balance for their lack of for-mal accountability 'downwards' and were puzzled at calls for more direct accountability to patients. The chair of one agency repeatedly maintained that the agency had central-government set targets, demonstrated that it had met or exceeded them in the glossy brochures produced by his organisation (which indicated its 'public accountability') and got extremely annoyed when pressed on how the public might hold his organisation responsible (interviews, 1997). Like Sir Robin Butler, he apparently sees 'giving an account' as synonymous with 'being called to account'.

Of course, there is not only 'downwards' and 'upwards' accountability in and between organisations; Elcock notes there is also accountability 'outwards', that is, towards colleagues and partner organisations (see Elcock, 1998, p. 31). 'Outward' accountability can lead to a closed and ineffective decision-making network. For Adrian Murray, Director of Planning in Staffordshire, a 'very strong network' of planning officers across the whole of the Midlands coordinate 'common policies… we look at one another's activities in terms of the overall picture' (interview, 1997). On occasions, the policy network that professionals inhabit can lead to a consensus on the types of decisions that need to be taken. Often this can lead to an unquestioning mind-frame that means bad decisions (such as the growth in building inner-city tower blocks during the 1960s) are taken because opinion from outside the network remains unconsidered. In such cases, there is a failure of accountability to both central policy makers and local communities. By the time the consequences of such decisions are discovered it is far too late to hold anyone responsible.

Although (as noted) concerns about declining accountability preceded the Thatcher years and would have posed a problem of legitimacy whatever government was in power during the last two or three decades, there is no doubt that the success of the new right agenda accelerated the departure from traditional measures of accountability. The transfer of public assets to private hands meant the removal of accountability from elected national and local representatives for services (such as water) that in many cases remained 'collective' and 'public'. The creation of regulatory agencies such as OFWAT to oversee the newly privatised water companies was an essential if inadequate counterbalance for the resultant failure of government to control private monopolies providing these public services. However, effective public accountability through elected representatives for the delivery of an essential service has been lost and the creation of regional monopolies means that public accountability has not been replaced by accountability through market mechanisms. Many of these privatised industries are important players in regional networks, and drawing them back into the fold of political accountability poses problems. More effective scrutiny of their actions by local representatives would be a start.

Neither a general concern with the needs of a local community, nor an adherence to professional standards, nor the publishing and dissemination of reports and accounts, are sufficient measures of accountability for quangos. 'Accountability' implies more than a general feeling of responsibility on behalf of the decision-maker. When public money is being spent, whatever the nature of the organisation spending that money, there must be public, participatory, transparent and effective mechanisms by which 'the public' (or their local representatives) can hold individuals and organisations to account for their failure to deliver the goods; removal from office must be an option.

The Blair government's concern with 'targets' for public sector organisations may be seen as offering a further measure of public accountability, but quite apart from the problems of holding anyone to account (apart perhaps from central government) for a failure to meet the output targets, there is concern that such targets are set where they present little problem to implementors. As one quango member intimately connected with the bid for a Health Action Zone (HAZ) told me, the HAZ would reach its target 'by any means possible' (interview, 1999). The Child Support Agency provides an example of how targets can work against the public interest; the result was untold misery for many second families while the original targets of legislation, those completely abdicating their parental responsibility, went unpursued (see Chapter 4). The emphasis on cutting waiting lists in the NHS also illustrates the problems of targets. This became *the* priority, with the result that easily treated and non-urgent cases were prioritised, often at the expense of those with a serious illness.

The new community governance: a lack of accountability

I have already suggested that the new and extensive range of agencies now involved in the public policy process at sub-national level represent an essentially private, non-transparent and elite network form of community governance. I argued that the stated values and practices of local democracy – used by political and bureaucratic elites to justify their decision making processes – are in themselves misrepresentative of the real exercise of sub-national power. Representatives of the private sectors, both voluntary and profit making, are also 'shielded' from criticism by their involvement in the unarguably unsatisfactory democratic and representative processes at local level. Practitioner network decisions, with the involvement of very senior local government personnel providing the necessary sheen of legitimacy, are effectively endorsed by a relatively compliant local political–bureaucratic process. Many local politicians and council officers express concern about the process. One chief officer admitted he felt 'uneasy' about his involvement in the decision-making network involving TECs and Health Authorities and was 'troubled' by the weak accountability of such powerful organisations. However, it was essential that his council took an active role in such networks (interview, 1997).

There is increasingly an expectation that traditionally reactive civil servants should exercise 'leadership' (Pym, 1996). That expectation clearly exists at local level when applied to chief officers, and especially widely respected and proactive chief executives such as Brian Smith. Mr Smith's observation that politicians have a 'vision' and it is his job to 'try to translate that vision, *and a fair amount of vision of my own as well, and other officers vision*…into the art of the possible' (interview, 1997, my emphasis) emphasises this challenge to conventional notions of political accountability. Conventionally, chief officers are not supposed to exercise leadership or 'vision', they are supposed to respond to it. However much the rubric that 'officers advise, councillors decide' is clearly 'logically untenable' (Collins, 1984, p. 45), lip-service is normally paid to this convention, despite its manifest falseness. Politicians are still supposed to take the public credit and blame for the policies of their administration. However, following an embarrassing over-spend of £7m by Stoke's unitary council on their creation of a 'Cultural Quarter' (money that will probably have to be made good by local community charge payers) it was Brian Smith who was publicly fielding media questions rather than his elected leader and deputy leader, who were both apparently unavailable (Radio Stoke, evening news programme, Friday 9 July, 1999). Mr Smith was given a grilling which clearly often left him uncomfortable. However, he had felt that as the most senior available member of the council's management team it was his responsibility to defend the administration; indeed, Radio Stoke had, he says, insisted on the need for a senior representative to answer questions and he felt it was his duty to do so (conversation with author, 13 July, 1999). Imagine the same situation at national level, with New Labour wheeling out the Cabinet Secretary to defend financial miscalculations rather than a senior politician. It would not happen, indicating both the magnitude of Brian Smith's action and the stretching of traditional notions of responsibility. Agency chiefs, such as Derek Lewis when head of the Prison Service, are expected to face the flak; perhaps local authority chief executives are adopting the behaviour of the new magistracy as local authorities move to becoming just another local agency for central policy objectives?

As the previous chapter indicated, the lack of effective accountability does not necessarily mean that the decisions made are against the public interest or remain uninformed by the 'traditional' concepts of public service; one aim of NPM was that private sector values would affect the decision-making environment of the public sector but the values of the public service have also had an impact on actors in the private sector. However new the phenomenon may or may not be, both this and other research suggests there is a clear community/social dimension affecting the decisions made by business leaders. As I have said, this *may* be reflecting a necessary (that is, pragmatic) adjustment in the new world of public–private partnerships and it may be largely focused on the need for business and profits rather than being altruistically driven. Whatever the motivating factors, public interest clearly plays an important role in the decision-making processes of the new practitioner communities. A request to 'trust our motives' is obviously an insufficient accountability but it is often all we have.

Which sector? The impact of ethos on perceptions of accountability

I have already mentioned the difficulty of classifying many of the new organisations and the consequent problems this could pose for ascribing responsibility. One example is the crisis of accountability caused by the Training and Enterprise Councils' view of themselves as private sector bodies and their adherence to private sector ethics, despite being predominantly funded from central government. The officers of the Staffordshire TEC vehemently deny both that they are a public sector body and that their accountability is flawed. Richard Ward, chief executive of the Staffordshire TEC, points out that the TEC is a limited company by guarantee and cites the receivership of South Thames TEC as evidence that TECs 'are in the private sector', as such an action would be unthinkable for a quango. However, Richard Ward accepts that TECs might be more accurately seen as a 'hybrid animal', neither public nor private (interview, 1997). Whatever the rhetoric, TECs are adjuncts of central government and, as such, they are public sector bodies. Despite this, their conceptions of accountability, their various 'mission statements', and the perception officers sometimes give of 'us and them' with regard to local government (Haughton *et al.*, 1997; interviews with author, 1997), indicate an ethos in which the language and behaviour of the private sector tend to predominate and in which the interests of business seem paramount (Peck and Emmerich, 1993). However, TECs see themselves as intrinsically more accountable than local governments as well as essential to local partnerships:

> TECs are far more accountable than local authorities, and local authorities don't like that…once in [councillors] can do what they…like. You can't censure them in any shape or form…you can't influence a decision…[Unlike local authorities] the TEC has a performance related contract for everything they deliver…The TEC is a partner in all eleven SRB bids, in the two regional challenge bids and is leading some of them itself because local government can't do without us, it needs our dimension in economic terms to address the software. They've got the authority and the statutory role of delivering the hardware of economic development and we, as the key strategic partner of government in the private sector have got the role of delivering the software side [i.e. educational and technical skills].
>
> (interview with Richard Ward, 1997)

So, for Richard Ward, the suggestion that the TEC is unaccountable is ludicrous. Not only is the TEC accountable under the Companies Act and accountable to Parliament though the Secretary of State, Ward also argues that the broadening of community representation on his TEC's board equates with a broadening of accountability. What this does demonstrate is that the notion of accountability is complex and given the realities of the new system of governance, is unlikely to be solely confined within the singular strand of representative accountability.

There are clearly competing demands between a requirement for political accountability and the increasing need for public services to operate as efficiently as private sector businesses supposedly do. Also, attempts to replace political accountability with some sort of pseudo-market accountability through mechanisms such as the Citizen's Charter have increased public expectation about their ability to demand better services (Elcock, 1998), without necessarily weakening public belief in the need for democratic accountability. Services have been removed from local authority control and single-purpose local agencies such as TECs have no formal responsibility to local decision-makers. Indeed, TEC officers often display a contempt for local councillors and businessmen; one leading TEC official's view was that most councillors were egotistical and 'out for what they can get' and he lamented the 'desperately poor industrial management in this county' (interview, 1997). This is not a view that my interviews with leading businessmen in Staffordshire leads me to share (see also Haughton *et al.*, 1997). It must also be admitted that, contrary to some of the negative impressions given of TECs in this and other research, some actors feel there has been a marked improvement in their local TEC's attitude towards partners and a more collaborative and friendly relationship has developed which may be a reflection of the change of government in 1997 (discussion with head of further education college, 1999).

Elite views on the *loci* of responsibility

It is commonly argued that the accountability of public servants differs fundamentally from that of business management and the multiple and frequently conflicting demands made of public accountability contrast with an accountability rooted in the single end of making a profit (see, for example, Elcock, 1998; Bogdanor, 1994). If one accepts this, a model of political accountability applicable to all governance organisations might be an unrealistic proposition. However, this oversimplifies the accountability of managers working in the private sector who, just like actors (both political and bureaucratic) in the public sector, appear to feel a need to respond to a far more diverse set of 'responsibilities' than such a simplistic conception of private sector accountability and responsibility envisage. It also overlooks the fact that public sector accountability is likewise rooted in a single overriding base, in that case 'the democratic ideal'. When public and private sector actors are asked about the interests they serve it appears to be private sector actors who feel a more diverse set of responsibilities.

Table 7.1 demonstrates that, for both bureaucrats and politicians in the elected public sector the primary (and overwhelming) responsibility was felt towards the local community, although officers also felt a strong responsibility towards the policy of the controlling party, just as democratic theory says they should do. A far more complex picture emerges when the responses of senior managers in the private sector are analysed.

As Table 7.2 shows, it is clear that in the private sector the interests served by actors are not just those of profit-making. While formal responsibility is felt mainly towards shareholders, senior decision-makers feel personally most obligated to serve the interests of shareholders, customers and staff in roughly equal measure. Brian Patterson

Table 7.1   Elected public sector (politicians and chief executives) – interests served, formally and personally ($n=21$)

Interest served	1. Formal	2. Personal
Local community/constituents	23	22
Controlling party policy	10	2
Integrity/public interest	3	6
'The Party'	0	6
Legal requirements	2	1
Other	3	7
Local business	2	1

Notes: Questions asked were:
(1) In *formal* terms, which is the main interest (or interests) you and your organisation must serve?
(2) Which interest (or interests) do you *personally* feel most obligated to serve?

Table 7.2   Private sector (profit-making) – interests served, formally and personally ($n=37$)

Interest served	1. Formal	2. Personal
Shareholders/board	32	16
Customers	22	15
Staff	21	18
Local community	13	6
Central government	2	2
Regulatory agencies	3	3
Banks	7	1
Suppliers	3	1
Interests of the industry	2	1
Society in general	1	0
Profitability	0	4
'The Brand'	0	4
Distributors	0	1
Professional organisation	0	1
Professional/ethical standards	0	2

Notes: Questions asked were:
(1) In *formal* terms, which is the main interest (or interests) you and your organisation must serve?
(2) Which interest (or interests) do you *personally* feel most obligated to serve?

of Wedgwood agreed it was difficult to balance the needs of such disparate interests but competitiveness must dominate:

> the thing that keeps me sane in the middle of all of that in my belief in market forces … because if in trying to reconcile those needs, often difficult, I lead the company in a direction which makes it uncompetitive in market terms then ultimately the company and all the stakeholders who depend on it are going to suffer.
>
> (interview, 1997; see also Chapter 4)

However, it remains a common criticism of private sector provision of welfare services that the private company's pursuit of profit is incompatible with the achievement of collective social goals (see Le Grand, 1998). To some extent, the 'quasi-markets' established by the Thatcher governments, most notably in health care, social services and education, in which the state finances independent companies competitively bidding (supposedly) to provide collective services to regional health authorities, were an attempt to tackle this problem and, of course, to 'roll back the frontiers of the state' (Le Grand and Bartlett, 1993). With the arguable exception of the limited education quasi-market, where parents are 'purchasers', 'agents' such as health authorities and local social service departments buy the services. Whether they act in the interests of the ultimate consumer or in pursuit of their own agenda is difficult to establish especially given the absence of downward accountability structures. Qualities of service may suffer because of the financial conflict of interests (cheapest cost to agent, maximum profit to the provider) at the core of the agent–provider relationship.

As I have argued above (see Chapter 6), while there may be neither formal accountability to the public nor a common ethical code, managers and executives in the private sector clearly have a set of generalised ethical objectives, which they pursue in their daily life and against which they judge the operational activities of their organisations. Local family concerns (especially) have deep roots in the community. For Gerald Tams, the Chairman of Staffordshire pottery manufacturers John Tams, underlying the goal of 'maximising the company's profits', the personal interest he felt obligated to serve was 'to provide a stable business for our … work force'. His 'vocation' was to 'set a good example with regard to all employment matters and in maintaining a Christian attitude in this regard' (questionnaire response, 1996). The safety and environment of the work force dominated his considerations when making operational decisions. Nor is

Gerald Tams alone; while acknowledging that the main interest they must serve formally is generating profits, both the chairman and the managing director of Steelite International argue that this is necessary in order to enable the organisation 'to serve customers, shareholders, employees and the community' (questionnaire response, 1996). Such multiple obligations were commonplace, and a strong commitment to the local community was the norm. Are such comments and beliefs to be treated as just public relations, paying lip-service to the needs of staff and local communities? Of course, they could be just that, but my interviews and discussions with senior private sector decision-makers – and an examination of their actions – leads me to believe otherwise. We must not overstate the case. Profit is still the priority, but it is clearly not the only concern.

Table 7.2, above, indicates that the private sector 'ethos' includes a sense of responsibility to the public, and not just as customers. The realisation of the primary importance of shareholders felt by private sector managers did not mean they minimised the relevance of other factors; privately, the interests of their staff got top priority. Concerns about the monolithic accountability of private sector managers appear to be misplaced. Rooted in the multiple responsibilities of both private and public sectors is a solid commitment to one overriding principle – democracy for public servants, profit for private actors. However, the fact that private actors can recognise other responsibilities means that when they engage in formal or informal governance networks it is unlikely that collective motives and responsibilities will be ignored. Despite this, it is undeniable that such 'responsibilities' have no formal base and can be ignored when inconvenient, or perhaps it would be kinder to say that in the end the need to satisfy market requirements will override all other considerations. More positively, my findings on the contribution to a new public service ethos by private sector members of public–private partnerships suggests they feel strongly about their commitment to wider values.

The concerns of economic partnerships

Clearly, the introduction of CCT and the creation of arm's-length regional bodies have raised concerns about failures of accountability. However, it is in the area of economic partnership, now essential 'to unlocking competitively allocated resources from Brussels and Westminster' (Peck and Tickell, 1994, p. 263) that most concern was expressed by some interviewees. As in Staffordshire, private–public networks appear to be flourishing throughout Britain. Such networks cover a wide range of partnerships, between organisations with contrasting rationales and funding, raising concern about standards of accountability when public sector organisations are involved. One long-term county councillor detected sinister overtones of Freemasonry, saying 'I feel that the "old boy" network still works in local affairs – it is not what you know but who you know' (interview, 1997). However wide of the mark such comments may be, the usual secrecy of the relationships between public and private actors means such views are inevitable and fairly widespread. The cooperation between business and local councils in Staffordshire's bids for regeneration money was worrying to some. When contracts were awarded based on bids worked out with leading industrialists and entrepreneurs the danger of such close cooperation is apparent. It also raises the question of how far elected representatives should bear responsibility for the actions of their unelected 'partners' in local policy communities. These are tricky areas to investigate. The relationship between local public officials, councillors and businessmen engaged in what are essentially largely publicly funded projects with the potential to deliver massive profits to entrepreneurs, could not fail to raise concern, given the lack of transparency and accountability.

Such concern is often not appreciated by at least one side of the partnership. One leading Staffordshire entrepreneur (who had worked on a number of high profile projects with the council concerned) proposed a major joint development project. He was angered when a leading officer suggested the authority should actively encourage other major private sector interests to submit proposals based on his ideas because of the danger of allegations of favouritism:

> I said … we've worked together now for five years … I've come here with a grand idea, we're going to put our money down and our effort down … we've worked together with your local authority, a success story beyond the call of duty … and you say that to us!
>
> (interview, 1997)

From his outraged comments at what many might see as the normal practice of open and competitive bidding, it is clear that such close relationships between developers and politicians might 'subvert', however benevolently, the democratic process. What is clear from my interviews is that elite perceptions of accountability are flexible, although the overwhelming majority of local politicians clearly felt ultimately responsible to their local communities.

The new magistracy

The conflicting (or complementary?) loci of accountability shown by senior actors in the public and private sector are also found in most quangos. In a wide-ranging survey of the 'new magistracy' Skelcher and Davis (1996) found differences in the locus of accountability (for example, 'local community' or 'secretary of state'), dependent upon the type of quango. Table 7.3 details the responses of quango member to their 1994 survey into eight types of body which Skelcher and Davis broadly classified as 'quangos'.

Skelcher and Davis also found that, in general, members of local quangos had never given a great deal of attention to accountability; a private sector City Challenge director replied that 'I've never been asked who I'm responsible to' and then struggled to give an answer beyond 'the community, probably' (1996, pp. 16–17). Skelcher and Davis argued that local councillors (comprising 10 per cent of quango membership) 'go through a more complex recruitment process and have a greater level of local accountability' because of this. However, given that the process by which local councillors are appointed to the boards of quangos is still shrouded in secrecy, it is difficult to agree with this argument. More basically, legitimacy or accountability are, like bus tickets, *not* transferable from one institution to another. My study of Staffordshire-based quangos found similar variations to Skelcher and Davis regarding individual perceptions of accountability. Many quangos, such as Regional Health Authorities and Sports Councils, are not as responsive to the public as various Citizen's Charters have trumpeted, with chief officers feeling primarily accountable to their funding bodies

Table 7.3 Perceptions of accountability by local quango members (Base: 1481)

To whom do you consider yourself accountable?	% response
Chair and non-executives	60
Local community generally	59
People who use the organisation's services	52
Secretary of State/Regional Health Authority	45
Taxpayers nationally	39
Staff of the organisation	29
Chief executive	22
Nominating organisation or group	17

Source: Skelcher and Davis, 1996, p. 16

rather than their 'customers'. Removed from direct accountability to the public or their target groups, a major aim must be to satisfy their funders, while their target groups may have little influence over them. This suggests that more effective ways of monitoring their performance are needed and that greater accountability to the local community is overdue. Agreement between the Labour government and the Liberal Democrats on constitutional reform is said to include greater scrutiny and accountability for quangos (*The Independent*, 6 March, 1997), although there has been little indication that Tony Blair's government sees this as a priority. Anecdotal evidence suggests that the political persuasion of new appointments is the only significant change. New Labour apparatchiks now seem to be dominant, although the continuing lack of transparency makes this difficult to verify.

Public demands on the system for greater accountability have increased at the same time as the ability of local politicians to control the quality of services delivered at local level has declined and as ministerial control and responsibility has also diminished. However, a new government has aroused optimism among some long-time observers of local government. Initiatives such as action zones have encouraged the belief that the Blair government's reforms of the state are driven by a 'need to increase public participation and accountability' (Elcock, 1998, p. 29). While New Labour may be more inclined towards local discretion than the previous Conservative governments it must again be noted that the increasingly specific output targets set by Blair's government potentially inhibit local autonomy.

The Citizen's Charter

The majority of work formerly carried out by regional civil servants under the direct control of government departments headed by Ministers of State is now carried out by agencies headed by chief executives. Central government has created agencies which operate at arms-length from their former departments and hence at arms-length from ministerial control. Consequently, as we have seen, the lines of accountability back to citizens have become 'long and tortuous'. Elcock notes that:

> these changes have been accompanied by a reduction in public opportunities for participation in government decision-making because public services have been removed to the private sector by

privatisation or contracting out, or because consultation procedures have been removed or abridged in order to permit quicker and more entrepreneurial decision-making.

(ibid., p. 27)

The changes have been mostly driven by the various new right critiques of the over-centralised nanny state. The two main elements of the market critique of state service provision is that market reforms will increase efficiency (by which is usually meant financial efficiency) and provide greater direct accountability to the public (Cochrane, 1993). However, as with the Citizen's Charter, such accountability is only in the public's role as 'consumers', and thus only partially satisfactory at most. At one level, the Citizen's Charter was an attempt to rectify some of the deficits of local accountability and William Waldegrave (1993) argued that it offered greater accountability than the local electoral system to the consumer of services. However, for some observers the concept of the public service customer – implicit in the philosophy of the Citizen's Charter – is (amongst other things) 'profoundly undemocratic' (Chandler, 1996, p. 40) and full of contradictions (Hunt, 1996). Perhaps the most serious concern about Citizen's Charters is the implication they carry of a serious critique of liberal democracy. This is because such charters imply that choice in the market place is more effective than voting (Chandler, 1996, p. 50) but the 'tenets of liberal democracy give political accountability pride of place: it is not just a mechanism but *the* mechanism' (Rhodes, 1988, p. 403).

Of course, voting should not be the only activity synonymous with citizenship but neither is citizenship synonymous with being solely a consumer of services, which has been seen as a fundamental weakness of the Citizen's Charter (Rhodes, 1987, pp. 65–7). There are also services provided which most citizens do not consume, although they may be indirect beneficiaries of, such as community care and the Probation Service. However, at the very least, Citizen's Charters, revamped with measurable acceptable standards for delivery of services, could significantly augment the weak democratic accountability given by the current electoral system. As Marr points out 'if the individual cannot, as a voter, play a role in the way a hospital is run, then perhaps he or she can do it as a consumer' (Marr, 1996, pp. 264–5). However, it is far more important to address the weaknesses in current democratic accountability than it is to improve accountability in other ways, however desirable such improvements may be.

Public–private partnerships and accountability

For Marr, the major philosophical question for our democracy is now: 'can individual choice through the market be an effective alternative to individual choice through the ballot-box?' (1996, p. 265). Given the fundamental changes that have taken place in the delivery of local and regional services a more pertinent question is 'how can these two choices complement each other and help reinforce effective mechanisms of accountability'?

It must be stressed that, despite some local government actors admitting their initial hostility towards private sector actors, and acknowledging their consequent reluctance to allow private interests into the collective decision-making process, the merits of such involvement seem to be fully accepted by both local politicians and council officers. There appear to be few qualms from the public sector about the two sectors working more closely together. Indeed, in Staffordshire, most actors expressed a hope that the links between private and public sectors could become stronger. The example of Staffordshire supports the contention that the influence and access of private sector actors in public service markets has certainly increased (Deakin and Walsh, 1996, p. 46). This is in addition to the formal public–private partnership arrangements much lauded by governments; there is an informal network of decision making far removed from the formal avenues and that network is clearly composed of public and private interests working together, effectively in secret. A number of businessmen, chief executives and political leaders in Staffordshire were quite open about the way the network operated. When, for example, leading entrepreneurs met a problem over planning or development, such entrepreneurs would ring members of the public sector (planners, chief executives, politicians) in order to sort it out. As with Brian Smith's public grilling on a potential scandal for his administration, imagine a prominent national businessperson admitting to a 'private line' to central political actors such as Cabinet Secretary Richard Wilson or Tony Blair and the significance of such access becomes apparent.

Although privileged access is assuredly not a new phenomenon and there is no suggestion of impropriety in the public–private relationships examined in Staffordshire, it does raise serious questions about democratic principles. Local businessmen, councillors and chief officers are often accused of fixing deals in smoke-filled rooms. In Staffordshire, leading business people making large profits out of public projects have a direct line to local decision makers and vice versa. The surprising thing is not that it happens, but that the protagonists are so open about it to an outsider. The immediate question is 'what about other interests which don't have this direct line?'. The admission also raises serious questions about the decision-making capabilities of local bureaucrats, who are clearly potentially powerful individuals. Indeed, some local councillors see their chief executive as more important and influential than their political leader (Temple, 1996).

From trust to suspicion

As I noted in the previous chapter, central to the new culture of governance is a shift in ethical focus from process to end product, and from a professionally self-referencing definition of efficiency and effectiveness to one defined in terms of outcomes. This shift in focus informs the range of solutions available for the resolution of public service delivery problems, the way in which priorities are identified and set, and the style in which solutions are presented and justified. It is unsurprising that demands for greater access and accountability in the conduct of public affairs arise when 'the ends justifies the means' becomes a dominant philosophy. The clash with traditional notions of good practice is clear, arousing considerable disquiet about the new environment from a commonwealth raised on those traditions. In addition, unresolved questions – for example, who sets 'outcome targets', who measures whether these have been achieved, who takes responsibility if they fail to be achieved? – need to be addressed before one can have confidence in published output targets improving public accountability. As already noted (see Chapter 4), rather than the government deciding whether or not it has met its own targets, an independent audit team might be a good idea.

At the moment, increasing centralisation and the loss of functions to quangos and quelgos implies an anti-democratic tendency, as did (arguably) the extension of CCT (although the 'best value' process, with its stated commitment to meeting community needs, could redress the balance). In between, the elected local council, supposedly the focus of local democracy, is in danger of being by-passed (Hill, 1994, p. 230). Often, the 'choice' offered to local 'consumers' is illusory. The development of non-statutory service providers is largely justified in terms of greater choice, better quality service and value for money. Hill (1994) argues that without participation, choice is not empowering, and the consensus that quality of service is the main aim of local government calls into question the notion of representative local democracy.

Held (1996) maintains that democracy cannot be based on a simple market contract. Participation in decision making, not just an ability to claim often spurious compensation if government fails to meet self-defined targets, is essential for democracy. Developments such as citizen's juries, opinion polls and focus groups might be welcome as a means of informing decision making but Daly (1996, p. 61) fears such developments could lead to an even less accountable situation in which unaccountable quango members 'end up listening to individuals who represent no one'. One member of a citizen's panel told me, 'I'm asked my opinion on things I don't know anything about, but I still give my views' (interview, 1999). As Pfeffer and Pollack (1993) so eloquently put it, 'the unaccountable in pursuit of the uninformed', is hardly a suitable basis for policy formulation. As Hill notes, 'democratic politics must be reaffirmed as the legitimate base for choices if equity as well as service standards is to be realised' (1994, p. 203).

Public confidence in governing institutions is declining. Of course, just as I argued that the new system of governance has not usurped an estimable system of local government, as some writers imply, we must be careful not to imply a 'golden age' of accountability. For example, the accountability of the former nationalised industries was largely spurious, their boards generally having both a great deal of freedom from ministers and Parliament and also precious little sense of responsibility to their customers.

However, it is hard not to agree with the contention that the confusion for the end users of the changes in the way public or quasi-public services are provided has probably contributed to declining trust. As Greenaway points out we are in 'new constitutional territory' in Britain (1995, p. 373). The old certainties, while unsatisfactory under close examination, at least led to some ultimately responsible (and usually elected) public figure, who could be relied upon to fall on their sword if the occasion demanded it. However nonsensical historians rate the resignation of Minister of Agriculture Sir Thomas Dugdale in 1954 over the 'Crichel Down affair', following criticism of civil service conduct which took place *before* Dugdale became the minister, it at least reassured the public that someone was not only responsible but prepared to accept responsibility; it also 'clearly established standards for ministerial responsibility which have not always been honoured since' (Comfort, 1993, p. 135). In more recent times, a number of ministerial refusals to accept responsibility have contributed to the public perception that politicians are unwilling to accept responsibility for matters supposedly under their control. These have included the failure of

Conservative Home Secretary Michael Howard to resign after serious errors in the running of prisons, resulting in the sacking of the Director-General of the Prison Service in contentious circumstances, and the failure of Labour Home Secretary Jack Straw to take responsibility for the Home Office overseeing the unfortunate publication of confidential witnesses' names in the Macpherson Report into the Metropolitan Police's mishandling of the inquiry into the murder of Stephen Lawrence.

Not all bad news, but…

In some respects it could be argued that local accountability has actually increased. Against expectations, the establishment of the Audit Commission (1982) has significantly improved financial accountability and the quality of many services, and the Commission has not hesitated to support local authorities whose spending priorities reflect local preferences. Although it remains essentially a creature of central government, the Audit Commission has also been regularly critical of central government policy (Wilson and Game, 1998, p. 105). Whatever its weaknesses, the Citizen's Charter has at least given some recognition to the elector as a consumer of services, although the promise by John Major's Conservative government to the citizen that the Citizen's Charter would improve 'choice, quality, value and accountability' was ill-defined. Hunt notes the ambiguity of such a promise and regrets the 'casual use' of terms and phrases such as 'quality' and 'accountability' and 'giving more power to the people' without telling the public what such rhetoric really means (Hunt, 1996, pp. 55–6). Hunt points out that the redress of faults offered by the Citizen's Charter is 'offered principally at the lowest level of the hierarchy', ignoring the possibility that organisational difficulties, which are ultimately the responsibility of ministers, may be the source of problems (ibid., p. 66). Therefore, how much can consumers (citizens) really affect the quality of service they receive? It must be noted that, however inadequately, the electoral accountability of central government partly balances this concern. The citizen as voter can punish the governing party for organisational and policy failures and seek redress as a consumer at the point of delivery but this is a convoluted and unsatisfactory means of holding representatives to account.

Despite a greater commitment to specific performance outputs in recent years, there are some things that can't be measured in this way and indefinite promises continue to dominate government proposals. The 1998 White Paper on modernising local government trumpeted 'a bigger say for local people' and 'a better deal for local people' as its 'twin aims' (DETR, 1998). Such vagueness precludes any effective measurement of the success or failure of what will be extremely costly and disruptive processes. It is therefore impossible for the central government to be held *accountable* for this policy. How can we tell if local people have a 'better deal' or even a 'bigger say'? If they don't, central government will blame local government for failing to enforce its policies, however vague they might be and however unlikely they are to achieve the stated aims. On the other hand, the government's 1999 White Paper on health makes a number of extremely specific output promises, including cutting deaths from cancers by a fifth and deaths from heart disease and strokes by a third (Department of Health, 1999). Unfortunately, the inevitably long-term nature of such projects (the date to achieve these figure by is 2010) militates against a future government taking responsibility for failing to achieve the targets set, although you can be sure they will take the credit if the targets are met.

Conclusion

If we believe that groups or individuals exercising public power should be accountable to 'society' then there is a double requirement on those holding power. There should be 'a means of holding to account' and 'the giving of an account' (Stewart and Davis, 1994, p. 32) so that merely 'giving an account' is not a sufficient measure of accountability. Richard Ward's TEC brochures, useful though they may be, are not enough. The claim that such services are now far more responsive to the consumer and that such responsiveness is far stronger than traditional electoral accountability (Waldegrave, 1993) is an argument which overlooks the requirement that public bodies should be accountable not just for the quality of service they deliver but also, *and far more fundamentally*, for the policies that produced such services in the first place.

As far as appointed boards go, both local and central accountability has to be improved. Better local accountability requires some education of local populations who do not know the functions carried out by quangos – for example, the 1986 Widdicombe Report found that most people thought hospitals were run by local councils. However, even the knowledgeable have no way of holding such bodies to account. The members of a health authority which permits a hospital medical ethics committee to allow clinical trials of new procedures on premature babies in the hospitals it oversees without adequately explaining this to parents (as North Staffordshire's health authority apparently did, with tragic consequences; *The Independent*, 1 September, 1999) would probably not survive direct electoral accountability. When the lines of accountability are as obscure as at present, the public does not know the identity of those responsible and, even if they did, has no measures for removing them from office. The argument that such bodies are accountable through the control of ministers who operate under the Parliamentary scrutiny of directly elected members is laughable. The notion of 'ministerial responsibility' has been weakened by ministers who refuse to accept responsibility for matters directly under their control, let alone those matters separated from them by a 'long and tortuous line' of accountability (Stewart and Davis, 1994, p. 33).

At one time, 'the burden of public service accountability was previously spread between local authorities and Parliament' (ibid.) but quangos are now wholly responsible through these convoluted lines of responsibility to central government, a fundamental change in the operation of the British state. All such bodies could now be seen as under central control. They fail to meet the most basic forms of public scrutiny. Most of them hold their meetings in private, many make their own audit arrangements, there is no effective 'ombudsman' for some (including TECs and Colleges of Further Education) and, unlike local government councillors, no member of any appointed body is liable to surcharge (Davis and Stewart, 1993).

However, quangos are part of the process of governance in their areas and there are a number of ways to improve local democratic control. Either there could be direct elections to such bodies, which would give each fragmented system of the local governance network its own elected base of legitimacy, or local government could become the focus of accountability for such bodies by taking over responsibility for their functions (Stewart and Davis, 1994; Daly, 1996). Alternatively, local authorities could act as the principal means of holding such bodies to account. A mechanism for removing the members of public boards from office when they fail in their duties is an essential tool for this. There is, quite naturally, some concern over increasing the power of local councils (or more accurately, restoring some of their former powers) and any such move would also require a strengthening of local elected accountability by such means as referenda, citizens' panels and a citizen's charter which emphasised citizen's rights. Such moves would create a genuinely more responsive, accountable and democratic system of local governance, but despite the rhetoric there is little sign that central government wishes to see a vibrant local democratic system with a competing base of legitimacy.

8
Governance and the Third Way

Introduction

When New Labour swept to power in May 1997 the party's lack of a clear ideological framework was not foremost in the minds of voters; it was enough for many that New Labour was not the Tories. However, the continuing criticism that New Labour conceals a 'principle free zone' (Maude, 1998) and that many of the party's principles are 'something worse than vagueness' (Crick, 1999, p. 26) is potentially damaging if allowed to gain a foothold in the public mind. For many reasons, the party needs to be seen to stand for something concrete.

This chapter explores the relationship between the changes I have identified in local government and the ideological predilection and policy agenda of the post-1997 Labour government. I begin by examining New Labour's search for a defining ideology and then outlining Tony Blair's vision of the Third Way. The various criticisms of the concept are examined and some of the dangers that a fixed ideological position could bring for New Labour are assessed. As I have already proposed, something genuinely new may be happening in British politics, in that outputs and not ideology appear to be driving the agenda of governance under New Labour. This concentration on outputs rather than ideological purity reflects the direction taken by the party at local level throughout the 1990s. The chapter then looks at the problems the Third Way poses for the Tories and offers the possibility of their electoral salvation through local government, where many of the principles and policies associated with Third Way have become common practice, resulting, as shown in Chapter 6, in a change of ethos among service providers. Finally, an interpretation of what the Third Way *should* be is offered – that is, experimental, pragmatic and decentralised decision-making – and the local governance network (with the elected local council as the pivotal and legitimising actor) is presented as potentially the ideal agent.

New Labour: the search for a defining ideology

The Third Way is not the party's first choice of a defining ideology. After a brief flirtation with communitarianism during the early 1990s, Labour launched the 'stakeholder society' (Hutton, 1995, and others). However, this turned out to be unsaleable – the 'stakeholder society' (in short, a mix of government offering opportunities to the individual citizen in return for a larger measure of individual responsibility) was both vague and essentially and uncomfortably inegalitarian, as well as being misunderstood or not understood by both the political elite and the wider polity. For critics, the imprecision of stakeholder government was a major factor in its appeal for New Labour (Maltby and Wilkinson, 1998, p. 197) but that imprecision may also have contributed to its failure to catch the imagination.[1] Despite the failure of Hutton's stakeholding and Etzioni's communitarianism to inspire public and party, the party still longs for a 'Big Picture' (Tonkin, 1998). As a trenchant American critic puts it, 'Europe's intellectuals' after 'generations of denigrating capitalism' (Novak, 1998, p. 3) have come to doubt much of their traditional understanding. Dionne perceptively points out that voters clearly like and want capitalism, so in order to win elections 'parties on the left … have to prove they're comfortable with the market and accept its disciplines'; however, voters want capitalism tempered by other values, such as community and compassion. Therefore, New Labour felt it necessary to launch a Third Way which embraced capitalism but also addressed the need for 'realism with a heart' (Dionne, 1999, p. A17).

The problem for New Labour is that its process of ideological overhauling came to be seen by many influential commentators as purely (or predominantly) for electoral purposes; playing the 'politics of catchup' when what was needed was an 'alternative vision' to Thatcherism (Hay, 1994, p. 701). Those political scientists who attended the session at the Political Studies Association Conference (Durham, 1990) where Peter Mandelson responded to the question, 'is there any policy of Labour's that you would not be prepared to abandon if you thought it would gain votes?', with the one word answer 'no', will never forget that moment. To the massed ranks of largely cynical political scientists, it seemed to sum up the agenda of Neil Kinnock's Labour party precisely. Professor David Denver then, to general amusement, asked Mandelson whether he had ever read the work of Anthony Downs, to which

Mandelson also replied simply 'no'. Since then, the party elite appears to have realised that simply 'not being the Tories' is not enough in the long term. So, at the same time as the party trumpets its new pragmatism and its willingness in both seeking funds from business and presenting itself as capable of managing a modern economy without resort to the old shibboleths of cloth-cap Labour, the search for a new model to put 'theoretical flesh' (Giddens, 1998, p. 2) on the bones of its policies has assumed great importance. Pragmatism may be a factor for all ideologues, especially for Thatcher, but at least she had a clear idea where she was going; Richards argues that 'in openly elevating pragmatism above ideology [New Labour] will always be navigating a course which is harder to define' (1999, p. 7). To be fair, it is important to note that what became known as 'Thatcherism' would have similarly resisted definition in the early stages of the first Thatcher government.

What is clear is that the concept of the Third Way has become more important to Tony Blair and New Labour than previous attempts to redefine the party ideologically. Among other things the Third Way project has contributed to raising Blair's international profile (Michel and Bouvet, 1998). World-wide, other 'modern Labour leaders', including Bill Clinton and Gerhard Schröder, have also been searching for a doctrine than can distinguish their parties from Reaganite/Thatcherite neo-liberalism (Brittan, 1999, p. 25) and too much is now invested in the Third Way for it to be jettisoned as quickly as stakeholding was.

Tony Blair: the Third Way as the unification of liberalism and social democracy

Before assessing Tony Blair's account of the Third Way, it is necessary to point to the debt his brief Fabian pamphlet clearly owes to the ideas of Anthony Giddens. As Bryant (1999, p. 18) points out, 'most of the concepts and ideas in [Blair's] pamphlet are simple versions' of Giddens' ideas. However, and perhaps of necessity, Blair's vision is 'less radical' and while they have much in common 'they do not represent a single vision' (ibid.). As with previous plunderings of relatively complex intellectual positions, New Labour has extracted and simplified the concepts that it needs.

Tony Blair says that governments need a 'powerful commitment to goals and values' but that in order to become 'popular and widely understood' ideas need labels; in his opinion, the Third Way is the best label for 'new politics' being forged by 'the progressive centre left' in Britain and elsewhere (Blair, 1998a, p. 1). Despite Vincent's claim that the new socialism 'appears to see itself as a form of "middle way" between the New Right and the old socialist concerns' (Vincent, 1998, p. 52; see also Brittan, 1999, p. 25: Novak, 1998), Blair maintains the Third Way is *not* an attempt to split the difference between right and left; it stands for a 'modernised social democracy...founded on the values which have guided progressive politics for more than a century – democracy, liberty, justice, mutual obligation and internationalism'. Blair maintains that the Third Way moves *beyond* the 'old left' and the 'new right', drawing its vitality from its attempt to unite the two great streams of left-of-centre thought, that is, social democracy and liberalism, 'whose divorce this century did much to weaken progressive politics across the West' (Blair, 1998a, p. 1). The Prime Minister's decision to involve the Liberal Democrats in the committees of cabinet government, despite Labour's huge parliamentary majority rendering this apparently unnecessary (and incomprehensible to some of his senior colleagues), fits completely with this ideological aim.

There is no doubt about the social democratic project at the heart of The Third Way. For Giddens as for Blair, the Third Way (despite the title of an earlier work of his, *Beyond Left and Right*) is essentially about the updating of social democracy rather than a synthesis with new right ideology or even a movement away from ideology. Northern European countries (Germany, Holland, Sweden), where state involvement in all spects of society is generally more formalised than within the United Kingdom, are frequently cited by Giddens as examples of such ideas in practice.

So – the values are clear, if rather universal, and the goal is a revitalised social democracy. Can the prime minister be a little more specific about his goals? It is here that the cynic or sceptic could have a field day, especially given the almost evangelical flavour of his pronouncement that: 'our mission is to promote and reconcile the four values which are essential to a just society which maximises the freedom and potential of all our people – equal worth, opportunity for all, responsibility and community' (Blair, 1998a, p. 3). The Third Way does have core values (however vague and universal they may be) but Blair admits a great deal of pragmatism is essential to give those values practical effect. As the Prime Minister acknowledges:

> some commentators are disconcerted by this insistence on fixed values and goals but pragmatism about means. There are even claims that it is unprincipled. But I believe that a critical dimension of the Third Way is that policies flow from values, not vice versa. With the

right policies, market mechanisms are critical to meeting social objectives, entrepreneurial zeal can promote social justice, and new technology represents an opportunity, not a threat.

(Blair, 1998a, p. 4)

As Blair himself says, New Labour's approach to policy is based upon 'permanent revisionism' (ibid.), a continual search for better means to meet the party's goals. Most commentators have missed the implication of this and of Tony Blair's comment that policies flow from values rather than vice versa. Robert Harris points out that this is:

one of the most startling propositions I have ever heard advanced by any British politician ... What Mr Blair is stating, in effect, is that he doesn't intend to play politics by the old rules any more. He reserves...the right to change his policies as circumstances change, and he will do so not merely as matter of expediency but *as a matter of principle.*

(Harris, 1998, emphasis in original)

Smith (1998) argues that given that part of the Third Way's appeal to Tony Blair may well have been its general lack of precision (room for manoeuvre being a valuable political tool) there is a danger that Blair may come to regret his reliance on 'left-of-centre sociologists' such as Giddens. However, as Harris has observed, the imprecision of the Third Way allows New Labour almost unlimited ideological flexibility while the right to change polices 'as a matter of principle' also affords the party a defence against accusations of U-turns.

Some influences on the Third Way

I do not propose a detailed examination of the theoretical and empirical foundations of the Third Way but it is essential to examine a few of the key influences in the transition from Labour to New Labour. The idea that the Third Way is merely a label to shroud pragmatism is not tenable. Pragmatism is a key element of the Third Way but Labour has a long history and the party's association with ideas of fairness and egalitarianism is a valuable resource. In discussions of the Third Way, little reference tends to be made to Labour's own history, perhaps because New Labour is so often characterised as an 'ideological departure' from the party's past (Buckler and Dolowitz, 2000, p. 27); when Labour's commitment to nationalisation was ditched, Blair declared 'today a new

Labour party is being born' (in King and Wickham-Jones, 1999b, p. 268). The 'modernisation' project goes back at least to the jolt Labour received from the creation of the Social Democratic Party (SDP) in 1981, and the General Election defeat of 1987 led Neil Kinnock to implement a policy review which 'left virtually no aspect of policy unexplored' (Blackburn and Plant, 1999, p. 1). Earlier, the public–private ownership debate was a feature of both Tawney's (1952) and Crosland's (1956) work, both influential works in centre-left thinking. That said, although Home Secretary Jack Straw cites Tawney's *Equality* as an influence (McElvoy, 1998), it would be a mistake to link the Third Way too closely to the concerns of the traditional British centre-left (see Buckler and Dolowitz, 1999). For example, Crosland's central argument for demand management to ensure full employment, an effective welfare state and economic growth, contrasts with New Labour's rejection of Keynesianism (King and Wickham-Jones, 1999a).

Margaret Thatcher is a more obvious contributor to the Third Way. Quite apart from Blair and Thatcher's mutual admiration (Blair, 1996), some of the roots of the Third Way lie in the response to the local governance reforms she introduced. Also, Cabinet Secretary Richard Wilson recognises the importance of perhaps the most significant reform instituted during Thatcher's era, the introduction of Next Steps agencies. The creation of arms-length agencies allowed the executive to concentrate on policy matters and also introduced a newly 'rationalised' local 'quasi-civil service' more receptive to meeting centrally set targets. As Richard Wilson notes, there is 'now a much sharper focus on the outcomes that the government wishes to deliver in the community' (Wilson, 1999). Although pragmatism about means was a key factor, the driver of the Thatcherite revolution was ideological; it achieved necessary change but that change was also dysfunctional. In the words of a senior local Labour politician, 'what it did was achieve the dislocation required to allow things to be put together again' (interview, 1999). This prompts the thought that, rather than the Third Way's stated aim of a reformulation of social democracy, Blair's true 'historic project' might be adjusting us to Thatcherism (Hall, 1998).

There have also been attempts to place the Third Way in a broader philosophical perspective. Buckler and Dolowitz (2000, p. 1) argue that Rawlsian social justice 'provides a philosophical position suitable to characterising [New Labour's] agenda' (ibid.). However, Blair himself, despite admitting its 'elegance and power' specifically rejected Rawls' 'highly individualistic view of the world' (in King and Wickham-Jones, 1999a). Robert Putnam's concept of social capital was utilised by Labour insiders to ensure the 'new party' would be 'built on firm intellectual foundations' (Gould, 1998, p. 231). As Putnam put it 'the greater the level of trust within a society, the greater the likelihood of co-operation' (Putnam, 1993, p. 171). However, there are problems with Blair's utilisation of social capital; 'high levels of social capital assume consent, informal spontaneous arrangements and limits to the marginalisation of groups' (King and Wickham-Jones, 1999a, p. 21) but Blair maintains that 'duties of citizenship', if neglected, will need to be enforced (1998a, p. 12). 'Enforced' social capital is a contradiction and Blair's exposition of the Third Way is 'elusive' about the substance of his commitment to social capital (King and Wickham-Jones, 1999a, p. 20). The clash of Blair's continuation of Thatcher's centralisation of power (Jenkins, 1999) with communitarian ideas and attempts to build social capital in the sense of wider citizen involvement is apparent. An essential element of rebuilding trust in government is to foster community decision making (Wilkinson and Applebee, 1999), but this conflicts with the need for local actors to meet centrally determined outputs.

King and Wickham-Jones (1999b) make a convincing case for the debt owed by New Labour to Bill Clinton's repositioning of the Democratic Party. Labour strategist Philip Gould produced a powerful argument that in order to win Labour needed to repackage itself in the same way but his paper with Patricia Hewitt was not well received by Smith's leadership team (Gould, 1998, p. 175; see also King and Wickham-Jones, 1999b, pp. 264–70). It was only when Smith was succeeded by Blair in July 1994 'that the thrust of the modernisation project was resumed' (Kavanagh, 1997, p. 217).

What is apparent is that the influences on New Labour have been varied, some of the components that inform the Third Way are in potential conflict, and there are ambiguities in Blair's position. For example, one of the ideas adopted from President Clinton, welfare to work, contains elements of coercion conflicting with communitarian ideas, as does Blair's argument that a modern notion of community recognises 'individual choice and personal autonomy' (in Buckler and Dolowitz, 2000, p. 10). However, such contradictions are inevitable in the complex process of formulating a new position (King and Wickham-Jones, 1999a).

Criticisms of the Third Way

The argument that Blair's Third Way is more about imprecise sound bites than a coherent philosophical position can often be given substance by his own exposition of the phrase. To say that the Third Way is fundamentally about 'traditional values in a changed world' (Blair, 1998) is essentially trite – almost any political leader could say the same. New Labour's search for a 'new model' is, its critics say, an attempt to dignify its lack of ideology with a high sounding label. Tony Blair openly admits the centrality of pragmatism to his project, so is the Third Way merely an attempt by him to justify this pragmatism? Tonkin notes that what is really new about the Third Way is the Blair government's belief that:

> pragmatism cannot justify itself. Even the art of the possible must dress itself up as an idealist's abstract dream. New Labour seeks an overarching theory to explain its not having an overarching theory. And you can't get much more post-modern than that.
>
> (Tonkin, 1998)

Tonkin makes an amusing point, but overlooks the necessity of 'ideology' to a party. Political parties cannot be at heart Machiavellian – or if they are they cannot make a virtue of it. It is essential for many reasons that parties stand for 'something'. Electorates like parties with 'principles', activists at all levels are largely driven by 'principles', and predominantly office-seeking politicians (as Harold Wilson was sometimes alleged to be) lack a coherent agenda when governing which can translate into an appearance of drift and vacillation, or even corruption. A belief in the primacy of the state as a provider of a universal welfare system 'from the cradle to the grave' may be something you agree or disagree with, but at least you know where you stand with a party that espouses such a view. Labour's apparent ideological imprecision is both its strength and its weakness – on the one hand, it gives the party enormous freedom of movement, but on the other hand, whatever the influence of post-modernist thought both elites and the electorate still expect a party to stand for easily identifiable positions on the relative roles of the state and civil society. So, inevitably, especially given the traditionally adversarial nature of British politics, such ideological imprecision has led to criticism from what it might now be more accurate to term 'the old new right'.

Francis Maude, in a speech to the Social Market Foundation (London, August 1998), ridiculed the notion of the Third Way as a 'principle free zone' in which Labour attempts to have its cake and eat it. For Maude, the Third Way is 'inchoate…even its most ardent advocates are at a loss to define it' and the 'mystically significant' Third Way is non-existent. Of course, it is not only 'the old new right' who attack the perceived emptiness of the Third Way; many on the left are equally concerned about a lack of substance behind the shiny facade of New Labour. Bernard Crick wonders what the 'public philosophy' of the party is, fearing that 'pluralism has lost out to centralism' (1997, p. 349) and Vincent worries that the 'new socialism' lacks 'theoretical gravitas' (1998, p. 57). Dionne comments that the strongest critique of the Third Way is that 'its careful balancing act sounds too good to be true' (1999, p. A17). Clearly aware of the potential for such criticisms, Giddens argues that:

> in the UK as in many other countries at the moment, theory lags behind practice. Bereft of the old certainties, governments claiming to represent the left are creating policy on the hoof. Theoretical flesh needs to be put on the bones of their policy-making – not just to endorse what they are doing, but to provide politics with a greater sense of direction and purpose.
>
> (Giddens, 1998, p. 2)

So for Giddens and others, without the essential theoretical underpinnings the New Labour project will continue to be seen by many people as 'no more than election rhetoric, a marketing ploy with little substance' (Vincent, 1998, p. 48).

Warning: there must be no return to social democracy!

Giddens maintains that New Labour is not just about image and that 'a substantive agenda is emerging' (Giddens, 1998, p. 155). Critics from both the left (Sengupta, 1998) and right (Smith, 1998) argue this agenda represents a distinct shift to the left ideologically. If this is the case, and if the 'substantive agenda' is broadly 'social democracy' (as both Blair and Giddens insist) many observers feel it is doomed to fail. It is not only that the structural and managerial reforms of previous governments 'are too well advanced to go backwards' even if Labour wished to do so (Massey, 1997, p. 24); there is no desire for the project electorally. John Gray argues that while the new social democratic consensus is an improvement on the 'sterile and atavistic debate between new right and old left' it is a 'backward-looking perspective' because one of the 'irreversible consequences' of Thatcherism (despite Thatcherism's failure to diminish poverty or roll back state expenditure) is 'the impossibility of any return to the policies and institutions of social democracy' (Gray, 1997, p. 327). This is both for historical reasons (the collapse of the class base of such parties) and because of the unsustainability of a large state 'in which neither taxpayers nor leaders can be relied upon to finance public deficits' (ibid., p. 328). Just as the New Right could not return to a lost 'old moral world', so the belief that just because Thatcherism became unpopular there will be a 'renaissance of collective sentiment' is unrealistic. We live in a more individualistic and pluralist culture, and Gray believes that what is important is to recognise this and understand that as a society:

> we will seek ways to make our economic culture friendlier to the needs of the people it exists to serve. We will aim to provide institutions and policies which moderates its risks for them … we will strive for a fairer distribution of skills and opportunities. We can hope in these ways to make our individualism less possessive and more convivial.
>
> (Gray, 1998, p. 334)

For Gray, this process will be necessarily incremental. There appears to be no essential conflict between the views of reformed Thatcherites like Gray and the erstwhile socialists and Marxists who have embraced the New Labour project. Despite their stated commitment to social democracy, experimentation and not adherence to some rigid ideological framework is the guiding characteristic of Blair and Giddens' Third Way. However, and apparently unconsidered by Giddens, there is the possibility that given the necessarily incremental nature of such a process, 'social democracy' will not be the end product. For example, in Austria, traditionally far-right wing politicians like Jorg Haider also propose a Third Way as a flexible and pragmatic approach to problems and as an attempt to break out of the left-right 'ideological straitjacket' (Haider, 1997, p. 93). It is fair to assume that, in this case, such pragmatism is not intended to deliver 'social democracy'.

Problems for New Labour

Giddens' book is a stimulating and often persuasive argument but his attempt to provide a succinct summary of the Third Way illustrates the pitfalls of trying to reduce what is essentially a pragmatic response towards problem-solving to a catchy phrase: 'if I had to describe it to the man in the pub, I would say it was an attempt to create a society that is inclusive and fair but competitive in the global market' (quoted in Chittendon and Williams 1998, p. 12). This does not describe the Third Way, but merely summarises some of its aims. 'The man in the pub' will be no wiser about the *way* this admirable goal is to be achieved and Francis Maude's assertion that Labour wants to both have its cake and to eat it appears to have some foundation. Of course, stating the basic premise of the Third Way is a potentially dangerous practice; Emperor Pragmatism may appear to be wearing no clothes. As Tony Blair has noted, one problem is the pejorative nature of 'pragmatism' to politicians and political commentators, as the practice implies a lack of principles. New Labour has suffered enough such accusations from both within and without the party for this to be adequate enough explanation of their attempts to dress flexibility with some philosophical overgarments, if this is indeed what they are trying to do.

The inherent need for experimentation and flexibility poses an immediate and more concrete problem in the Third Way project for Britain and relates directly to some of the dilemmas identified by this book – such an approach appears to demand a less centralised political and bureaucratic state than we currently have. Will British central politicians and civil servants allow such flexibility? As Labour MP Dennis MacShane points out, the Third Way 'is all about letting localities decide their tax rate, encouraging mutuality, and requiring companies to accept social responsibilities'. MacShane asks, can Britain 'adapt to the demands of post-socialist politics as defined by Anthony Giddens?' (MacShane, 1998, p. 5).

For MacShane, Britain, despite being the 'birthplace of third-way politics', may be the most difficult country for the Third Way to prosper. He has a point. Networks of local cooperation exist partly as a response to the restrictions central government has attempted to place on local autonomy. Despite the rhetoric, there is concern that New Labour ministers are as disinclined as their Conservative predecessors to allow local actors to take decisions in high profile areas such as education and health, or to allow local authorities to introduce genuinely radical programmes to decentralise their own decision making, where Labour's responses have sometimes demonstrated an 'enormous gap' between rhetoric and practice (Sumners, 1996, p. 206). The national business rate will stay says the 1998 White Paper on modernising local government. Councils will be compelled to prepare plans to bring in new models of local government (DETR, 1998), one of which apes the 'cabinet with a leader' model which largely accounts for the failure of accountability at the centre of government: little sign there that local experimentation will be allowed to prosper except within rigidly controlled boundaries.

Tony Blair offers devolution for Scotland and Wales as an example of his party's willingness to decentralise power. As Crick points out, these measures of devolution can be seen as 'exceptions born of political necessity' rather than 'a general desire to devolve as much government as possible from Whitehall and Westminster' (Crick, 1997, p. 349). Scotland and Wales may have their own assemblies now, but their powers (especially the Welsh Assembly) are limited. Other measures of constitutional change, such as reform of the House of Lords, are characterised less by pragmatism than by uncertainty. There is an incremental process taking place, whereby reforms are being instituted without any clear idea of a desirable outcome, other than a vague hope that what will emerge will be 'more democratic' (or less troublesome to the executive?) than what previously existed. In many ways, this mirrors the new government's activities in other more substantive policy areas, especially in educational reform. The aim of Action Zones is a hope for higher standards but quite how they will be achieved remains uncertain.

Put aside your cynicism: something new is happening ...

French prime minister Lionel Jospin has said that 'if the Third Way lies between ultra-liberalism and state socialism I'm interested. If the Third Way locates itself between (neo-) liberalism and social democracy, count me out' (quoted in *The Independent*, 16 September 1998, p. 5). Quite apart from the problem of defining 'ultra' and 'neo' liberalism, this implies a fixed position upon an ideological continuum, from which remedies for all problems can be found. As we have seen, if the Third Way is to be about anything, it is that the best way to achieve the goal, no matter what its ideological baggage, is the way that should be chosen. For example, Labour has a goal for junior and secondary education – high standards, largely measured by examination results. If the local education authorities fail to deliver higher standards then David Blunkett will allow private companies to bid to run schools. Such a decision would have been inconceivable for previous administrations, even for the 1979–90 Conservative governments. Trade Unions (while still largely hostile to programmes such as the Private Finance Initiative) have also announced they will bid to run schools inside the Education Action Zones, in which private companies or consortia can bid to run groups of 'failing' schools.

David Blunkett, who as shadow education minister once famously told a Labour party conference 'read my lips, no selection', now in office accepts that Action Zones may well produce privately controlled state schools who select pupils on the basis of ability. Responding to concerns that such developments will also lead to private firms making profits from running state schools, Blunkett declares that 'in the end, it's outcomes that matter' (*File on Four*, BBC Radio 4, 2 February 1999).

For New Labour, if a private company can deliver the same 'essential' services more cheaply than the state *and* make a profit, where is the problem? As this book has argued throughout, such attitudes have long been common in local government; however much Thatcherite local initiatives were initially opposed by many councillors, the realities of central control soon ensured a healthy dose of pragmatism among Labour and Liberal Democrat councillors.

Clearly, something genuinely *new* is happening in British politics. The agenda is not ideologically driven, but output driven. Those outputs are of course, political, but as journalists have loved to point out, everyone can agree about the aims; the huge import of this has been ignored by many commentators. Here we have a series of aims by a British government that everyone can broadly agree with. Not only that, the government is prepared to listen to suggestions on achieving those aims from any source, even to the extent of allowing private companies or trade unions to run our state schools and to allowing another political party to contribute formally within government to that debate. Despite Francis Maude's belief that 'the great battle of political ideas is just beginning' (1998), it could be proposed from the evidence that the end of ideology – much trumpeted but unseen since Daniel Bell's first tentative proposal – is arguably in sight. As Robert Harris points out, 'the removal from the political scene of the whole notion of "left" and "right" and its replacement by some endlessly shifting "third way" – that would be a revolution' (Harris, 1998; see also Marr, 1999).

At the beginning of the twenty-first century, while ideology may not be dead yet, looking around the world at a host of governments from both 'right' and 'left' one could be forgiven for thinking so – for example, the governments of France, Britain, Germany, the USA and Japan, run by individuals and parties from apparently widely differing social, political and historical perspectives, occupy largely the same ground. Politics is becoming about managing events rather than directing them. Arguably, and the pragmatism implicit in the Third Way recognises this, the best governments can hope to do is respond incrementally to external pressures, selecting the best available 'partial-solution' to the problem at hand in a managerial style based on 'facilitation, accommodation and bargaining' (Rhodes, 1996, p. 666). But how can this be reconciled with the fact that within Blair's statement of the Third Way there remains a concern for ideology? Indeed, his decision to involve the Liberal Democrats in government fits completely with his desire to unite social democracy and liberalism. It can only be that, just as he says he is trying to do, Tony Blair is seeking a new and more permanent consensus.

The electoral consequences of building such a consensus are considerable for the erstwhile natural party of government. With commendable consistency, many senior Conservatives still cling to the notion that one mechanism, the market, should be given primacy wherever possible; as one insider (a speech writer for a senior shadow minister) told me, 'if the party doesn't stand for the primacy of the free market, it is no longer the Conservative party'. One is unavoidably reminded of a stumbling Major government in its death throes desperately searching for functions to privatise before the inevitable loss of office. If there is a core to the Third Way it is that such certainties concerning the delivery of products and services have gone – direct government action is only one of many means (including private sector provision) that may be used to deliver New Labour's policies.

Public pronouncements from senior party figures show the Conservative party is clearly watering down its commitment to the free market; the last time the party had to make such a fundamental shift in beliefs it took them just a few short post-war years to agree the primacy of the state in welfare and service provision. A 'leaked' internal party report posits 'the market is a useful tool [but] Conservatives do not worship the market as an end in itself: they value it as a useful means to an end' and the report proposes that a future Conservative government would intervene in the market if the nation's 'well-being' depended on such action (Grice 1999a). More directly, amidst accusations from critics that he was betraying Margaret Thatcher's legacy and (allegedly like Labour) being driven by focus groups rather than ideological conviction (Grice, 1999b), the one-time far-right Tory and then deputy leader Peter Lilley announced in a 1999 Carlton Club speech that the party could only restore public confidence in its commitment to the welfare state if it emphatically accepted that 'the free market has only a limited role in improving public services like health, education and welfare'. Lilley added that Conservatives must be 'prepared to accept that there is more to Conservatism than defending and extending the free market' (Webster, 1999). Such a fundamental retreat from the basic principles of Thatcherism shocked many of the party faithful and stimulated some vicious invective directed mostly at leader William Hague from right-wingers (Gabb, 1999). After initially supporting his deputy, a panicking Hague sought to reassure his critics by the sacrificial removal of Lilley from the Conservative front-bench team. Given that public–private partnerships are now readily accepted by Labour and the Liberal Democrats and are endorsed by the far-right Conservatives who were shocked by Lilley's speech (ibid., p. 5), quite why the leadership have to make such provocative announcements is unclear. A more measured tone could have allayed public fears of Conservatives as anti-welfare state without provoking the party faithful. Whatever, as in the post-war era, a Conservative party is pragmatically preparing itself for another major ideological change of direction in response to perceived electoral necessity.

The Third Way: all things to all people?

There have been tentative suggestions (for example, Tonkin, 1998) that New Labour and the Third Way can be seen as a natural consequence of a media-saturated post-modern society; a party driven by focus groups (Grice, 1999b) and for whom image is all-important. Can the Third Way be seen as a 'post-modern political ideology'?

As might be expected in a post-modern world, there is not one but many post-modernisms, some more hopeful for the future of politics than others. However, there are some dominant themes in the literature. Howarth emphasises three post-modern themes: (1) the critique of what Jean-François Lyotard called 'meta-narratives' such as Marxism; (2) Richard Rorty's rejection of objective standpoints; and (3) Jacques Derrida's criticism of essentialist thinking; that is, in any concept there is always ambiguity and 'undecidables' (Howarth, 1995, pp. 116–18). The implications of living in a post-modern world (if we *do* live in a post-modern world; see Rhodes, 1997, p. 182; Giddens, 1990) are that relativism and subjectivity reign. As a consequence, mass parties now:

> have to appeal generally and not be tethered to sectional groups and classes…perhaps most significantly of all, they cannot afford to be too ideological. They need to be flexible, pluralistic, and appeal across classes and to many identities, and be prepared to change as people change.
>
> (Adams, 1998, p. 210)

Without being cynical, this sounds like a perfect description of New Labour's national strategy both in action and rhetoric. It also corresponds with the flexible strategic approach local political actors have adopted in order to respond to their own economic and social problems and partly explains the willingness of voters to trust Labour in power at local level.

If Adams is correct, then modern political parties will also need slogans that are flexible and pluralistic and it might be suggested that the 'Third Way' could be seen as an 'empty signifier' (Laclau, 1995, p. 171).

That is, rather as the slogan 'Viva Peron' was once used to galvanise Argentinean society with each supporting section of society attaching different meanings to the phrase, so the Third Way is an essentially empty phrase that signifies different things to different people. In the language of British politics, the Third Way becomes an effective and polysemic soundbite (not unlike 'New Labour'?) capable of a variety of interpretations. To give just a few possible interpretations: for corporate business the Third Way means 'establishing win-win situations…the third way challenge is…about integrating the principles of social responsibility, accountability and inclusivity within business basics' (Lloyds TSB, 1998); to ideologues it is shorthand for a 'rebirth of social democracy' (Blair; Giddens); to the electorate it implies that New Labour really are 'new and different' and not like either the old sleazy Tories or the old trade-union dominated Labour party; to a local political elite it implies a more prominent role as a pivot for the new patterns of regional collaboration implied by public–private partnerships. To political journalists, whether pro, anti or in-between, it acts as a useful device to hang their current ponitificatings upon. For Andrew Marr in the *Express* the Third Way is about the 'need for us all to put something back into society' (27 January 1999), for Kim Sengupta in *The Independent* it is welcomed as 'a socialism that dare not speak it's [sic] name' (24 April, 1998), and for David Smith in *The Sunday Times* the Third Way is a potential millstone around the political neck of the essentially pragmatic Tony Blair (13 September, 1998). Bizarrely, for distinguished cultural commentators like Bryan Appleyard, the 'whole point' of the Third Way is to 'soften the effects of the free market on the culture', a project he regards as doomed because of New Labour's wholesale adoration of pop culture; for Appleyard, pop culture is 'the globalised free market in its most raw and rampant form' (1999, p. 4). Truly, the Third Way appears to be all things to all people.

Some thinkers have attempted to place New Labour firmly in the liberal tradition. Andrew Vincent (1998, p. 57) points out that both Thatcherism and the new socialism are 'underpinned by a heavy baggage' of nineteenth-century liberal theorising, while Michael Lind (1998) offers the Third Way a 'Third Man' to replace Marx and Keynes, and he doesn't mean Harry Lime; Lind believes the nineteenth-century German–American Friedrich List's version of liberalism can give the new centre left consensus both a theoretical base and a programme of action. I would maintain that any such search is futile, and perhaps especially one that seeks to resurrect an almost forgotten thinker as the intellectual inspiration for the new politics.

Incremental decision making

There can be no clearly delineated 'Third Way', and efforts to dignify the new pragmatism of Labour with an easily digested and appropriate label are therefore doomed to fail. What there is what both Tony Blair and Francis Maude perversely call the First Way (big government/ socialism) and Second Way (the Thatcherite market revolution). More accurately, in Western democracies such as Britain and the United States, the first way was the market, the second way the various attempts grouped under Keynesianism (the New Deal in 1930's America, post-war nationalisation and later post-war consensus in Britain) to cope with the perceived 'failures' of the market in advanced industrial societies. Whatever the rhetoric, Thatcherite social and economic policies were merely another attempt to draw a new line along the unidimensional ideological continuum. Crucially, there is no all-embracing Third Way which will somehow marry the best of both these templates into a framework for government action. Methods depend on the problem – a bottom-up rather than a top-down framework, which of course demands a policy process in which the expertise of the pejoratively termed 'street level bureaucrat' has a bigger role to play. Local government could play a crucial role in informing central decision makers of the viability of certain courses of action and of the need to build effective local decision-making and implementation alliances. Giddens believes that 'bottom-up alliances … can provide a basis for radical policies' (1998a, p. 45) but bottom-up policy making is by nature an essentially incremental process.

Given the extremely broad nature of New Labour's goals, the party does not have, in policy theory terms, a rationally based strategy; it could best be characterised as 'muddling through' or 'disjointed incrementalism' (Braybrooke and Lindblom, 1963). Disjointed incrementalism involves a continual process of assessment and policy emerges as the result of 'partisan mutual adjustment', that is, a process of give-and-take between the actors (who both compete and co-operate) engaged in a particular policy area. Over the last 20 years, central government policy has created fragmented and multiple 'service delivery networks' (Rhodes, 1998, p. 260). In such an environment, partisan mutual adjustment – implying an essentially neo-pluralist political process – is essential to the successful outcome of central government policies. As Rhodes puts it:

> policy outcomes are not the product of actions by central government. There is order in the policy area but it is not imposed from on high: it

emerges from the negotiations of the several parties. No single actor has the information or expertise to solve complex problems. No one actor has the influence or policy instruments to decide unilaterally. All the actors in a particular policy area need one another.

(Rhodes, 1998, p. 26)

Crucially, in such a policy process, as means change so do goals, which perfectly describes Tony Blair's stated policy of 'permanent revisionism'. Such a policy process is also a pragmatic response to the realities of the British state; the power of the centre to control the periphery is often overstated, with the central–local relationship being more accurately described as one of mutual dependency (Rhodes, 1988). The pragmatic response by local politicians to the attempts by Conservative governments to weaken their local power base has created an ideal environment for New Labour's policy aims to thrive; whether Tony Blair is happy with such potentially powerful local actors is less clear.

Local government: the foundation of the Third Way?

Simon Jenkins (1998) argues that Tory salvation lies in the town halls they once ruled, as eventual disquiet with New Labour gets translated into protest votes for Conservative candidates in local elections. One problem for this strategy is that it is in local authorities, still largely Labour controlled, where the Third Way as public–private partnerships and networks is most vigorously practised. Labour councillors, despite their initial hostility and scepticism, have over the past decade come to appreciate the need for flexibility to achieve their aims. If they want a revitalised local economy, and especially if they want European Union support or money for Education Action Zones, they need to involve all sections of the community – political, voluntary, community, business, quangocracy – in coordinating a coherent strategy. The pragmatism of the Third Way is already day-to-day reality at local level, with public–private partnerships often directed by public sector actors, and the central party must have the confidence to allow local Tories to continue with policies many believe are the most appropriate solution to regenerating local economies. It could be argued that the success of Labour in local government politics has been the driving force of Third Way politics. As I have outlined, central to the new culture of 'governance' at local level is a shift in ethical focus from process to end product. As Chapter 6 showed, a great many local authorities have moved from a radical public sector driven ethos towards more outcome-orientated approaches where the ethical consideration is expressed in terms of an optimum outcome for those receiving the services.

Some of the constraints and conditions which the previous government placed upon local actors need to be relaxed. As noted, critics argue that New Labour has so far shown little decentralising tendencies (Crick, 1998) but this may be unfair. The establishment of new regional forums (such as the West Midlands Regional Chamber) and the newly created (1999) Regional Development Agencies are alleged to be a first step towards regional home rule. However, it must be noted that these are appointed bodies; the lack of transparency in appointments to these boards also raises concern. Another major step is the replacement of CCT by a 'best value' system where *every* local authority service will have to satisfy three basic requirements: '(1) efficiency (that is, value for money); (2) quality; (3) acceptability (to the community)' (McNaughton and McNaughton, 1999, p. 32). As Clarke notes, the idea of a fixed and *compulsory* process such as CCT is anathema in the new environment of governance where presumptions about whether public or private provision is superior should be immaterial; what should matter 'is that the means of delivery should be fit for the purposes being pursued' (Clarke, 1997, p. 17). The idea of subjecting every local authority service to the 'best value' process might also be seen as over-directive, but there is no compulsion under the 'best value' scheme to offer services out to tender. Also, 'best value' fits Clarke's criterion, as whether a private firm or the council's own workforce operate a service, 'all that matters is that the criteria for best value are met' (McNaughton and McNaughton, 1999, p. 33).

Whatever one feels about the element of compulsion in CCT, one of the benefits of central government legislation initially badly received by local actors (such as CCT) is that local authorities of all political persuasions have had to become far more flexible in their solutions to local problems. Local councils now seek private sector help to improve standards in schools, as in the once staunch stronghold of municipal socialism, Lambeth (Rafferty, 1998); conversely, councils also engage as commercial partners in business ventures, as in East Staffordshire's stake in Uttoxeter racecourse. Not surprisingly, then, responses from local councillors to the proposals for 'best value', although there are naturally some concerns, are largely favourable (McNaughton and McNaughton, 1999, p. 33).

The pivot: local government's legitimacy

For Jenkins (1998), if there is a Third Way in modern politics 'it is through dispersed democracy, the subsidiary accountability practised in Germany, Scandinavia, the Netherlands and even France, yet still anathema to Britain's metropolitan politics'. Local communities, led by local authorities and a business community which is more than willing to allow a social dimension to enter into their economic calculations, are already practising this Third Way; indeed, the process has been occurring, largely unnoticed outside of the practitioner and academic communities, for at least the last decade. Public–private partnerships are flourishing at local level, led by a new breed of mostly Labour and Liberal Democrat politicians because local Conservatives lost control of all but a handful of councils over the course of 18 years of Conservative national government. Operating within constraints placed upon them by a central government distrustful of alternative power sources, Labour politicians in particular were forced to look for new ways of delivering the service provision they felt their communities needed. Inevitably, bids for European Union money demanded a coherent response which drew together all sections of a community and the process of forming partnerships was instrumental in changing long-term preconceptions on all sides.

I have already argued that this new culture of cooperation has partly contributed to a change in the ethos of those involved in service delivery, a change which reflects the public–private partnerships movement away from procedures towards a concentration on outcomes; what matters is the end result (for example, more patients treated more effectively) and not how it is achieved. To reiterate, the managerial characteristics this shift has produced includes a more pragmatic and relatively non-ideological approach to problem solving and a concern with the needs of consumers, including (at least tentatively) the notion that consumers of services should be involved in setting priorities and therefore need to be better informed about all stages of decision making. Throughout local and regional government, both elected and non-elected, there is clear evidence of such a change in attitudes, as my research has shown. The growing concentration on outcomes rather than ideology noted at local level is also a defining characteristic of New Labour at the national level, a focus noted by commentators on the right (Blundell and Gosschalk, 1997) and seen as essential by some on the left (Perri 6, 1998b). It has to be acknowledged that the use of the terms 'right' and 'left' feels increasingly anachronistic when examining the flexible and pragmatic politics which now largely characterises our regions.

If the Third Way is to be more than just a sound bite, decision making has to be as local as possible. Given that improving community involvement is one of the Third Way's stated aims, greater democratic control needs to be established over what is, at present, a largely unaccountable network of local governance. The divisions between public, private and voluntary sectors are uncertain, and public (both elected and appointed) and private actors are now implementing (and sometimes developing) strategic policy together. Such changes emphasise that the public sector needs the involvement of private sector organisations to provide expertise to tackle social problems beyond the control of a single agency, but the relationship is one of mutual benefit:

> public agencies foster stable communal relations and the mediation of conflicting interests. The functional importance of local governments thus stems from their strategic position in the group universe, their pivotal position in bringing groups together within legitimate public institutions and their possession of financial and other resources.
>
> (Jacobs, 1996, p. 133)

So, local government is the pivotal actor and provides legitimacy to the involvement of other actors, and local government involvement is actively sought in order to provide that legitimacy to commercial schemes. Given this, there is a strong argument for increasing the coordinating role of local government.

For example, Clarke (1997) argues that a local authority could be given a 'power of local competence' to do anything not explicitly forbidden by statute. A clearer definition of a council's local leadership role will 'emphasise the links between the local authority and the other agencies and actors on the local governmental stage' (Clarke, 1997, p. 18). The legitimising role local councils perform means there should be a requirement on publicly funded agencies to publish their strategic statements and policy plans and to consult the local authority on them. Implicit in this is the need to enhance local democracy, providing 'immediate opportunities for the exercise of citizenship' (ibid.). A number of changes could be proposed to enhance the democratic legitimacy of local government. For example, there is a clear requirement to increase turnout at local elections; the introduction of proportional representation (PR) might not only increase turn-out (Rallings *et al.*, 1994), there are also indications that hung councils (the likely outcome of PR) produce more open and receptive local authorities (Temple, 1996). Other suggestions to increase community involvement (and hence legitimacy) include citizens' juries, panels, forums, public meetings and referenda. It has to be recognised that any new agenda for local government:

> must create new confidence at the local level for councils...to take charge of their service and regulatory responsibilities and for them to lead their communities, engaging with the variety of organisations in local governance and drawing them into their democratic processes.
>
> (Clarke, 1997, p. 20)

The local governance network can, if empowered, be more pragmatic and experimental than central government; in any policy area a number of alternatives can be tried, according to local perceptions of need, and the consequences of inappropriate policies will be less disastrous. The clear requirements of the Third Way – a more experimental and pragmatic decision making process – would be ideally met by governance networks which had local government institutions at their core, provided of course that democratic accountability was enhanced by some or all of the methods discussed above. Unhappily, the centralising tendencies of Blair and New Labour which I have noted militate against such a process.

Conclusion

Post-modernists reject the conceit of 'meta-narratives' like Marxism – crudely, how can one view of the world claim primacy as an explanation of the myriad relations existing between human beings? Similarly, how can one position on the ideological spectrum – that is, 'social democracy' – have all the answers for the problems raised by the complex network of interactions that is our post-modern society? There is an opportunity to forge something genuinely different and a label like the Third Way may not only fail to describe the process, it may also carry the danger (despite the 'principled pragmatism' observed by Robert Harris) of potentially limiting the Labour government's range of responses to policy problems.

There are aspects within the Third Way which may be uncomfortable for Tony Blair. In a new and flexible problem-solving environment where much is made of the need for transparency and accountability at the point where services are delivered, observers express doubts about the nature of executive accountability towards parliament and hence to the electorate (Weir and Beetham, 1998). If the process of modernising local government reproduces such cabinet structures in councils the problem will be reproduced at local level; this seems likely to happen, as over 80 percent of local authorities report that it is their intention to introduce such a prime ministerial/cabinet system (Leach, 1999). If the Third Way does mean greater democracy and decentralisation (as both Blair and Giddens maintain) then such gaps in the chain of accountability pose potentially serious questions about the seriousness with which New Labour views the entire project. For example, to have confidence in ministerial control of private provision of 'public' services (as David Blunkett expects), we need to have our representatives equipped with the power to question and ultimately censure the executive, and there is little sign of Tony Blair being willing to grasp that particular nettle. The impression persists that New Labour ministers see victory in a general election as sufficient mandate to do almost anything, including introducing new policies (for example, student fees) which have not received even this indirect voter approval. Such 'democratic accountability' amounts to little more than a request by public actors to 'trust our motives and ethics' rather than offering anything concrete and useful to the consumer of public services: it also reinforces the perception of 'semi-authoritarianism' that clings to New Labour (Brittan, 1999, p. 27).

Essentially, the Third Way represents a rebuttal of old certainties – neither the market nor collective provision has all the answers. The answer depends, not on the provision if universal mechanisms from a relatively fixed ideological position but on the best way to achieve a desired end. Giddens may wish to locate the Third Way in some space upon the continuum broadly equating with 'social democracy', but to be truly different from preceding 'Ways' the Third Way must be about the willingness to try new means of doing things. If private provision (or any combination of voluntary, public and private) can provide better schools, then let it. If companies can provide a better medical insurance scheme for their workers, let them. If the state can provide better provision of essential services such as water, let it. And 'better' cannot mean fitting an ideological model which insists on either individual or collective solutions; nor can it mean some mix of the two (such as 'social democracy') as the starting point for discussion. Rather, the best decision is one that, as 'best value' insists, produces more efficient and higher quality services as judged by the communities who receive those services. Of course, such flexibility demands a willingness to allow small-scale local experiments rather than wholesale and potentially disastrous change such as the poll tax and our over-prescriptive national curriculum.

Therefore, local government has a crucial role to play in the process. If it is not just rhetoric that a revival of civic culture is a 'basic ambition of Third Way politics' (Giddens, 1998a, p. 127), then local councils are ideally placed to aid such a process. Also, in the public–private partnerships so essential to the success of the 'new politics' it is necessary to ensure that 'the public interest remains paramount' (ibid., p. 124). Local government provides legitimacy to the involvement of other actors, and local government involvement is actively sought in order to provide that legitimacy; that input can help to ensure that the driving force of all such projects is in the public interest. To succeed in realising its stated aims of 'equal worth, opportunity for all, responsibility and community' (Blair, 1998a, p. 3), the Third Way must *trust* local policy-making communities and embrace local autonomy, rejoice in encouraging a variety of responses to difficult problems and, most importantly, encourage and support local government as a pivot of legitimacy for policy-making networks. How enthusiastic New Labour is about enhancing the powers and responsibilities of local elected actors will be a measure of how serious a project the Third Way really is.

9
Prime Manager – but What For?

Introduction

This book has outlined some of the important changes to the operation of local governance, especially since Margaret Thatcher's prime ministership. Throughout my examination, a number of suggestions have been offered for coping with some of the problems (and opportunities) thrown up by fundamental change and I do not propose to repeat or enlarge on all of those suggestions in this final chapter. After outlining the way in which my research indicates Britain now works at the local level, I make some observations and suggestions on the most central problem for democracy; that is, the weakness of democratic accountability. Based on my study of the new local governance system, I propose that, far from a more pluralist political culture under Blair and New Labour, the government's response to changes in local and regional governance suggests a more centralised process than under Margaret Thatcher. Unlike the oppositional years of the 1980s, and the moral and political uncertainty of the Major years, at the start of the new millennium the British people appear to embody widespread consensus for the public–private provision of services, endorsement of the Third Way's inherent pragmatism and support for the need of government to deliver measurable improvements to its services. The fundamental characteristic of governance in Britain can best be characterised by a movement from a predominant concern with ideology and process towards a more output-driven politics.

Some writers argue that the effect of the changes in governance mean the state is being 'hollowed out', in that functions are being passed 'upwards to the European Union, downwards to special-purpose bodies and outwards to agencies' (see Rhodes, 1997, p. 17). For others, the 'hollowing-out' thesis is not supported by the evidence, in that the central state has largely disposed of functions it no longer wanted. The systems of governance emerging are a new conception of the state bureaucracy, and the decentralisation of some functions to regional state actors has actually strengthened the regulatory powers of the state and allowed it greater flexibility (for example, see Saward, 1997; Majone, 1994). This may well have been a conscious reshaping of government by central actors (but see Rhodes, 1994). The move to output dominated politics by New Labour has consolidated central control. If it is not too fanciful an analogy, this new governance most resembles a business model in which one dominant figure (along the lines of a Branson or Murdoch) runs the conglomerate *UK plc* for the 'stakeholders' (the electorate), issues annual reports, sets clear targets with the managers (ministers) of the various departments and subsidiary companies (quangos, agencies) and employs a variety of different organisations to deliver the conglomerate's objectives. Helped by the changes Thatcher so bloodily introduced, Tony Blair dominates this new British governance system in a way she can only have imagined possible. He is its 'prime manager'.

An overview: the new local governance system

The multi-agency nature of modern local government is not new. An historical overview of the development of local government shows that there has always been a wide range of actors involved in delivering local services. However, at least since the late nineteenth century the need for a democratically elected tier of local government was broadly accepted. The arrival of Margaret Thatcher's government in 1979 changed that; her hostility to local government was unequivocal. She saw local government as in hock to public sector trade unions and, too often, under the control of 'extremist' local politicians hostile to the interests of business. The new right attack on the all-powerful state saw local actors as a key reason for the failure to reduce public spending and a major contributory factor in the growth of the post-war state. Whether or not the state was rolled back during the Thatcher years or merely had its boundaries redistributed, our fundamental assumptions about what the state and civil society should or should not do were successfully challenged. Many of the changes her governments introduced, driven by her belief in the importance of market forces, are now broadly accepted. However, the impact of those changes has raised concerns in a number of areas of local governance, notably in the effect the introduction of private sector practices has had on public sector accountability and ethics.

The apparent move since 1979 towards a more pluralistic local political environment conceals a centralising process. This has benefited Tony Blair's New Labour government in its pursuit of its goals but conflicted with his stated desire for greater community involvement in local politics (1998a). Output targets set by national government demand strong central control over service delivery. Apparently competing sets of actors are all more or less working towards the achievement of targets largely set by central government, with Blair managing that process. Local actors have an input into that process – Blair is aware that the art of the possible demands the setting of attainable goals and, therefore, at least some process of 'partisan mutual adjustment' – but once those centrally-determined targets are set it appears to have become the major occupation of ministers to ensure they are met. Arguably, Blair's interest in domestic policy 'is chiefly in meeting statistical targets and brokering deals between the Treasury and focus groups [and] spending departments are little more than agencies of this brokerage' (Jenkins, 1999, p. 24). Ministers have been largely relieved of the administrative burden of over-seeing huge government departments and can concentrate their energies on delivering those targets. At least ministers and the 'important' local organisations have *some* input into setting the targets. Despite the Third Way's trumpeting of empowerment, community involvement in the new governance system is peripheral and tends to occur late in the process, if at all. Too strong an upward demand for certain types of service would clash with the centrally determined outputs which arrangements like the health and education action zones are geared to satisfy. Community empowerment is unlikely to be delivered in such an environment.

For many observers, changes such as compulsory competitive tendering and private sector provision of public services have had a detrimental effect on the ethos of public service. I would argue otherwise. The move to output based politics and away from a concern with 'due process', or to put it another way, the acknowledgement that the private sector may often be a better mechanism to deliver some public services than the public sector, has more likely enriched the ethos of the public sector. Not only that, the impact of public service commitments on private sector actors may have also had a beneficial effect. Arguably, there has been a synthesis of public and private values in the new governance, creating a new ethos of public *service*. Following Thatcher, an often hidebound and essentially elitist perception of public sector behaviour has been challenged by the notion that it is what works that matters, rather than clinging to a conviction in the superiority of one ideological framework over another or in the benefits of a process of service delivery such as the nationalised industries. Accompanying this, there has emerged a rather more positive perception of the public from local service deliverers, especially by local councils.

Overriding the concern with outputs, however, there have increasingly been reservations about the lack of accountability of quangos and agencies. Ministerial accountability for agencies, for example, is fundamentally flawed by the weakness of Parliament in holding the executive to account. Effectively, there is no real scrutiny of the actions of quangocrats. Prime ministerial accountability, welcome though it is that Tony Blair takes responsibility for the targets his government sets, is an extremely blunt instrument for holding a huge governmental organisation to task. New Labour's general election victories will only partly depend (if at all) on Blair's success at achieving his targets; the quality of the opposition will probably be a more potent factor.

Inevitably, New Labour's concentration on outputs has prompted accusations from friends and foes alike that such pragmatism conceals a lack of principles, accusations that the development of the philosophy of the Third Way to succeed 'communitarianism' and 'stakeholding' has not abated. The Third Way is certainly an attempt, as Giddens (1998a) admits, to put some flesh on the bones of 'output politics', a process that while it preceded Blair, has been given a new status by New Labour's overwhelming concentration on outputs rather than ideology. Less acknowledged is the debt that the formulation of the Third Way owes to the compromises made by local politicians with the new political environment engendered by Thatcherism. Local Labour and Liberal Democrat politicians have been practising 'the Third Way' for a decade or more, searching for partners to deliver their goals wherever they can find them. Formerly left-wing councils like Sheffield long ago bit the bullet of pragmatism.

The need for democratic accountability

Perhaps the major concern to arise as a direct result of the changes to local service provision is the perceived crisis of democratic accountability. The accountability of public servants to democratically elected politicians and through them to the citizen is the principle that fundamentally distinguishes public administration from private administration (Elcock, 1988, p. 23). When private administrators become the deliverers of public services they must also be bound by the same principle and our elected representatives must have the power to put things right. It is not enough that private deliverers of public services are held responsible though a citizen's charter ineffectively mimicking the market mechanisms whereby consumers can exercise choice – 'if Rover make bad cars I'll buy Toyota' is a greater incentive to private administrators than 'if you fail to deliver your charter aims I am entitled to an apology' – they must be responsible to politicians who are answerable to the voter and those lines of responsibility must be clear and unambiguous. As Gilmour and Jensen note, while new methods of service delivery may offer greater efficiency they can also enable governments to escape responsibility 'for actions that are permitted, encouraged, controlled or paid for by the state' (Gilmour and Jensen, 1998, p. 247). Their findings that such transfers had led to a loss of governmental accountability in the USA prompted Gilmour and Jensen to note the necessity of 'a reinvention of accountability' to accompany this reinvention of government (ibid., p. 255). The way in which the private sector has been drawn into a web of local decision makers outside of conventional frameworks of accountability (see Pike, 1997, p. 6) means similar problems of accountability arise in Britain; unelected members of the partnerships may have no experience of seriously considering the preferences of local populations when making decisions. Indeed, when such networks are informal and unofficial, the preferences of local people cannot be directly represented. Private sector actors can also be uneasy with the need to establish the consensus that public sector decision making generally involves.

Our traditional accountability mechanisms 'were never designed to cope with multi-organisational, fragmented policy systems' (Rhodes, 1997, p. 21). Not only that, traditional local democratic accountability was both indolent and ineffective even when local government was more strongly in control. This does not mean local government cannot be the key actor in establishing effective mechanisms of accountability. While it is accepted that 'messy problems' might sometimes necessitate 'messy solutions', Rhodes' idea that 'accountability can no longer be specific to an institution but must fit the policy and its network' (ibid.) challenges (as Rhodes acknowledges) the concept of representative democracy which I would argue needs to be at the centre of any system of public accountability. I agree with Rhodes that the traditional mechanisms of representative democracy must be adapted to fit the workings of 'the new differentiated polity' (ibid., p. 22). However, when public money is being spent similar standards of accountability must apply no matter in what 'form' the bodies which provide that public service are constituted (see Davis, 1996, p. 3). Given the new consensus I have identified among the public, private and voluntary agencies delivering public services (see Chapter 6) where consumer judgement of quality and consultation and procedural transparency are central (if often unrealised) aims, this task may be difficult but it should not be impossible.

Proposals for reform

There are many possibilities for reform. Given the wide-ranging interests needing reconciliation in a root and branch reform of the way local and regional services are delivered (an unlikely event), in the spirit of the Third Way I suggest that an incremental approach is the most effective way to deliver the essential requirement that spenders of public money are democratically accountable. Local councils as currently constituted face a major problem in their desire for community leadership in that they are only one of the powerful groups involved in local governance. A number of intriguing suggestions have been made to draw those other groups into the democratic system but they tend to be unrealistic. Pike's suggestion that local authorities be divided into two houses, the existing elected council and a community senate, part directly elected but with co-opted representatives of the main local quangos, private sector and voluntary organisations (Pike, 1997, p. 6) is ingenious and plausible. However, the reaction of the current local government system to a legitimate and largely democratically elected 'competitor' can readily be imagined, as can the machinations of local interests to be co-opted (or not) into the senate. Perhaps more realistically, the introduction of proportional representation would hopefully mean a more representative local council, but it fails to address the accountability problems of quangos and private sector actors delivering public services.

Suggestions to improve openness in non-elected public bodies, for example, codes of conduct, co-opted elected representatives and a more transparent appointment system to quangos, rather than one 'good chap' tentatively sounding out another 'good chap', might be better than the current flawed system but none of these resolves the democratic deficit. Directly elected quangos are one suggestion. One potential problem for directly elected health authorities is that electoral processes could lead to the party politicisation of such quangos, but this is not an inevitable outcome; representatives need only stand on health issues. To the more fundamental problem that such elections would lead to local control over nationally funded services, Daly (1996) points out that such a consideration could equally be applied to local council elections!

Greater citizen involvement is seen as one answer and the aim of giving the public a bigger say is foremost in the minds of those advocating community regeneration and empowerment. For example, Community Regeneration Units, local partnerships of public-private and voluntary sectors led by community groups, could be responsible for generating plans 'consistent with local development and regional plans and which reflected the community's views, aspirations and needs' (Nevin and Shiner, 1995, p. 318) but the history of community participation programmes does not suggest such development are panaceas (Mayo, 1994, p. 19). Measures such as citizen juries and referenda have been a limited success due to a combination of citizen apathy and reluctant councils, who often cite apathy as a defence for their failure to involve the wider community. Community participation has to be supported by adequate resources (like money and training) if communities are to develop the expertise to cope with demands. A much stronger political will for empowerment (from both central actors and apathetic communities) and 'major cultural changes both within central and local government' (ibid.) is needed. Despite the sometimes touching faith that New Labour's election represented a new dawn (Elcock, 1998), it is unlikely that the necessary process of change in attitudes has started.

In the midst of all this concern with accountability, are we worrying too much? Young maintains that accountability has 'not withered, nor is it in crisis. It has simply begun to develop along lines which complement the elective mechanisms' (in Pratchett and Wilson, 1996, p. 9). Young, a distinguished observer of local government for many years, is dismissive of the belief that simply because an agency at local level is unelected it is unaccountable; 'accountability is not an "either/or" question; it is a "how much and in what ways" question' (ibid.). However, while recognising 'the subtle complexity of accountability' of both elected and unelected bodies in the local governance system, I would agree with Daly that 'no amount of tinkering with the present arrangements can act as an adequate substitution for local democratic accountability' (1996, p. 61).

This does not automatically mean that local councils are best placed to deliver democratic accountability, if only they were once again given control of their lost services. One does not need to share Bulpitt's somewhat dyspeptic view of the failures of local government to actually deliver 'local democracy' or agree with his belief that local democracy may no longer be a necessary part of the British constitution (1993) to recognise some truth in the argument that local governments have often been more concerned with protecting the interests of local service producers than with improving the lot of their electorate. Local government may no longer be the only actor that really matters in the local governance system and it is not always the most important (Cochrane, 1993, p. 124) but its elected mandate brings authority. Critics challenge that authority on the grounds that low electoral turnout indicates both a lack of public interest in local politics and a lack of legitimacy for those elected. However, supporters of local government have no doubts about the central position it should occupy in the local governance environment.

Local government as a focus of accountability

Driven by the belief that while 'fragmentation of agencies has not helped elected local authorities to articulate a common agenda for a local-ity ... no other body can easily assume this role' (Pratchett and Wilson, 1996, p. 14) there is considerable support for local government as the pivotal actor in local and regional service delivery. Perhaps this reflects an unspoken acceptance that the new (and essentially undemocratic) governance system is here to stay. While the public sector needs the involvement of private sector organisations to provide expertise to tackle social problems beyond the control of a single agency, the relationship is one of mutual benefit; local government's legitimating role strengthens the argument for increasing their coordinating role over regional networks and projects.

The Commission for Local Democracy's in-depth examination of the state of local democracy concluded with a report which suggested that:

> local authorities should be given a clear community leadership role with rights to have access to information on, to monitor and to comment on other local government bodies and public agencies operating locally, and with a right to represent the interests of the local community in any manner they think appropriate.
>
> (CLD, 1995).

This would certainly find favour with most local government actors, who tend to share the view of the Staffordshire chief executive who felt 'an awful lot of the functions of quangos do…could be done better and with more accountability by the elected public sector'. Even some Conservative MPs felt that 'one of the worst things that we've done as a party is to erode the power of local government' (Patrick Cormack, MP, interview, 1997) but Tony Blair appears unlikely to reject that legacy. Central government is understandably reluctant to empower an alternative source of authority and its responses have, as usual, concentrated on matters of officer-councillor ethics and the internal reorganisation of local councils rather than serious consideration of the role of other actors in the local governance system (for example, DETR, 1998).

A number of local government officers and councillors (interviews, 1997, 1999) support giving councils a power of local competence to do anything not explicitly forbidden by statute, which would be a 'symbolic way of endorsing the local leadership role' (Clarke, 1997, p. 18). However, it may be that less formal mechanisms of control will arise. New organisational forms, 'based on co-operative relationships between formally autonomous bodies' (Prior, 1996, p. 103) are beginning to develop and implement local policies. Local authorities are often taking the lead in creating 'local alliances, consortia and partnerships across the public, private and community sectors' and it is possible that in such activities 'the potential for a reassertion of the necessity of strong local government can be realised' (ibid.).

The concern with accountability is not just academic; effective mechanisms of accountability are essential to democratic government. From the United States, comes a warning for the British executive. Franklin Roosevelt's New Deal creation of a myriad of new federal agencies operating under delegated powers from central government raised similar concerns about accountability, which generated a 'bewildering array of…constraints on administrative discretion' (Gilmour and Jensen, 1998, p. 255). While acknowledging that central–local politics in the USA is fundamentally different, unless the accountability problem in our local governance system is tackled the same 'reformist response' (ibid.) might be engendered. If so, the eventual result would be that the much vaunted flexibility of the new policy networks would be gradually eroded as measures designed to satisfy public concern over the lack of clear democratic control of public spending were gradually introduced. Such measures would also inhibit central control, weakening Tony Blair's ability to manage the new governance.

Blair paints a picture for local government's future which supports the changing emphasis in central–local relationships, with local government 'in partnership with public agencies, private companies, community groups and voluntary organisations'. Its 'distinctive leadership role' will be to bring 'cohesion and co-ordination' to the fragmented governance system (Blair, 1998b, p. 13), thereby delivering 'joined-up government'. Blair's words support the belief of a more collaborative public service discourse but this is somewhat 'tempered by the threats also emanating from central government' (Clarence and Painter, 1998, p. 20). My investigation of New Labour's Third Way (Chapter 8) was somewhat sceptical of the seriousness of the government's intentions for local autonomy. Blair's request for local government to provide joined-up government (1998b) potentially facilitates even greater central control of local actors. In a modern and dynamic company everyone has to be 'on board', focused on the company's goals. The 'collaborative discourse' will not survive any serious disagreement with Blair's plans by local actors.

Any attempt to improve local autonomy must face up to the challenge that reform of central government is an essential prerequisite to successfully invigorating local democracy. The urge of the centre to intervene in local decision-making and to effect constitutional changes which tend to have unintended consequences 'down the line' must be constrained by effective scrutiny of the executive. If we are to get a pluralistic and community focused local governance system for the more individualised polity of the twenty-first century, central government's power of unilateral action is no longer appropriate. However, in an output dominated governance system, central government control is a prerequisite. Indeed, insider Philip Gould (1998) argues that Blair has too little control over local (and central) actors and that his powers need increasing if he is to deliver his aims. A Labour MP (briefly a Blair minister) told me that the concentration of power that has gradually accrued to the executive combined with its centralist tendencies meant that he could not see a Blair government giving power back to local authorities and other institutions. The MP also noted the lack of ideological direction in the government but believed that despite lacking inspiration it would, at its best, 'be a very good, efficient manager of this country' (interview, 1997). He may have put his finger on the central characteristic of New Labour's government style.

Conclusion: centralisation and prime managership

How does Britain work? Increasingly, like a large business with many subsidiaries, but 'controlled' by one senior manager, ultimately answerable to 'we the people' as stakeholders in the company. I do not mean to be flippant when I characterise Blair as the 'prime manager' within this system; the term describes his role precisely. Of course, he does not have total control (or anything like it) within his 'organisation'. As with any business, the 'boss' cannot direct the actions of all his or her underlings but that isn't necessary. The belief that 'Tony wants it' is the magic lubricant of government may be overstating the case (although it is what lobby correspondents and political commentators appear overwhelmingly to think) but it cannot be disputed that a tight grip is kept on his fellow board members of the Cabinet. Constrained to deliver their outputs, that imperative is carried down the company *UK plc* and into its 'suppliers'. At local and regional level, quangos and agencies charged with delivering the goods make it clear that partners who can help deliver the output targets are favoured.

The effective centralisation of political control in Britain, begun by Thatcher, has been continued by her true descendant (see Blair, 1996). While not wishing to stretch credulity, they are more similar than first impressions indicate. For example, neither appears to have any time for arguments with senior colleagues. No one disputes Thatcher's authoritarian streak, and Blair also displays at least 'semi-authoritarian' tendencies (see Brittan, 1999). Both have built much of their power on their undoubted charisma. Both are pragmatic, Blair openly so and Thatcher much more than her public statements (such as 'the lady's not for turning') might indicate. Portraying Thatcher as a narrow and inflexible ideologue would be inaccurate. When she said that economics were the method but her object was to change the soul, she clearly signalled her intentions. When attempts to control the money supply failed to deliver, privatisation took over as the primary means of changing our souls. She may have stumbled into the policy, she may have been (as Blair appears to be) lucky, but clever politicians use their luck. Privatising assets (whether through, for example, council house sales, CCT, share options on public utilities or deregulation) grabbed the popular mind in a way monetarism never could have and proved extraordinarily popular with the British public. Extending and encouraging privatisation into the heart of service delivery, the local governance system, took guts and determination. Throughout, however, and whatever the realities of state spending, the object to roll back the frontiers of the state and smash socialism never wavered. Similarly, Blair's belief in a reformulation of social democracy may be more than the rhetoric unkind souls have suggested. A renewal of social democracy may appear a futile pursuit, but Thatcher's wish to change our attitudes to the private sector once appeared similarly futile. In some ways, Blair's ideological goal appears easier than Thatcher's because surveys indicate we like the idea of the Third Way's 'caring capitalism'; we had to be forced to take the Iron Lady's medicine.

Helped enormously by the widespread creation of agencies controlled from central government departments and manned by ministers whose political career he largely controls, Tony Blair has quickly stamped the apparatus of government with his individual personality in a way unprecedented in Britain except in wartime. Margaret Thatcher was constrained by fierce opposition throughout the British state, especially from local government and its employees. Even within her own cabinet, she was forced to include men she disagreed with personally and ideologically. Nearly every important policy she introduced was bloodily opposed by competing forces in politics and society. Lacking her ideological battles, generating precious little opposition in the new post-Thatcherite world, Blair is able to rule almost unchallenged (for now) in the new consensual politics that has finally emerged, with his help, from the predominantly conflict-ridden Thatcher revolution.

Tony Blair *is* New Labour. Possessing charisma, a lot of luck, intelligence and political nous, and a realisation that the reformed governance system offers him the opportunity to introduce a more presidential or managerial way of governing, he can do almost anything. A *Labour* prime minister can privatise state assets, introduce student fees, attack the public sector, endorse the Thatcher legacy, and, crucially, set targets for improved public service outputs and expect to see them delivered. Then, he can ask the public to judge him on his government's record. Tony Blair is something new. The first peacetime 'elected dictator' (albeit with popular support) in Britain's democratic history. The debt he owes to his predecessors, notably Neil Kinnock and Margaret Thatcher, is one he is well aware of. Kinnock delivered a malleable party, Thatcher prepared a malleable local governance system and a reformed central administration, but to re-stress the importance of individuals, while he built upon those legacies his strong managerial control is indisputably *his* achievement. Blair has what are effectively presidential powers but, unlike American presidents, he is relatively unconstrained by competing democratic institutions. His parliamentary majority and control of his MPs means he never has to struggle to build a coalition to pass legislation and our unitary system facilitates control over local actors. He has enormous potential managerial power, and he is utilising this to deliver output-orientated politics. Judged by its actions, local government in general appears to have broadly accepted its new role as another agency, although that will probably change as Conservatives gradually regain power locally. However, given that Blair's policies largely fit the new consensus of public–private cooperation, that opposition may struggle to cohere.

The scale and depth of Blair's achievements, just like Thatcher's, will not be accurately assessed until he has gone from office. It may be that they are far deeper and longer lasting than the beginning of the twenty-first century gives credit for. Although many writers made prescient analyses, it took until the end of the twentieth century, ten years after she had gone from office, for the scale of Thatcher's reformulation of the British state to be understood. Final judgement on Blair may have to wait a similar amount of time. Is he delivering 'joined-up government' for a new age or 'joined-up dictatorship' (Jenkins, 1999) which an essentially pluralist local political culture will ultimately react against? His emphasis on deliverable outputs and his co-option of local actors to deliver them means Tony Blair's control of both central government and the local governance system is greater than any prime minister before him; to what end is still uncertain.

Notes

1 Thatcher's Legacy to Blair

1 Throughout this book I have used as illustrations the opinions of a decision-making elite from the private and public sectors, surveyed during 1996 and interviewed at length during the first half of 1997 as part of an in-depth study into local elite decision making in Staffordshire. A public opinion poll in December 1994 established those individuals the public thought were important (see Table 5.3). Using this information to augment my own list of 'important' people in Staffordshire, 231 senior people in the public and private sectors were surveyed or interviewed with open-ended questions between February and May 1996 and asked (among other things) to nominate the people they thought were important to Staffordshire decision making; the response rate was 52.4 per cent. Following their nominations, an elite list of 25 senior people in a range of organisations was compiled; one MP and one senior industrialist refused to be interviewed, although the industrialist allowed me to talk with one of his senior management team. In all, 24 people were personally interviewed (interviews ranging from 1 to 4 hours) between January and April 1997. The 24 comprised senior individuals in local government (officers and councillors), civil servants, members of quangos, chairs and chief executives of agencies, senior churchmen, media chiefs, heads of educational establishments, members of parliament, members of the European parliament, leaders of industry and commerce, and entrepreneurs. Many are cited in the text but some preferred to speak off-the-record. To identify the elite of 24 people here would provide considerable clues to 'who said what' in the text. Further interviews with senior figures in the local governance system took place during 1999, and some of the nominated elite of 24 people were also re-interviewed to clarify or update points they had made.

3 Drowning, not Waving: Local Government under Attack

1 Although Hill attributes this warning to Peter Shore (Hill, 1994, p. 183), Comfort (1993) also attributes the remark to Crosland but dates it 1974.

5 The Apathetic Community?

1 MORI's survey of Staffordshire was based on 2916 face-to-face interviews conducted at 235 sampling points between 27 October and 29 November, 1993.
2 Social classification is a tricky question, and a number of definitions exist. The classification adopted by MORI was the widely-used Institute of Practitioners in Advertising definition: Class A – higher managerial, administrative or

professional; Class B – intermediate managerial, administrative or professional; Class C1 – supervisory or clerical, and junior managerial administrative or professional; Class C2 – skilled manual workers; Class D – semi-skilled and unskilled manual workers; Class E – state pensioners or widows with no other income, casual workers and long-term unemployed.

8   Governance and the Third Way

1   It must be pointed out that Hutton's conception of stakeholding is not, as 'is often wrongly assumed', the same as the prime minister's version; 'Hutton's ideas are connected to his Keynesian beliefs', which Gordon Brown and Tony Blair do not share (Adams, 1998, p. 150). Also, elements of both stakeholding and communitarianism can be found in the Third Way (see Brittan, 1999).

Bibliography

Adams, Ian (1998) *Ideology and Politics in Britain Today* (Manchester: Manchester University Press).

Alexander, A. (1982) *The Politics of Local Government in the United Kingdom* (London: Longman).

Appleyard, Bryan (1999) 'Labour's pop culture project is doomed', *The Independent*, 25 January.

Ascher, K. (1987) *The Politics of Privatisation* (London: Macmillan).

Ashford, Douglas E. (1989) 'British Dogmatism and French Pragmatism Revisited' in Crouch, Colin and David Marquand (eds) *The New Centralism: Britain Out of Step in Europe?* (Oxford: Basil Blackwell).

Ashford, Nigel (1999) 'New Labour and the end of the welfare state', *Good Society*, Vol. 8 (2), pp. 32–6.

Askew, Judith (1991) 'Public and private sector partnerships for urban regeneration in Sheffield and Wakefield', *Local Government Policy Making*, Vol. 17 (4).

Audit Commission (1997) *Representing the People: the Role of Councillors* (Abingdon: Audit Commission Publications).

Axelrod, Robert (1984) *The Evolution of Co-operation* (New York: Basic Books).

Bagehot, Walter (1963) *The English Constitution* (London: Collins Fontana).

Ball, Rick and Jon Stobart (1996) 'Community identity and the local government review', *Local Government Studies*, Vol. 22 (1), pp. 113–26.

Barber, S. and T. Millns (1993) *Building the New Europe: the Role of the Local Authorities in the United Kingdom* (London: Association of County Councillors).

Baume, Jonathan (1991) *In Defence of the Civil Service*, Fabian Discussion Paper No. 8.

Benington, John (1994) *Local Democracy and the European Union: the impact of Europeanisation on Local Governance* (London: Commission for Local Democracy).

Benington, John and Vivien Lowndes (1993) Editorial, *Local Government Policy Making*, Vol. 20 (1), p. 1.

Birch, Anthony H. (1964) *Representative and Responsible Government* (London: Allen & Unwin).

Blackburn, R. and R. Plant (eds) (1999) *Constitutional Reform: the Labour Government's Constitutional Reform Agenda* (London: Longman).

Blair, Tony (1996) 'How I will follow her', *Daily Telegraph*, 11 January.

Blair, Tony (1998a) *The Third Way: New Politics for the New Century* (London: Fabian Society).

Blair, Tony (1998b) *Leading the Way: a New Vision for Local Government* (London: Institute for Public Policy Research).

Blair, Tony (1999) Speech to the Institute for Public Policy Research, London, 14 January.

Blake, Robert (1985) *The Conservative Party from Peel to Thatcher* (London: Fontana).

Blom-Hansen, J. (1997) 'A "new institutional" perspective on policy networks', *Public Administration*, Vol. 75 (4), pp. 669–93.

Blundell, John and Brian Gosschalk (1997) *Beyond Left and Right: the New Politics of Britain* (London: Institute of Economic Affairs).

Boaden, N., M. Goldsmith, W. Hampton, and P. Stringer (1982) *Public Participation in Local Services* (Harlow: Longman).

Bobbio, Norberto (1994) *Left and Right* (Cambridge: Polity Press).

Bogdanor, Vernon (1994) *Can Government Be Run Like a Business?* (London: Public Finance Foundation).

Bovens, M.A.P. (1996) 'The integrity of the managerial state', *Journal of Contingencies and Crisis Management*, Vol. 4 (3), pp. 125–32.

Braybrooke, D. and C.E. Lindblom (1963) *A Strategy of Decision: Policy Evaluation as a Social Process* (New York: Free Press).

Brereton, Michael and Michael Temple (1999) 'The new public *service* ethos: an ethical environment for governance', *Public Administration*, Vol. 77 (3), pp. 455–74.

Brittan, Samuel (1999) 'A wrong turning for the Third Way?', *New Statesman*, 1 January, pp. 25–7.

Brooke, Rodney (1989) *Managing the Enabling Authority* (Harlow: Longman).

Bruce, Alan (1993) 'Prospects for local economic development: a practitioner's view', *Local Government Studies*, Vol. 19 (3), pp. 319–40.

Bryant, C. (1999) 'The Third Way, two Tonies – and a single vision?', *ECPR News*, Vol. 10 (2), pp. 17–18.

Buckler, S. and D. P. Dolowitz (2000) 'Theorising the Third Way: New Labour and social justice', *Journal of Political Ideologies*.

Budge, Ian, Ivor Crewe, David McKay and Ken Newton (1998) *The New British Politics* (Harlow: Longman).

Bulpitt, Jim (1967) *Party Politics in English Local Government* (London: Longman).

Bulpitt, Jim (1972) 'Participation and local government: territorial democracy' in Parry, G. (ed.) *Participation in Politics* (Manchester: Manchester University Press).

Bulpitt, Jim (1983) *Territory and Power in the United Kingdom* (Manchester: Manchester University Press).

Bulpitt, Jim (1989) 'Walking back to happiness? Conservative party governments and elected local authorities in the 1980s' in Crouch, Colin and David Marquand (eds) *The New Centralism: Britain Out of Step in Europe?* (Oxford: Blackwell).

Bulpitt, Jim (1993) (1997) Review of S. Leach (ed.) *Strengthening Local Government in the 1990s*, *Public Administration*, Vol. 71 (4), pp. 621–3.

Burbidge, John (ed.) *Beyond Prince and Merchant: Citizen Participation and the rise of Civil Society* (New York: Pact Publications).

Butcher, Hugh (1993) 'Introduction: some examples and definitions'; 'Why community policy? Some explanations for recent trends' in Butcher, Hugh, Andrew Glen, Paul Henderson and Jerry Smith (eds) *Community and Public Policy* (London: Pluto Press).

Butcher, Tom (1998) 'The case for local involvement in urban regeneration' in Dobson, Andrew and Jeffrey Stanyer, *Contemporary Political Studies* (PSA 1998 Conference Papers).

Butler, David, Andrew Adonis and Tony Travers (1994) *Failure in British Government: the Politics of the Poll Tax* (Oxford: Oxford University Press).

Byrne, Tony (1994) *Local Government in Britain* (Harmondsworth: Penguin).

Cairns, D. (1996) 'Rediscovering democratic purpose in British local government', *Policy and Politics*, Vol. 24 (1), pp. 17–27.

Chandler, J.A. (1996) 'Citizens and customer care' in Chandler, J.A. (ed.) *The Citizen's Charter* (Aldershot: Dartmouth Press).

Chapman, Richard A. (1996) 'Standards in public life: a valediction', *Teaching Public Administration*, Vol. 16 (1), pp. 1–19.

Chittendon, Maurice and Alexandra Williams (1998) 'Third Way? It has to be a chocolate bar', *Sunday Times*, 27 September.

Christiansen, Peter Munk (1998) 'A prescription rejected: market solutions to problems of public sector governance', *Governance*, Vol. 11 (3), pp. 273–95.

Clarence, Emma and Christopher Painter (1998) 'Public services under new Labour: collaborative discourses and local networking', *Public Policy & Administration*, Vol. 13 (3), pp. 8–22.

Clarence, Emma and Christopher Painter (1999) 'Area based partnerships: UK action zones and collaborative purpose', paper presented to the International Conference on Multi-Organisational Partnerships and Co-operative Strategy, Tilburg University, 8–10 July.

Clark, Wayne (1998) 'Tenants' Associations and community activism', *Local Economy Quarterly*, Vol. 5 (3), pp. 15–23.

Clarke, Michael (1997) 'An agenda for re-inventing local government', *Public Money and Management*, Vol. 17 (2), pp. 17–20.

Clarke, Michael and John Stewart (1994) 'The local authority and the new community governance', *Local Government Studies*, Vol. 20 (2), pp. 163–76.

Cochrane, Alan (1993) *Whatever Happened to Local Government?* (Buckingham: Open University Press).

Cockburn, C. (1979) *The Local State* (London: Pluto Press).

Cole, Alistair and Peter John (1996) 'Economic policy networks in Leeds and Lille: emerging regimes or public sector alliances?', paper presented to the Association Francaise de Science Politique, Université de Paris IV at IEP Paris.

Colenutt, Bob and Austin Cutten (1994) 'Community empowerment in vogue or vain?', *Local Economy*, Vol. 9 (3), pp. 236–50.

Collins, Paul (1984) 'Local prime ministers' *Teaching Public Administration*, No. 4.

Comfort, Nicholas (1993) *Brewer's Politics: a Phrase and Fable Dictionary* (London: Cassell).

Commission for Local Democracy (1995) *Taking Charge: the Rebirth of Local Democracy* (London: Municipal Journal/CLD).

Connolly, Michael ((1996) 'Lessons from local government in Northern Ireland', *Local Government Studies*, Vol. 22 (2), pp. 77–91.

Cook, Yvonne (1999) 'Never mind the windfalls – look more closely at the "third way"', *The Independent*, Open Eye section, 1 June, p. 7.

Coulson, Andrew (ed.) (1998) *Trust and Contracts: Relationships in Local Government, Health and Public Services* (Bristol: The Policy Press).

Crick, Bernard (1997) 'Still missing: a public philosophy?', *The Political Quarterly*, Vol. 68 (4), pp. 344–51.

Crosland, Anthony (1956) *The Future of Socialism* (London: Jonathan Cape).

Crouch, Colin and David Marquand (eds) (1989) *The New Centralism: Britain Out of Step in Europe?* (Oxford: Basil Blackwell).

Daly, Guy (1996) 'Public accountability in today's health service', *Local Government Studies*, Vol. 22 (2), pp. 52–63.

Darke, R. and R. Walker (eds) (1977) *Local Government and the Public* (London: Leonard Hill).

Darwin, John (1996) 'New thunderbolt management', *Teaching Public Administration*, Vol. 16 (1), pp. 76–88.

Davis, Howard (1996) 'Quangos and local government: a changing world', *Local Government Studies*, Vol. 22 (1), 1996, pp. 1–7.

Davis , Howard and John Stewart (1993) *The Growth of Government by Appointment* (Luton: Local Government Management Board).

Deakin, Nicholas and Kieron Walsh (1996) 'The enabling state: the role of markets and contracts', *Public Administration*, Vol. 74 (1), pp. 33–48.

Dearlove, John (1973) *The Politics of Policy in Local Government* (Cambridge: Cambridge University Press).

Dearlove, John (1979) *The Reorganisation of British Local Government: Old Orthodoxies and a Political Perspective* (Cambridge: Cambridge University Press).

Deleon, L. (1998) 'Accountability in a 'reinvented' government', *Public Administration*, Vol. 76 (3), pp. 539–58.

Department of Environment, Transport and the Regions (1998) *Modernising Local Government: in Touch with the People* (London: Stationery Office).

Department of Health (1999) *Saving Lives: Our Healthier Nation* (London: Stationery Office).

Dionne Jr., E.J. (1999) 'Mr Marx, meet Mr Friedman' *The Washington Post*, 23 March.

Dobson, Andrew and Jeffrey Stanyer (1998) *Contemporary Political Studies* (PSA Conference Papers).

Doig, Alan (1984) *Corruption and Misconduct in Contemporary British Politics* (Harmondsworth: Penguin Pelican).

Doig, Alan (1995a) 'Continuing cause for concern? Probity in local government', *Local Government Studies*, Vol. 21 (1), pp. 99–114.

Doig, Alan (1995b) 'Mixed signals? Public sector change and the proper conduct of public business', *Public Administration*, Vol. 73 (2), pp. 191–212.

Dowding, Keith (1994) 'Policy networks: Don't stretch a good idea too far' in Dunleavy, Patrick and Jeffrey Stanyer (eds) *Contemporary Political Studies*, Vol. 1 (Political Studies Association).

Dowding, Keith (1995) 'Myth or metaphor? A critical review of the policy network approach' *Political Studies*, Vol. 43 (1), pp. 136–58.

Dowding, Keith, Patrick Dunleavy, Desmond King and Helen Margetts (1995) 'Rational choice and community power structures', *Political Studies*, Vol. 43 (2), pp. 265–77.

Duffy, K. and J. Hutchinson (1997) 'Urban policy and the turn to community', *Town Planning Review*, Vol. 68 (3).

Duke, Karen, Susanne MacGregor and Lynne Smith (1996) *Activating Local Networks: a Comparison of Two Community Development Approaches to Drug Prevention* (London: Home Office).

Dunleavy, Patrick (1980) *Urban Political Analysis* (London: Macmillan).

Dunleavy, Patrick (1997) 'The constitution' in Dunleavy, Patrick, Andrew Gamble, Ian Holliday and Gillian Peele (eds) *Developments in British Politics* 5 (London: Macmillan).

Elcock, Howard (1998) 'The changing problem of accountability in modern government: an analytical agenda for reformers', *Public Policy & Administration*, Vol. 13 (3), pp. 23–37.

Elcock, Howard with Michael Wheaton (1986) *Local Government: Politicians, Professionals and the Public in Local Authorities* (London: Methuen).

Etzioni, Amitai (1997) *The New Golden Rule: Community and Morality in a Democratic Society* (London: Profile Books).

Foley, Paul (1999) 'New Labour: A new deal for communities?', *Public Money & Management*, Vol. 19 (1), pp. 7–8.

Forrest, Ray and Ade Kearns (1999) *Joined-up Places? Social Cohesion and Neighbourhood Regeneration* (York: Joseph Rowntree Foundation).

Forsyth, M. (1982) 'Winners in the contracting game' *Local Government Chronicle*, 10 September.

Gabb, Sean (1999) 'Peter Lilley and the welfare state: why the Tories may be doomed after all', *Free Life Commentary*, 22 April, old.whig@virgin.net

Gaffney, Declan and Allyson M. Pollock (1999) 'Pump-priming the PFI: Why are privately financed hospital schemes being subsidised?', *Public Money & Management*, Vol. 19 (1), pp. 55–62.

Gamble, Andrew (1990) 'The Thatcher decade in perspective' in Dunleavy, Patrick, Andrew Gamble and Gillian Peele (eds) *Developments in British Politics*, 3 (London: Macmillan).

Game, Chris (1997) 'Unprecedented in local government terms – the Local Government Commission's public consultation programme', *Public Administration*, Vol. 75 (1), pp. 67–96.

Game, Chris and Steve Leach (1995) *The Role of Political Parties in Local Democracy* (London: Commission for Local Democracy).

Garmise, Shari and Gareth Rees (1997) 'The role of institutional networks in local economic development: a new model of governance?', *Local Economy*, Vol. 12 (2), pp. 104–18.

Giddens, Anthony (1990) *The Consequences of Modernity* (Cambridge: Polity Press).

Giddens, Anthony (1994) *Beyond Left and Right: the Future of Radical Politics* (Cambridge: Polity Press).

Giddens, Anthony (1998a) *The Third Way: the Renewal of Social Democracy* (Cambridge: Polity Press).

Giddens, Anthony (1998b) 'The future of the welfare state' in Novak, Michael (ed.) *Is There a Third Way? Essays on the Changing Direction of Socialist Thought* (London: Institute of Economic Affairs).

Gilmour, Robert S. and Laura S. Jensen (1998) 'Reinventing government accountability: public functions, privatisation, and the meaning of "state action"', *Public Administration Review*, Vol. 58 (3), pp. 247–58.

Glennester, H. and J. Midgely (eds) (1991) *The Radical Right and the Welfare State* (London: Harvester Wheatsheaf).

Gordon, Pamela (1997) *New Start? Local Government's Agenda for the Incoming Government* (London: CIPFA).

Gostick, Chris, Bleddyn Davies, Robyn Lawson and Charlotte Salter (1997) *From Vision to Reality in Community Care: Changing Direction at the Local Level* (Aldershot: Arena).

Gould, Philip (1998) *The Unfinished Revolution* (London: Little Brown).

Gray, John (1997) 'After social democracy' in Mulgan, Geoff (ed.) *Life After Politics: New Thinking for the Twenty-first Century* (London: Fontana).

Greenaway, John (1995) 'Having the bun and the halfpenny: can old public service ethics survive in the new Whitehall?', *Public Administration*, Vol. 73 (4), pp. 357–74.

Greenwood, John and David Wilson (1984) *Public Administration in Britain* (London: George Allen & Unwin).

Greer, Alan and Paul Hoggett (1996) 'Quangos and local governance' in Pratchett, Lawrence and David Wilson (eds) *Local Democracy and Local Government* (London: Macmillan).

Greer, Patricia (1994) *Transforming Central Government: the Next Steps Initiative* (Buckingham: Open University Press).

Gregory, Sarah (1998) *Transforming Local Services: Partnership in action*, in *Findings in Focus*, May 1999, Joseph Rowntree Foundation.

Grice, Andrew (1999a) 'Hague unveils his "caring Conservatism"', *The Independent*, 10 February.

Grice, Andrew (1999b) 'Hague accused of betraying legacy', *The Independent*, 22 April.

Griffiths, P. and A. Lawton (1992) 'Community councils in Wales', *Local Government Studies*, Vol. 18 (3), pp. 34–43.

Gyford, J. (1991) *Citizens, Consumers and Councils: Local Government and the Public* (London: Macmillan).

Habeebullah, Mohammed and Dave Slater (1993) 'Community government' in Butcher, Hugh, Andrew Glen, Paul Henderson and Jerry Smith (eds) *Community and Public Policy* (London: Pluto Press).

Haider, J. (1997) *Befreite Zukunft Jenseits von Links und Rechts: Menschliche alternativen fur eine brucke ins neue jahrtausend* (Wien: Ibera & Molden).

Hain, Peter (1976) *Community Politics* (London: Platform Books).

Hall, Stuart (1998) 'Nowhere man', *The Sunday Times*, 18 October.

Hampton, William (1987) *Local Government and Urban Politics* (London: Longman).

Harding, Alan (1989) 'Central control in British urban economic development programmes' in Crouch, Colin and David Marquand (eds) *The New Centralism: Britain Out of Step in Europe?* (Oxford: Basil Blackwell).

Hargreaves, Ian and Ian Christie (1998) *Tomorrow's Politics: the Third Way and Beyond* (London: Demos).

Harris, Robert (1998) 'Blair's third way to elected dictatorship', *Sunday Times*, 20 September.

Harrison, Brian (1996) *The Transformation of British Politics 1860–1995* (Oxford: Oxford University Press).

Haughton, Graham, Jamie Peck and Ian Strange (1997) 'Turf Wars: the battle for control over English local economic development', *Local Government Studies*, Vol. 23 (1), pp. 88–106.

Hay, Colin (1994) 'Labour's Thatcherite revisionism; playing the politics of "catch-up"', *Political Studies*, Vol. 42 (4), pp. 700–7.

Heatley, Rachel (1990) 'Partnership and economic regeneration: the Kirklees approach', *Local Economy*, Vol. 5 (1), pp. 70–3.

Held, David (1996) *Models of Democracy* (Cambridge: Polity Press).

Higgins, G. and J. Richardson (1976) *Political Participation* (The Politics Association).

Hill, Dilys M. (1970) *Participating in Local Affairs* (Harmondsworth: Penguin).

Hill, Dilys M. (1974) *Democratic Theory and Local Government* (London: George Allen & Unwin).

Hill, Dilys M. (1983) 'Decisions, decisions…', *Parliamentary Affairs*, Vol. 36 (1), pp. 121–5.

Hill, Dilys M. (1994) *Citizens and Cities: Urban Policy in the 1990s* (London: Harvester Wheatsheaf).

Hoggett, Paul (1996) 'New modes of control in the public service', *Public Administration*, Vol. 74 (1), pp. 9–32.

Holland, P. (1981) *The Governance of Quangos* (London: Adam Smith Institute).

Holliday, Ian (1997) 'Territorial politics' in Dunleavy, Patrick, Andrew Gamble, Ian Holliday and Gillian Peele (eds) *Developments in British Politics* 5 (London: Macmillan).

Hollis, G., G. Ham and M. Ambler (1992) *The Future Role and Structure of Local Government* (London: Longman).

Hood, Christopher (1991) 'A public management for all seasons' *Public Administration*, Vol. 69 (1), pp. 3–19.

Horton, S. (1990) 'Local government 1979–89: a Decade of Change' in Savage, S. and L. Robins (eds) *Public Policy Under Thatcher* (London: Macmillan).

Horton, S., and J. Jones (1996) 'Who are the new public managers? an initial analysis of 'Next Steps' chief executives and their managerial role', *Public Policy and Administration*, Vol. 11 (4), pp. 18–44.

Howarth, David (1995) 'Discourse theory' in Marsh, David and Gerry Stoker (eds) *Theory and Methods in Political Science* (London: Macmillan).

Hughes, Elizabeth (1998) 'Health Action Zones', *Local Economy Quarterly*, Vol. 5 (3), pp. 41–6.

Hunt, P. (1995) 'Accountability in the National Health Service', *Parliamentary Affairs*, Vol. 48 (2), pp. 297–305.

Hunt, Michael (1996) 'Accountability, openness and the Citizen's Charter' in Chandler, J.A. (ed.) *The Citizen's Charter* (Aldershot: Dartmouth Press).

Hutchinson, Jo (1994) 'The practice of partnership in local economic development', *Local Government Studies*, Vol. 20 (3), pp. 335–44.

Jackson, W.E. (1963) *Local Government in England and Wales* (Harmondsworth: Penguin).

Jacobs, Brian D. (1992) *Fractured Cities: Capitalism, Community and Empowerment in Britain and America* (London: Routledge).

Jacobs, Brian D. (1993) 'Economic developments and political interests in Manchester and Birmingham', paper presented to Local Government Finance Seminar, University of Neuchatel, Switzerland, 25–28 June.

Jacobs, Brian D. (1996) 'A bureau-political model of local networks and public/private partnerships: responses to crisis and change', *Journal of Contingencies and Crisis Management*, Vol. 4 (3), pp. 133–48.

Jacobs, Brian D. (1997) 'Networks, partnerships and European union regional economic development initiatives in the West Midlands', *Policy and Politics*, Vol. 25 (1), pp. 39–50.

Jacobs, Brian D. (1998) 'The regional city: governance and competitiveness in Pittsburgh' in Peele, G., C. Bailey, B. Cain and B.G. Peters (eds) *Developments in American Politics*, 3 (London: Macmillan).

Jay, Anthony (1994) 'What shall we do about local government?' Unpublished lecture to the Institute of Economic Affairs, London, June.

Jenkins, Simon (1995) *Accountable to None: the Tory Nationalization of Britain* (London: Hamish Hamilton).

Jenkins, Simon (1996) 'Accountable to none', *Public Money & Management*, Vol. 16 (2), pp. 3–4.

Jenkins, Simon (1998) 'Hague's local heroes' *The Times*, October 7.

Jenkins, Simon (1999) 'Joined-up dictatorship' *The Times*, July 30.

John, Peter (1997) 'Local governance' in Dunleavy, Patrick, Andrew Gamble, Ian Holliday and Gillian Peele (eds) *Developments in British Politics* 5 (London: Macmillan).

John, Peter and Alistair Cole (1995) 'Models of local decision-making networks in Britain and France', *Policy & Politics*, Vol. 23 (4), pp. 303–12.

Jones, George (1977) *Responsibility and Government* (London: London School of Economics).

Jones, George (1988) 'Against regional government', *Local Government Studies*, Vol. 14 (5), pp. 1–11.

Jones, George and Tony Travers (1994) *Attitudes to Local Government in Westminster and Whitehall* (London: Commission for Local Democracy).

Joseph Rowntree Foundation (1999) *Findings in Focus*, May.

Judge, D. (1993) *The Parliamentary State* (London: Sage).

Kavanagh, Dennis (1997) *The Reordering of British Politics: Politics after Thatcher* (Oxford: Oxford University Press).

Keith-Lucas, B. and P. Richards (1978) *A History of Local Government in the Twentieth Century* (London: Allen & Unwin).

King, D. and M. Wickham-Jones (1999a) 'Social capital, British social democracy and New Labour', *Democratization*, Vol. 6 (4).

King, D. and M. Wickham-Jones (1999b) 'Bridging the Atlantic: the Democratic (Party) origins of welfare to work' in M. Powell (ed.) *New Labour, New Welfare State? The 'Third Way' in British Social Policy* (Bristol: The Policy Press).

Kingdom, John (1991a) *Local Government and Politics in Britain: an Introduction* (Hemel Hempstead: Philip Allan).

Kingdom, John (1991b) 'Reappraising local government: the political dimension', *Politics Review*, Vol. 1 (2), pp. 2–7.

Kirkpatrick, Ian and Miguel Martinez Lucio (1996) 'The contract state and the future of local management', *Public Administration*, Vol. 74 (1), pp. 1–8.

Knox, C. (1998) 'The European Model of service delivery: a partnership approach in Northern Ireland', *Public Policy and Administration*, Vol. 18 (2), pp. 151–68.

Laclau, E. (1995) 'Why do empty signifiers matter to politics?' in Weeks, J. (ed.) *The Greater Evil and the Lesser Good* (London: Rivers Oram).

Lawton, Alan and Aidan Rose (1991) *Organisation and Management in the Public Sector* (London: Pitman).

Leach, Steve (1996) 'The indirectly elected world of local government', *Local Government Studies*, Vol. 22 (2), pp. 64–76.

Leach, Steve (1999) Presentation at Local Government Management Board, London, 18 February.

Le Grand, Julian (1990) *Quasi-Markets and Social Policy: Studies in Decentralisation and Quasi-Markets* (Bristol: School for Advanced Urban Studies).

Le Grand, Julian (1998) 'Ownership and social policy', *The Political Quarterly*, Vol. 69 (4), pp. 415–21.

Le Grand, Julian and Will Bartlett (eds) (1993) *Quasi-Markets and Social Policy* (London: Macmillan).

Levett, R. (1993) *Agenda 21: a Guide for Local Authorities in the U.K.* (Luton: Local Government Management Board).

Lind, Michael (1998) 'The time is right for the Third Man', *New Statesman*, 13 November.

Ling, Tom (1998) *The British State Since 1945: an Introduction* (Cambridge: Polity Press).

Lipsky, Michael (1980) *Street Level Bureaucracy: Dilemmas of the Individual in Public Service* (New York: Russell Sage Foundation).
Littlewood, Stephen and Aidan While (1997) 'A new agenda for governance? Agenda 21 and the prospects for holistic local decision-making', *Local Government Studies*, Vol. 23 (4), pp. 111–23.
Lloyd, John (1998a) 'Serf no more' in Novak, Michael (ed.) *Is There a Third Way? Essays on the Changing Direction of Socialist Thought* (London: Institute of Economic Affairs).
Lloyd, John (1998b) 'Third way? They'll do it their way', *New Statesman*, 4 December, pp. 8–9.
Lloyds TSB Group plc (1998) 'Third Way – The Road to Damascus' Advertisement, *New Statesman* supplement, 11 December.
Loughlin, Martin (1996) 'The constitutional status of local government' in Pratchett, Lawrence and David Wilson (eds) *Local Democracy and Local Government* (London: Macmillan).
Loughlin, Martin and Colin Scott (1997) 'The regulatory state' in Dunleavy, Patrick, Andrew Gamble, Ian Holliday and Gillian Peele (eds) *Developments in British Politics*, 5 (London: Macmillan).
Loveland, Ian (1999) 'Local authorities' in Blackburn, Robert and Raymond Plant (eds) *Constitutional Reform: the Labour Government's Constitutional Reform Agenda* (London: Longman).
Lowndes, V. and C. Skelcher (1998) 'The dynamics of multi-organisational partnerships: an analysis of changing modes of governance', *Public Administration*, Vol. 76 (2), pp. 313–33.
Lynn, P. (1992) *Public Perceptions of Local Government: its Finances and Services* (London: HMSO).
Mabileau, A., G. Moyser, G. Parry and P. Quantin (eds) (1989) *Local Politics and Participation in Britain and France* (Cambridge: Cambridge University Press).
McElvoy, Anne (1998) 'What's the Big Idea? I don't know that we need one', *The Independent*, 29 September.
McGuinness, Tony (1991) 'Markets and managerial hierarchies' in Thompson, G., J. Frances, R. Levacic and J. Mitchell (eds) *Markets, Hierarchies & Networks: the Coordination of Social Life* (London: Sage).
Macintyre, Donald (1999) 'Mr Blair is right to demand results in return for public money', *The Independent*, 22 July.
Mackenzie, W.J.M. and J.W. Grove (1957) *Central Administration in Britain* (London: Longmans).
Macnaghten, Phil, Robin Grove-White, Michael Jacobs and Brian Wynne (1995) *Public Perceptions and Sustainability in Lancashire: Indicators, Institutions, participation* (Lancaster: Lancashire County Council).
McNaughton, Neil and Rob McNaughton (1999) 'Best value: a fresh start for local government', *Politics Review*, February, pp. 31–3.
McRae, Hamish (1997) 'It is hard to play by the rules when there are none left' *The Independent* 19 March.
MacShane, Dennis (1998) 'Can we adapt to the third way?', *The Independent*, 16 September.
Majone, G. (1994) 'The rise of the regulatory state in Europe', *West European Politics*, Vol. 17 (1), pp. 77–101.
Malde, Bharat (1994) 'The return of the public servant', *Local Government Studies*, Vol. 20 (1), pp. 7–15.

Maloney, William A. and Jeremy Richardson (1994) 'Water policy-making in England and Wales: policy communities under pressure?', *Environmental Politics*, Vol. 3 (4), pp. 110–38.

Maltby, Josephine and Roy Wilkinson (1998) 'Stakeholding and corporate governance in the UK', *Politics*, Vol. 18 (3), pp. 197–204.

Marks, Naomi (1999) 'The global village still needs its parish pump', *The Independent*, 23 March.

Marr, Andrew (1996) *Ruling Britannia: the Failure and Future of British Democracy* (London: Penguin).

Marr, Andrew (1999) 'Blair reveals his vision of real hope', *Daily Express*, 27 January, p. 13.

Marsh, David and R.A.W. Rhodes (eds) (1992) *Policy Networks in British Government* (Oxford: Clarendon Press).

Marsh, David and Gerry Stoker (eds) (1995) *Theory and Methods in Political Science* (London: Macmillan).

Massey, Andrew (1995) 'Ministers, the agency model and policy ownership', *Public Policy & Administration*, Vol. 10 (2), pp. 71–87.

Massey, Andrew (1997) 'Management, politics and non-departmental bodies', *Public Money & Management*, Vol. 17 (2), pp. 21–6.

Maud, J.P.R. (1932) *Local Government in Modern England* (London: Thornton Butterworth).

Maude, Francis (1998) 'No such thing as a Third Way', *The Independent*, 4 August.

Mayo, Marjorie (1994) *Communities and Caring: the Mixed Economy of Welfare* (London: Macmillan).

Mellors, Colin (1989) 'Non-majority British local authorities in a majority setting' in Mellors, Colin and Bert Pijnenburg *Political Parties and Coalitions in European Local Government* (London: Routledge).

Metcalfe, Les and Sue Richards (1990) *Improving Public Management* (European Institute of Public Administration: Sage).

Michel, Fredric and Laurent Bouvet (1998) 'Paris, Bonn, Rome: a Continental Way?' in Hargreaves, Ian and Ian Christie (eds) *Tomorrow's Politics: the Third Way and Beyond* (London: Demos).

Miller, W.L. (1988) *Irrelevant Elections? The Quality of Local Democracy in Britain* (Oxford: Clarendon Press).

Moore, Chris (1988) 'Models of local authority economic policy: markets and interventionism in local economies', Paper presented to Political Studies Association Conference, Plymouth Polytechnic, 12–14 April.

MORI (1994) *Community Identity in Staffordshire* (London: MORI).

Morris, J. and C. Brigham (1993) 'Filling the information gaps', *Local Government Chronicle*, 17/24 December.

Morris, Robert (1981) 'Education' *Local Government Studies Annual Review '81'*, Vol. 7 (2).

Morris, Robert (1990) *Central and Local Government After the Education Reform Act 1988* (Harlow: Longman).

Morris, Robert (1994) 'New magistracies and commissariats', *Local Government Studies*, Vol. 20 (2), pp. 177–85.

Mountfield, Robin (1997) 'The new Senior Civil Service: managing the paradox', *Public Administration*, Vol. 75 (3), pp. 307–12.

Mulgan, Geoff (ed.) (1997) *Life After Politics: New Thinking for the Twenty-first Century* (London: Fontana).

Nevin, Brendan and Phil Shiner (1995) 'Community regeneration and empowerment: a new approach to partnership', *Local Economy*, Vol. 9 (4), pp. 308–22.

Nevin, Brendan and Phil Shiner (1996) 'The left, urban policy and community empowerment: The first steps towards a new framework for urban regeneration', *Local Economy*, Vol. 10.

Newman, Janet (1998) 'The dynamics of trust' in Coulson, Andrew (ed.) *Trust and Contracts: Relationships in Local Government, Health and Public Services* (Bristol: The Policy Press).

Nichols, Geoff and Peter Taylor (1995) 'The impact on local authority leisure provision of Compulsory Competitive Tendering, financial cuts and changing attitudes', *Local Government Studies*, Vol. 21 (4), pp. 607–22.

Niskanen, W.A. (1973) *Bureaucracy: Servant or Master?* (London: Institute of Economic Affairs).

Nolan Report (1995) *Standards in Public Life; First report of the Committee on Standards in Public Life* Cmnd. 2850–51 (London: HMSO).

Nordlinger, E.A. (1981) *On the Autonomy of the Democratic State* (Cambridge, MA: Harvard University Press).

North Staffordshire Health Authority (1999) *Health and Well Being Improvement Programme* (Stoke-on-Trent: NSHA).

Novak, Michael (1998) 'The crisis of social democracy' in Novak, Michael (ed.) *Is There a Third Way? Essays on the Changing Direction of Socialist Thought* (London: Institute of Economic Affairs).

O'Toole, Barry J. (1993) 'The loss of purity: the corruption of public service in Britain', *Public Policy and Administration*, Vol. 8 (1), pp. 1–6.

Osborne, David and Ted Gaebler (1992) *Reinventing Government* (Reading: Addison-Wesley).

Painter, Christopher and Emma Clarence (1999) 'New Labour and Inter-governmental Management: Flexible networks or performance control?' paper presented to Third International Research Symposium on Public Management, Aston University Business School, 26 March.

Palfrey, C. and P. Thomas (1996) 'Ethical issues in policy evaluation', *Policy & Politics*, Vol. 24 (3), pp. 277–85.

Parry, G. and G. Moyser (1989) 'Community, locality and political action: two British case studies compared', in Mabileau *et al.* (eds) *Local Politics and Participation in Britain and France* (Cambridge: Cambridge University Press).

Parry, G., G. Moyser and N. Day (1992) *Political Participation and Democracy in Britain* (Cambridge: Cambridge University Press).

Pattison, Stephen (1994) 'The value of ethics', *Local Government Studies*, Vol. 20 (4), pp. 547–53.

Peck, Jamie and Mike Emmerich (1993) 'Training and Enterprise Councils: Time for a change', *Local Economy*, Vol. 8 (1), pp. 4–21.

Peck, Jamie and Adam Tickell (1994) 'Too many partners … the future for regeneration partnerships', *Local Economy*, Vol. 9 (3), pp. 251–65.

Percy-Smith, Janie (1996) *Discussing Democracy: the Response to 'Taking Charge: The Rebirth of Local Democracy'* (London: Municipal Journal/CLD).

Perri 6 (1998a) 'Problem-solving government' in Hargreaves, Ian and Ian Christie (eds) *Tomorrow's Politics: the Third Way and Beyond* (London: Demos).

Perri 6 (1998b) 'Ownership and the new politics of the public interest services', *The Political Quarterly*, Vol. 69 (4), pp. 404–14.

Peters, Glyn (1999) *Waltzing With The Raptors: a Practical Roadmap to Protecting your Company's Reputation* (Chichester: John Wiley).

Peters, Thomas and Robert Waterman (1982) *In Search of Excellence* (New York: Harper & Row).

Pfeffer, N. and A. Pollack (1993) 'Public opinion and the NHS: The unaccountable in pursuit of the uninformed', *British Medical Journal*, 25 September.

Phillips, Anne (1996) 'Why does local democracy matter?' in Pratchett, Lawrence and David Wilson (eds) *Local Democracy and Local Government* (London: Macmillan).

Phillips, Louise (1996) 'Rhetoric and the spread of the discourse of Thatcherism', *Discourse and Society*, Vol. 7 (2), pp. 209–41.

Pickvance, Chris (1991) 'The difficulty of control and the ease of structural reform: British local government in the 1980s' in Pickvance, Chris and Edmond Preteceile (eds) *State Restructuring and Local Power: a Comparative Perspective* (London: Pinter).

Pike, Alan (1997) 'Why a new local governance is needed', *Public Money & Management*, Vol. 17 (1), pp. 5–6.

Pirie, Madsen (1981) *Micropolitics* (London: Institute of Economic Affairs).

Plamping, Diane, Pat Gordon and Julian Pratt (1998) *Action Zones and Large Numbers: Why Working with lots of People Makes Sense* (London: Kings Fund Publishing).

Pliatsky, L. (1980) *Report on Non-Departmental Bodies* (London: HMSO Cmnd 7797).

Pollit, C. (1993) *Managerialism and the Public Services* (Oxford: Oxford University Press).

Pollit, C., J. Birchall and K. Putnam (1998) *Decentralising Public Service Management* (London: Macmillan).

Poole, Michael, Roger Mansfield, Miguel Martinez Lucio and Bob Turner (1995) 'Change and continuities within the public sector: contrasts between public and private sector managers in Britain and the effects of the "Thatcher Years"', *Public Administration*, Vol. 73 (2), pp. 271–86.

Potter, Jenny (1988) 'Consumerism and the public sector: how well does the coat fit?', *Public Administration*, Vol. 66 (2), pp. 149–60.

Pratchett, Lawrence and David Wilson (eds) (1996) *Local Democracy and Local Government* (London: Macmillan).

Pratchett, Lawrence and David Wilson (1997) 'The rebirth of local democracy?', *Local Government Studies*, Vol. 23 (1), pp. 16–31.

Pratchett, Lawrence and Melvin Wingfield (1994) *The Public Service Ethos in Local Government: a research report* (London: Commission for Local Democracy).

Pratchett, Lawrence and Melvin Wingfield (1996) 'Petty bureaucracy and woolly-minded liberalism? The changing ethos of local government officers', *Public Administration*, Vol. 74 (4), pp. 639–56.

Prior, David (1996) 'Working the network: local authority strategies in the reticulated local state', *Local Government Studies*, Vol. 22 (2), pp. 92–104.

Putnam, Robert (1993) *Making Democracy Work: Civic Traditions in Modern Italy* (Princeton: Princeton University Press).

Pym, Mike (1996) 'Accountability and leadership in the prison service', *Teaching Public Administration*, Vol. 16 (1), pp. 36–53.

Quantin, P. (1989) 'In search of community spirit' in Mabileau, A., G. Moyser, G. Parry and P. Quantin (eds) *Local Politics and Participation in Britain and France* (Cambridge: Cambridge University Press).

Radcliffe, James (1993) *Executive Agencies and Changing Civil Service Working Practices* (Staffordshire University: Papers in Politics and International Relations, No.13).

Radcliffe, James (1996) 'Community care and new public management: the local government response', *Local Government Studies*, Vol. 22 (2), p. 153–66.

Radcliffe, James (1997) 'The Scott inquiry, constitutional conventions and accountability in British government', *Crime, Law & Social Change*, Vol. 7 (1), pp. 1–14.

Rafferty, Frances (1998) 'Lambeth asks business to help', *Times Educational Supplement*, 6 February.

Rallings, Colin and Michael Thrasher (1997a) *Local Elections in Britain* (London: Routledge).

Rallings, Colin and Michael Thrasher (1997b) 'Local elections' in P. Norris and N. Gavin (eds) *Britain Votes 1997* (Oxford: Oxford University Press).

Rallings, Colin, Michael Temple and Michael Thrasher (1994) *Community Identity and Participation in Local Government* (London: Commission for Local Democracy).

Rallings, Colin, Michael Temple and Michael Thrasher (1996) 'Participation in local elections' in Pratchett, Lawrence and David Wilson (eds) *Local Democracy and Local Government* (London: Macmillan).

Ranson, Stewart (1990) 'Education' in Deakin, N. and A. Wright (eds) *Consuming Public Services* (London: Routledge).

Ranson, Stewart and John Stewart (1998) 'Citizenship in the public domain for trust in civil society' in Coulson, Andrew (ed.) *Trust and Contracts: Relationships in Local Government, Health and Public Services* (Bristol: The Policy Press).

Redcliffe-Maud, Lord (1969) *Royal Commission on Local Government, Volume One, Report* (London: HMSO).

Rhodes, R.A.W. (1981) *Control and Power in Central–Local Relations* (London: Gower).

Rhodes, R.A.W. (1987) 'Developing the public service orientation; or let's have a soupcon of political theory', *Local Government Studies*, Vol. 13 (1), pp. 63–73.

Rhodes, R.A.W. (1988) *Beyond Westminster and Whitehall: the Sub-central Governments of Britain* (London: Unwin Hyman).

Rhodes, R.A.W. (1994) 'The hollowing out of the state', *The Political Quarterly*, Vol. 65, pp. 138–51.

Rhodes, R.A.W. (1996) 'The new governance: governing without government', *Political Studies*, Vol. 44 (4), pp. 652–67.

Rhodes, R.A.W. (1997a) 'From marketization to diplomacy: it's the mix that matters', *Australian Journal of Public Administration*, Vol. 56 (1), pp. 40–53.

Rhodes, R.A.W. (1997b) *Understanding Governance* (Buckingham: Open University Press).

Rhodes, R.A.W. (1998) 'Diplomacy in governance', *Politics Review*, Vol. 7 (3), pp. 24–7.

Richards, Peter G. (1973) *The Reformed Local Government System* (London: George Allen & Unwin).

Richards, Steve (1999) 'An earthquake strikes New Labour', *New Statesman*, 1 January.

Robson, W. (1954) *The Development of Local Government* (London: Allen & Unwin).

Rogaly, Joe (1993) 'Opportunists in waiting', *The Financial Times*, 17 September.

Rosenberg, David (1989) *Accounting for Public Policy: Power, Professionals and Politics in Local Government* (Manchester: Manchester University Press).

Roulier, Monte (1997) 'Local community: seedbed of civil society' in Burbidge, John (ed.) *Beyond Prince and Merchant: Citizen Participation and the Rise of Civil Society* (New York: Pact Publications).

Sanderson, Ian (1998) 'Beyond performance measurement? Assessing "value" in local government', *Local Government Studies*, Vol. 24 (4), pp. 1–25.

Sanderson, Ian and Anne Foreman (1996) 'Towards pluralism and partnership in management development in local government', *Local Government Studies*, Vol. 22 (1), pp. 59–77.

Saward, M. (1997) 'In search of the hollow crown' in Weller, Patrick, Herman Bakvis and R.A.W. Rhodes (eds) *The Hollow Crown* (London: Macmillan).

Seebohm, F. (chairman) (1967/68) *Report of the Committee on Local Authority and Allied Personal Social Services* (London: HMSO).

Sellar, W.C. and R.J. Yeatman (1930) *1066 And All That* (London: Methuen).

Sengupta, Kim (1998) 'Shhh, don't tell … Tony Blair is a *socialist*', *The Independent*, 24 April.

Sheaff, Rod and Michael West (1995) 'Marketization, managers and moral strain: chairmen, directors and public service ethos in the NHS', *Public Administration*, Vol. 75 (2), pp. 189–206.

Simon, Herbert (1957) *Administrative Behaviour* (New York: The Free Press).

Skeffington, A. (chairman) (1969) *People and Planning* (London: HMSO).

Skelcher, Chris and Howard Davis (1996) 'Understanding the new magistracy: a study of characteristics and attitudes', *Local Government Studies*, Vol. 22 (2), pp. 8–21.

Smith, C. and B. Anderson (1972) 'Political participation through community action' in Parry, G. (ed.) *Participation in Politics* (Manchester: Manchester University Press).

Smith, David (1998) 'Blair's third-way guru charts an ominous path', *Sunday Times*, 13 September.

Steele, Kevin (1992) 'Patients as experts: consumer appraisal of health services', *Public Money & Management*, Vol. 12 (4), pp. 31–7.

Stewart, John (1989) 'A future for local authorities as community government' in Stewart, John and Gerry Stoker (eds) *The Future of Local Government* (London: Macmillan).

Stewart, John (1996) 'Reforming the new magistracy' in Pratchett, Lawrence and David Wilson (eds) *Local Democracy and Local Government* (London: Macmillan).

Stewart, John and Howard Davis (1994) 'A new agenda for local governance', *Public Money & Management*, Vol. 4 (1), pp. 29–36.

Stewart, John and Gerry Stoker (eds) (1989) *The Future of Local Government* (London: Macmillan).

Stewart, John and Gerry Stoker (eds) (1995) *Local Government in the 1990s* (London: Macmillan).

Stoker, Gerry (1988) *The Politics of Local Government* (London: Macmillan).

Stoker, Gerry (1996) 'Redefining local democracy' in Pratchett, Lawrence and David Wilson (eds) *Local Democracy and Local Government* (London: Macmillan).

Sumners, Martin (1996) 'Only connect: towards a new democratic settlement' in Mark Perryman (ed.) *The Blair Agenda* (London: Lawrence & Wishart, 1996).

Tant, A.P. (1993) *British Government: the Triumph of Elitism* (Aldershot: Dartmouth Press).

Tawney, R.H. (1952) *Equality* (London: Allen & Unwin).

Taylor, A. (1997) 'Arm's length but hands-on – mapping the new governance: The Department of National Heritage and cultural politics in Britain', *Public Administration*, Vol. 75 (3), pp. 441–66.

Tebbit, Norman (1993) *Unfinished Business* (London: Weidenfeld & Nicholson).

Temple, Michael (1993) 'Devon County Council: a case study of a hung council', *Public Administration*, Vol. 71 (4), pp. 507–33.

Temple, Michael (1996) *Coalitions and Cooperation in Local Government* (London: Electoral Reform Society).

Thomas, Ian C. (1994) 'The relationship between local authorities and TECs in metropolitan areas', *Local Government Studies*, Vol. 20 (2), pp. 257–305.

Thompson, G. (ed.) (1991) *Markets, Hierarchies & Networks: the Coordination of Social Life* (London: Sage).

Travers, Tony (1986) *The Politics of Local Government Finance* (London: Allen & Unwin).

Troxel, James P. (1997) 'The recovery of civic engagement in America' in Burbidge, John (ed.) *Beyond Prince and Merchant: Citizen Participation and the Rise of Civil Society* (New York: Pact Publications).

Vincent, Andrew (1998) 'New ideologies for old?', *The Political Quarterly*, Vol. 69 (1), pp. 48–58.

Waldegrave, William (1993) *The Reality of Reform and Accountability in Today's Public Service* (London: CIPFA).

Walsh, Kieron (1989) 'Competition and service in local government' in Stewart, John and Gerry Stoker (eds) *The Future of Local Government* (London: Macmillan).

Walsh, Kieron (1995) 'Competition and service delivery' in Stewart, John and Gerry Stoker (eds) *Local Government in the 1990s* (London: Macmillan).

Wargent, Martin (1993) 'Marketing in the public sector – a Probation Service view', *Local Government Policy Making*, Vol. 20 (1), pp. 44–9.

Warren, J.H. and P.G. Richards (1965) *The English Local Government System* (London: George Allen & Unwin).

Webster, Philip (1999) 'Hague backs Lilley as Tory revolt erupts', *The Times*, 22 April.

Weir, Stuart and W. Hall (eds) (1994) *EGO Trip: Extra-governmental organisations in the United Kingdom and their Accountability* (London: Charter 88).

Weir, Stuart and David Beetham (1998) *Political Power and Democratic Control in Britain* (London: Routledge).

Weller, Patrick and Herman Bakvis (1997) 'The hollow crown: coherence and capacity in central government' in Weller, Patrick, Herman Bakvis and R.A.W. Rhodes (eds) *The Hollow Crown* (London: Macmillan).

Weller, Patrick, Herman Bakvis and R.A.W. Rhodes (eds) (1997) *The Hollow Crown* (London: Macmillan).

Wheatley, Lord (chairman) (1969) *Royal Commission on Local Government in Scotland, Report* (Edinburgh: HMSO).

Widdicombe, D. (1986) *Report of the Committee of Inquiry into the Conduct of Local Authority Business* (London: HMSO).

Wilkinson, David and Elaine Applebee (1998) 'Implementing holistic government: joined-up action on the ground', paper for the Local Government Management Board.

Wilks, Steven and Maurice Wright (eds) (1987) *Comparative Government–Industry Relations* (Oxford: Clarendon).

Willetts, David (1996) *Blair's Gurus* (London: Centre for Policy Studies).

Wilson, David and Chris Game (1998) *Local Government in the United Kingdom* (London: Macmillan).

Wilson, Richard (1999) 'Permanent revolution? Yes, minister', *The Independent*, 11 May.

Wolmar, Christian (1997) 'Unelected, unaccountable and still unchallenged', *The Independent*, 13 June.

Worcester, Robert and Roger Mortimore (1999) *Explaining Labour's Landslide* (London: Politico's Publishing).

Wright, Maurice (1988) 'Policy community, policy network and comparative industrial policies', *Political Studies*, Vol. 36 (4), pp. 593–614.

Young, K., B. Gosschalk and W. Hatter (1996) *In Search of Community Identity* (London: Local Government Commission).

Index